THE VERY BEST OF

FRASIER®

THE VERY BEST OF

FIFTEEN OF THE FINEST *FRASIER* SCRIPTS

First published 2001 by Channel 4 Books
an imprint of Pan Macmillan Ltd
Pan Macmillan, 20 New Wharf Road, London, N1 9RR
Basingstoke and Oxford
Associated companies throughout the world
www.panmacmillan.com

ISBN 07522 6179 7

1 3 5 7 9 8 6 4 2

A CIP catalogue record for this book is available from
the British Library.

Designed and typeset by Neal Townsend

Printed and bound by Mackays of Chatham, plc, Chatham, Kent

This book accompanies the television series FRASIER ®
produced by Paramount Pictures for Channel 4.

Jefferson Graham is the author of several books, including
Frasier: The Official Companion Book and covers the internet for *USA TODAY*.

CONTENTS

INTRODUCTION

Within these pages are collected thoughts, witticisms and rants from eight seasons of America's smartest and wittiest comedy, a collection of farce, physical comedy, sharp psychological exchanges, sophisticated familial strife and just plain funny writing.

These are "Frasier" scripts as they were filmed in front of the cameras at Paramount Studios in Hollywood, before the producers were forced to make trims for time to fit the show into the non-negotiable twenty-two minute network timeslot.

So readers "will read scenes here that never made the air," says David Lee, one of the three "Frasier" co-creators, who selected these fifteen episodes for publication with fellow co-creators Peter Casey and David Angell.

Included in this mix are episodes that won coveted Emmy, Writer's Guild and Humanitas awards for their writing. Lee says having a second edition of scripts in book form "honors the writers. Far too many people, to this day, think the actors make up the words."

Dan O'Shannon, an executive producer of "Frasier," says that when watching an episode of the show, we see the acting, direction, sound mix, music—everything that goes into the final mix. "On the page, the show is laid bare," he says. "And you can see it how it started. As words."

"Frasier" began in 1993 as a spin-off of "Cheers" about the pompous Boston psychiatrist who moved to Seattle to care for his ailing dad Martin, fight the sibling rivalry wars with uptight brother Niles, and accept a new job as a radio shrink.

The only TV show ever to win back-to-back Emmys five years in a row for best show has proved to be incredibly durable. The show's five core characters (with the addition of Frasier's producer Roz and Martin's care-giver Daphne) have remained intact, with one big story change: at the end of the seventh season, in a pivotal script included here, Niles and Daphne declared their love for each other.

Other highlights include:
My Coffee with Niles (season one)
Lee calls it "one of the great defining scripts for the show. We wanted to see if we could write about Niles and Frasier talking about whether they were happy—and David and Peter pulled it off." The last episode of the first season—unusual, in that most American TV shows opt for cliffhangers or special guest stars, "this was a big signal to the audience and critics that we were willing to try new things and break the sitcom formula. It was also a signal to us that we could do it."

Adds Lee: "David and Peter also did this episode in real time. Frasier and Niles met at Café Nervosa for twenty-two minutes. There were no artificial act breaks, no excuses to cut to commercial. In fact, when that time came, Niles said 'Will you excuse me for a moment, I have to go to the bathroom.'"

The Candidate (season two)
Frasier endorsed a candidate for election, only to learn that he believes he was abducted by aliens. "We got to comment not only on the insanity of politics, but also UFOs, in the very same episode," says Lee.

Seat of Power (season two)
"This was our revenge, from all of us who were picked upon by bullies when we were kids," says Lee of the show that found Frasier calling for a plumber, a team that happened to include a man who was Niles' sixth grade terrorizer. "I even named the bully after my sixth grade bully (Billy Kriezel,)" says Lee.

The Innkeepers (season two)
The producers were fans of director Blake Edwards and his skill with physical comedy, and attempted to match that kind of spirit in the sitcom, showing the chaos that happened when Frasier and Niles opened a restaurant. In the show, Roz's hair catches on fire, Daphne kills an eel by twirling it around her head and a car drives through the window.

Breaking the Ice (season two)
Winner of the Humanitas award, given out for uplifting stories about the human condition, about an ice-fishing trip with Frasier and his father. "A small story," says Lee. "About how difficult it is for parents and children to tell each other that they love them."

Death and the Dog (season four)
A friend of the producers told of his mother taking her dog to a pooch psychiatrist, and an episode was born, concerning Martin hiring a doggie shrink to treat pooch Eddie's depression. "It morphed into one of those shows that allowed our characters to sit around the living room and ponder death and depression for a good ten minutes," says Lee.

To Kill a Talking Bird (season four)
The writer, Jeffrey Richman, mentioned one day that when he was a child, he knew a man who got a bird attached to his scalp and couldn't get it off. Producers thought that was a wonderful situation for Niles to get into at a dinner party. Lee won an Emmy for directing this episode.

Frasier's Imaginary Friend (season five)
What if you were dating someone really terrific, but circumstances prevented your family from meeting him or her? That was the genesis of "Friend." Frasier was involved with a hot super model, played by Sela Ward ("Once and Again,") but couldn't tell Niles and Martin. What viewers didn't know was that this episode got filmed twice. Five days after the performance, producers discovered that the "A" camera malfunctioned in the second act, and had to reassemble everyone to re-shoot it.

The Dinner Party (season six)
Frasier and Niles attempt to stage a dinner party, and twenty-two minutes later, after arguing about the guest list, caterer and other particulars, they decide it's not worth the trouble. It's another "Frasier" episode played out in real time, a particular favorite of Lee's, because "real time is difficult, closer to a stage play. We often find when we have a particular set of rules to follow, it forces us to become more creative."

Dr. Nora (season six)
In this episode, KACL wanted to add a second radio psychiatrist, and

Frasier selects Dr. Nora, played by Christine Baranski ("Cybill,") only to find himself horrified by her views. To make amends for his decision, he attempts to reconcile Dr. Nora with her estranged mother, played by Piper Laurie. Both actresses were nominated for Emmys.

Merry Christmas, Mrs. Moskowitz (season six)
Frasier pretends to be Jewish when his girl friend Faye's (Amy Brenneman of "Judging Amy") Jewish mother visits. "This episode received the Emmy, Writer's Guild Award and Humanitas prize," says Lee. "Do we need any other reason for including it?"

Out with Dad (season seven)
Reprising the tone of season two's "The Matchmaker," when Frasier's new boss thinks he's gay, this one featured Martin pretending to be gay on Valentine's Day, with Niles as his lover. Written by Joe Keenan (who also penned "The Matchmaker").

Something Borrowed, Someone Blue (season seven)
After seven years, producers knew they couldn't keep Niles yearning for Daphne any longer and sought to break new ground with this episode. "It wasn't an easy decision," says O'Shannon. "There was concern about losing the romantic tension, but you can't keep showing them almost getting together. It's amazing it lasted as long as it did."

Sliding Frasiers (season eight)
Inspired by the 1998 film "Sliding Doors," the idea of **Sliding Frasiers** was to play off the phrase, "it is better to have lost at love than to have never loved at all," and show Frasier both finding and losing love. "We show both sides of the romantic equation for Frasier," says O'Shannon, who wrote the episode with Bob Daly. "All in the course of one show. We rose above the gimmick for a show that was very well received."

One of America's longest running shows, Frasier is just as popular in England, which Lee attributes to Britons appreciating "wit, farce, style and good humor. We love drawing room comedies, Noel Coward and P.G. Woodhouse. So while it's a thrill that Frasier feeds the hungry masses, we also take special delight that it appeals to Epicurean tastes as well."

Jefferson Graham

THE CAST

Frasier Crane	Kelsey Grammer
Martin Crane	John Mahoney
Niles Crane	David Hyde Pierce
Daphne Moon	Jane Leeves
Roz Doyle	Peri Gilpin
Bulldog Brisco	Dan Butler
Eddie	Moose

ADDITIONAL CAST MEMBERS

MY COFFEE WITH NILES
Waitress	Luck Hari

THE CANDIDATE
Waitress	Luck Hari
Little Boy	Christopher Walberg
Phil Patterson	Boyd Gaines
Jimmy	Jack Tate
Madman Martinez *(v.o.)*	Dan Gerrity
TV Announcer *(v.o.)*	Maris Clement

SEAT OF POWER
Elliott *(v.o.)*	Jeff Tucker
Danny Kriezel	John C. McGinley
Billy Kriezel	Mike Starr

THE INNKEEPERS
Gil Chesterton	Edward Hibbert
Owner	Mike Nussbaum
Otto	Nathan Davis
Maurice	Jay Bell
Sous-Chef	Alan Shearman
Waiter	Robert Jacobs
Bartender	Tom Hewitt
Brad	Diedrich Bader
Joan	Deborah Lacey

BREAKING THE ICE
Jake *(v.o.)* — Patrick Kerr
Ranger — Rick Cramer

DEATH AND THE DOG
Alice *(v.o.)* — Adrienne Hampton
Dr. Stephen Kagen — Tom Lagleder
Dr. Arnold Shaw — Zeljko Ivanek

TO KILL A TALKING BIRD
Stephanie — Patricia Wettig
Christine — Lisa Akey
Carol Larkin — Rosemary Murphy
Alfred Larkin — Jack Sydow
Wella — Brandi Burkett
Elaine Hensley — Nancy Linari
Peter Soutendeck — Wayne Alexander
Bird *(v.o.)* — Gregg Berger

FRASIER'S IMAGINARY FRIEND
Kelly Easterling — Sela Ward
Joanne — Lisa Coles
Felicity — Kim Oja
Waiter — Andrew Philpot
Stewardess — Leslie Ishii

MERRY CHRISTMAS, MRS. MOSKOWITZ
Jean — Carole Shelley
Faye — Amy Brenneman
Sal — Jihad Harik
Dell — Lombardo Boyar

DINNER PARTY
Allison Wolpert *(v.o.)* — Susanne Blakeslee
Harry Wolpert *(v.o.)* — James Cunningham

DR. NORA
Dr. Nora — Christine Baranski
Kenny — Tom McGowan
Mrs. Mulhern — Piper Laurie

George	Douglas McDonald
Jenny *(v.o.)*	Joanne Anderson
Jill *(v.o.)*	Pia Zadora
Tom *(v.o.)*	Yo-Yo Ma
Denise *(v.o.)*	Bonnie Raitt

OUT WITH DAD

Edward	Brian Bedford
Helen Browning	Mary Louise Wilson
Emily Browning	Marg Helgenberger

SOMETHING BORROWED, SOMEONE BLUE (PARTS I & II)

Donny Douglas	Saul Rubinek
Dr. Mel Karnofsky	Jane Adams
Simon Moon	Anthony LaPaglia
Mrs. Gertrude Moon	Millicent Martin
Mrs. Richman	Brooks Almy
Miss Carney	Teri Ralston
Tim Walsh	Ed Quinn
Nigel Moon	Patrick Hillan
Bartender	Rob Klingman
Waiter	A.T. Montgomery

SLIDING FRASIERS

Kenny Daly	Tom McGowan
Monica	Charlotte Ross
Mike	Jon Curry
Judy	Heather McDonald
Robert	JD Roberto
Emcee	Michael G. Hawkins
Phil *(v.o.)*	Cameron Watson
Rachel *(v.o.)*	Bernadette Peters
Announcer *(v.o.)*	Ilo Orleans

AND THE DISH RAN AWAY WITH THE SPOON (PARTS I & II)

Dr. Mel Karnofsky	Jane Adams
Simon Moon	Anthony LaPaglia
Adrianna	Karen Kondazian
Woman	Stephanie Nash

MY COFFEE WITH NILES

Written by
David Angell & Peter Casey

Created and Developed by
David Angell, Peter Casey, David Lee

Directed by
James Burrows

ACT ONE

SCENE A

> *A black screen. In white letters appears, "My Coffee With Niles."*

> *FADE IN:*

INT. CAFÉ NERVOSA — DAY — DAY 1

> *It's a busy afternoon crowd. All the tables are taken. Niles is at the counter, talking on a cellular phone as Frasier enters.*

Niles   *(into phone)* Now calm down, dear. Okay, take a left... now the second right... then take a left... Goodbye, sweetheart.

Frasier   Did Maris get lost again?

Niles   Yes, she wandered into the kitchen by mistake. I had to talk her back to the living room.

Frasier   *(scanning the room)* Busy today. Aren't there any tables?

Niles   Not at the moment. That table by the window received their check five minutes ago. But they've been just sitting there yammering away ever since. I've been shooting them dirty looks, but they haven't budged.

Frasier   Let me see the look.

> *Niles shoots Frasier a dirty look.*

Frasier   They'll be there for a while.

Niles   In the meantime, shall we go ahead and order?

Frasier   Why not?

> *Frasier flags down a passing waitress.*

Frasier   What are your coffees of the day?

Waitress   Zimbabwe and Kenya.

Frasier   I'll have a Zimbabwe latte.

Niles   And I'll have a Kenya cappuccino.

> *She moves off.*

Frasier   Something tells me that's the closest we're ever going to come to a safari. So, what's new?

Niles   Well, Yoshi our gardener finally won the battle of the wills. He got Maris to dig up her camellias so he could put in that precious Zen garden he's been hocking us about since last fall.

Frasier   How did it turn out?

Niles   Oh, it's completely authentic. The perfect place for meditation. Yesterday I found Maris smack dab in the middle sitting in the lotus position.

Frasier   Well, good for her. Apparently it's bringing out her spiritual side.

Niles   I'm not so sure. She was reading a Danielle Steele novel while making a nail appointment on her cellular phone.

They laugh.

Frasier   When you come right down to it, Maris is kind of a hoot, isn't she?

Niles   Oh she's a hoot and a half.

Frasier   Do you realize that today marks one year since I moved here from Boston?

Niles   Really? A year? My the time has flown. It seems like only yesterday Dad moved in with you.

Frasier   It's funny how two people can have distinct opposite impressions about the same event.

Niles shakes his head.

Niles   A year. It's amazing how a man's life can change.

Frasier   It's extraordinary. I mean, I'm divorced, I'm in a new city, I have a new job, and Dad's moved in with me.

Niles   Actually, I meant me. We've gone through three housekeepers and changed our china pattern.

Niles looks at the people still at the table by the window.

Niles   Look at them. They're still sitting there. Maybe if we both give them the look.

Frasier   Worth a try.

They both give a dirty look. The people rise.

Niles   It's working, it's working.

Frasier   I'll never doubt you again, Niles.

They high-five. When they turn back around, two other people have taken their table.

Niles   Try the look on that table. I'm going to the men's room.

Frasier turns to another table, as we:

FADE OUT.

SCENE B

> *FADE IN:*

INT. CAFÉ NERVOSA — EXACTLY THE AMOUNT OF TIME IT TAKES TO DO A COMMERCIAL LATER — DAY 1

> *Niles enters from the bathroom shaking his hands as he crosses to Frasier.*

Niles   Maddening.

Frasier   What is it now?

> *Niles pulls out a bunch of paper napkins and begins drying his hands.*

Niles   They have a new moisturizer dispenser in the men's room and it turns out the cream is entirely too oily so I had to re-wash my hands and wouldn't you know it, that's when the hot air hand dryer chooses to break down.

Frasier   How *do* you get through the day?

> *The waitress approaches with their coffees.*

Waitress   Here you go, Zimbabwe and Kenya.

Frasier   Excuse me, did I say decaf?

Waitress   No, you didn't.

Frasier   I'm sorry. If I drink the regular stuff it'll keep me tossing and turning all through my brother's conversation.

> *Niles gives him a look.*

Waitress   No problem.

> *The waitress takes the coffee and crosses away.*

Frasier   Thank you. *(To Niles)* It doesn't look like anybody's leaving. Shall we take a table outside?

Niles   Why not? I'm feeling al fresco.

Frasier   How does Mrs. Fresco feel about that?

> *They laugh. Niles picks up his coffee and they exit to the outside patio.*

> *RESET TO:*

EXT. PATIO AREA OF CAFÉ NERVOSA — CONTINUOUS

> *Niles and Frasier move to an empty table. Niles proceeds to wipe down the chair and the table with his handkerchief.*

Frasier	I'll bet you're a lot of fun on a camping trip.
Niles	If there's a God in heaven, I'll never find out.
	They sit down.
Niles	Well, now that chapter two of your life is in full swing, would you mind if I asked you something?
Frasier	Go right ahead.
Niles	Are you happy?
	Frasier doesn't answer.
Niles	Did you hear the question?
Frasier	I'm thinking about it. It's a deceivingly complex question.
Niles	No, it's not. Either you're happy or you're not.
Frasier	Are you happy?
Niles	No, but we're not talking about me.
Frasier	Well, let's not gloss past that. You, my only brother, just told me you're not happy and it pains me to hear it. I want to know why.
	Niles takes a deep breath.
Niles	I was watching PBS in my study the other night and they were showing a documentary about the Great Depression. Vintage Steinbeck. Desperately poor people escaping the dust bowl. Their meager possessions strapped to rickety old trucks heading to what they thought would be their salvation. Then there was this scene of a scruffy little boy being handed a pair of brand new shoes by the Salvation Army. Frasier, if you could have seen the look on his face. It was a look of pure and utter happiness. I've never experienced that kind of happiness. Not in my whole life. Not even when I bought these four hundred dollar Bruno Maglis. Do you like them?
	Niles holds up one of his feet to show Frasier his shoes.
Frasier	They're very nice.
Niles	What about the tassels?
Frasier	I'm not really a tassel guy.
Niles	Neither am I. Nevertheless, there they are.
	Niles and Frasier chatter back and forth for a while in overlapping riffs.
Niles	Of course, it's not that I have anything to be unhappy about. I mean, I have my health, a wonderful home, a beautiful wife…

(glances over at Frasier) Did your eyebrow move?

Frasier   I don't think so.

Niles   I have my practice. Although lately I've lost track of the ideals that led me into psychiatry in the first place. But then look who I'm talking to — psychiatry's answer to the drive-thru window. A healer with his picture on the side of buses.

SFX: A bus driving by.

Niles   Oh, there you go now. *(Re: picture on bus)* That's a new one — fangs and a beard.

Frasier   Damn kids.

Niles   You know, there are times I wonder if I'm not just in it for the money.

Frasier   Oh I'm sure that's not true. Especially since… Well, never mind.

Niles   Since what? What were you about to say?

Frasier   I'd rather not.

Niles   Actually there's no need to. I think I know what you're getting at. You've been wanting to ask me for years. Did I marry Maris for the money?

Frasier looks at him as if to say, "Well?"

Niles   I resent that. I did not marry Maris for her money. It was just a delightful little bonus.

Frasier   So you're saying you do love her.

Niles   Of course I love her. But it's a different kind of love.

Frasier   You mean it's not human?

Niles   *(not amused)* I mean it doesn't burn with the passion and intensity of a Tristan and Isolde. It's more comfortable, more familiar. Maris and I are old friends. We can spend an entire afternoon together, me at my jigsaw puzzle, she at her autoharp, not a word spoken between us and be perfectly content.

Frasier   I'm told it was a lot like that near the end in the Hitler household.

Niles   Why don't we turn the focus back to where it belongs. This whole thing started with me asking if *you* were happy. And don't think about it this time, just answer.

Frasier   Well…

Roz approaches.

Roz   Hey guys.

Niles   Hello, Roz. What are you doing here?

Roz   I always wanted to fly a jet and they're having a special on jet flying lessons so I thought I'd take advantage of it. *(Duh)* I came here to get coffee.

Niles   *(sarcastic)* Well, thanks for stopping by. I'd have been mad if you didn't.

Roz   *(to Frasier)* I'm also meeting someone here.

Frasier   Let me guess, a man?

Roz   *(pointedly)* Yes. It's that new guy, Andy Winslow, up in the news department. He's really cute. He caught me checking him out when he was bending over the water fountain.

Frasier   Ah, love at first sight.

Roz   Hey, there's all kinds of love. Anyway, he said, "Why don't we have some coffee and get to know each other?" I don't know, I've got a very strange feeling that this could be the one.

Frasier   Roz, honey, you say that about every guy you meet. Let's just see if this one calls back.

Roz   Yeah, I guess. *(Peering in the window)* I don't think he's here yet. I'm going to see if I can snag a table.

Frasier   Good luck.

As Roz starts to exit:

Niles   Bye, Roz.

Roz, not looking back, mumbles something and gives a half-hearted wave and exits into the coffee house.

Niles   I don't think she likes me.

Frasier   It's not a question of liking or not liking, Niles. She despises you.

Niles   *(considers)* Well, if it were important to me I'd do something about it.

Niles gets up from the table and looks through the café window.

Niles   You know, she *is* comely in a back alley sort of way.

Frasier   Roz? Yes, she's very attractive.

Niles   Have you ever thought about you two well, you know…

Frasier   Roz and me? Oh no. No, no, no.

Niles   Oh come on now. You've never fantasized of stealing away to some cheap little motel with her?

Frasier   Well, I am a man with normal urges. And she does have this blouse that tends to open up when she bends over the cart rack. But mixing romance and work, that can get pretty messy. Is it worth it?

Niles Don't ask me. You're the one who looked down her blouse.

The waitress approaches with Frasier's coffee.

Waitress Decaf Zimbabwe latte.

Frasier That's non-fat milk, right?

Waitress *(mad)* No.

Frasier I hate to bother you again, but I'm watching my fat intake and I…

Annoyed, she picks up the coffee and walks away. SFX: Rain. Some raindrops begin falling. They look up to the sky.

Niles Is that rain?

Frasier *(sarcastic)* No, God is crying.

Niles Can't I ask a simple question?

Frasier Do you ask any other kind?

Niles picks up his cup from the table and they exit into the coffee house.

RESET TO:

INT. CAFÉ NERVOSA — CONTINUOUS

They immediately notice that Roz is sitting alone at a table.

Frasier Hey, how the hell'd she get a table? We were here first.

She sees them, smiles and waves. They give her fake smiles and wave at her. At that moment, Niles notices two patrons leaving an upstage table.

Niles Frasier, Frasier!

They start for the table, but another couple beats them to it. Again, Niles notices people at the table by the window get up and leave.

Niles Frasier, Frasier!

At that exact moment another standing patron spots the same table. Suddenly they all bolt to the table. Niles throws himself at a patron, blocking his way, while Frasier slides into a seat first.

Frasier *(triumphantly)* Sorry.

The other person moves off. Niles sits.

Frasier	Nice block, Niles.

They sit for a beat. Frasier looks out the window and shakes his head.

Frasier	Unbelievable.
Niles	What is it?
Frasier	Oh, I was just thinking about something that happened the other morning. I asked Dad to pass me a bran muffin and do you know what he said to me? "What's the magic word?"
Niles	You're kidding.
Frasier	He didn't find it amusing when I said, "rest home."

Niles chuckles. A good looking man has entered and has crossed to Roz's table.

Niles	Ooh, look, look, look that must be Roz's coffee companion. Wow, he's really handsome, isn't he?
Frasier	"Wow?" Did you say "wow?"
Niles	Good Lord, I did. I don't think I've ever said "wow" describing another man before. I wonder if that means something.
Frasier	Of course it does. It means you're a gay man, living a charade with Maris and you should have come out of the closet years ago. Do you want to tell Dad, or shall I?
Niles	You know, Frasier, sometimes you're just too flip.

Martin, Daphne, and Eddie enter. Martin is in a foul mood.

Martin	It was stupid. Come on, admit it. This walk was stupid.
Daphne	It was not stupid. You needed to get your exercise. What was stupid was that you went out without your bumberchute.
Martin	It's called an umbrella. Speak English, will you?

The waitress approaches.

Waitress	Sorry, sir. No dogs allowed.
Martin	*(pretending to be blind)* What?
Waitress	*(realizing)* Oh, I'm sorry.
Martin	That's okay.

The waitress moves off.

Frasier	What are you guys doing here?
Daphne	I thought your father needed some exercise and I had to come down here to pick up some beans, so we walked. Well, two of us

walked. One of us had to be dragged by his collar.

Martin   Hey, I told you I didn't want to come. Look at me. I'll probably die of pneumonia.

Daphne   Oh you'll out-live us all. The cranky ones always do.

Daphne moves to the counter.

Frasier   Let's get you something hot to drink, Dad.

Frasier signals for a waitress.

Frasier   What would you like, cappuccino, latte?

Martin   *(to waitress)* Coffee. Black. And don't put anything fancy in it.

Waitress   We have two special coffees today…

Martin glares at her.

Waitress   I'll surprise you.

Martin pulls up a chair and sits down.

Martin   Look at us, we're soaked to the skin.

Frasier   Well, there's no need to get mad at Daphne. She's only doing this for your own good.

Martin   Why the hell do you always take her side?

Frasier   I don't. You're in a fine mood today.

Martin   By the way, you left a mess in the kitchen this morning.

Frasier   I just had a piece of toast.

Martin   And you didn't use a plate like I've asked you to. You buttered it on the counter. I know because you left a bunch of crumbs and toast sweat there.

Niles   Toast sweat?

Frasier   Yes. When you take hot toast and lay it on a surface, it leaves little droplets of dew. Haven't you heard Dad's lecture on the evils of toast sweat? It's the scourge of our times.

The waitress puts down a cup of coffee in front of Martin and one in front of Frasier.

Waitress   One coffee black and a decaf, non-fat, Zimbabwe latte.

Frasier   Oh dear, is that cinnamon on the foam?

Without missing a beat, she picks up the coffee and goes.

Frasier   As long as we're picking at each other's scabs, I found another one of Eddie's chew toys in my sweater cubby and there was hair all over my favorite pullover. I know he sleeps in there when I'm not home.

Martin   Serves you right for keeping your sweaters in something called a "cubby."

Frasier   From now on, my bedroom is off limits to that flea bag.

Martin   He is not a flea bag.

Niles   So, Dad, how about those Mariners?

Martin   Shut up, Niles. Look, who are we kidding here? This isn't working out. If my hip is in good enough shape to walk down here, maybe it's time I found a place of my own.

Frasier   Oh, no, not this again.

Niles   But where will you go?

Martin   Don't you worry about me. I'll find something. I've got a little money saved up. *(To Frasier)* Moving in with you wasn't my idea…

Frasier joins in on Martin's speech.

Frasier/Martin And the last thing I want to do is be a burden to anyone.

Martin   *(to Niles)* That's your brother's smart ass way of saying he's heard this before. Well, you won't have to hear it anymore.

Martin stands to go.

Martin   Come on, Eddie. *(To Frasier and Niles)* Tell Daphne to catch up with us.

Frasier   Come on, Dad. We play this little melodrama out at least once a week. Will you sit down? It's raining.

Martin   No, no. And I can pay for my own coffee. How much is it?

Frasier   A dollar fifty.

Martin   *(astounded)* For coffee? What kind of world are we living in?

Martin grabs a newspaper by the door and holds it over his head as he exits into the rain. Frasier heads off to the men's room in back as we:

FADE OUT.

END OF ACT ONE

ACT TWO

SCENE C

> *FADE IN:*

INT. CAFÉ NERVOSA — EXACTLY THE AMOUNT OF TIME IT TAKES TO DO A COMMERCIAL BREAK LATER — DAY 1

> *Frasier enters from the restroom and crosses back to the table.*

Niles Frasier, are you alright? You were in the bathroom forever.

Frasier I tried that damn hand cream. It was so oily I couldn't get a grip on the doorknob. I had to wait to be rescued. When some guy finally came in I said, "Oh my God, am I glad to see you." I can't even describe the look he gave me.

> *A man passes by, staring at Frasier.*

Frasier Oh, there it is.

> *Daphne comes to the table carrying a bag of beans.*

Daphne Where's your father?

Frasier We locked horns again over some piddly bit of nonsense and he left. He said for you to catch up with him.

Daphne I don't know what's wrong with him. Lately he's had a face as long as a wet weekend. Yesterday, when I insisted he do his stretching exercises, he told me I could stick my feet behind my head and spin like a top.

Frasier Oh, I'm sure he didn't mean it. When he gets like this you just have to ignore him. Right, Niles? *(No response)* Niles?

Niles I'm sorry, Frasier. For some reason I'm feeling a little dizzy.

Daphne I guess I better go after him.

Niles Here. Take my bumberchute.

Daphne Isn't that nice. At least someone appreciates my mother tongue.

> *Daphne exits.*

Niles Yes, I've always had an ear for your tongue.

Frasier Niles.

Niles What did I say? *(Then)* Would you like another coffee?

Frasier I haven't had my first one yet.

> *Niles signals the waitress, indicating that he'd like another coffee for himself. Frasier stares out the window.*

Frasier Why is it always so difficult for us?

Niles   Maybe you should try looking at it from Dad's point of view. As a policeman, he was in a position of authority. Now that's been taken away from him. Railing against the world is his way of trying to control his ever shrinking sphere of influence.

Frasier   I can appreciate his frustration. But that doesn't stop me from occasionally wanting to kick that cane out from under him. And hoping he lands on Eddie.

Niles   The simple truth is, it's hard. I know you're trying.

Frasier   I am. And every now and then I see the fruits of my labor. For example, just the other night Dad was watching TV and I'd fallen asleep on the couch. Suddenly I stirred. I could feel something on my head and I realized that Dad was standing over me stroking my hair.

Niles   Dad? Did he say anything?

Frasier   Yes. He said, "Why don't you get a haircut? You're starting to look like Bozo." I'm sure he was just covering. What do you think?

Niles   It probably wouldn't hurt to get a trim.

Frasier   No, I mean, do you think he was covering?

Niles   Of course he was covering. You know Dad. Tough as nails on the outside, but on the inside one big giant… spike.

The waitress comes over with Niles' coffee.

Niles   Gràzie.

Frasier   Excuse me, what about mine?

Waitress   We've got a team of specialists working on it.

She moves off.

Frasier   Do you mind if we get off the subject of Dad and talk about something else?

Niles   Not at all. Let's pick a new subject. Something light and frothy.

Niles begins to sip his coffee.

Frasier   I agree. Are you in love with Daphne?

Niles does a spittake.

Frasier   That takes care of the frothy part.

Niles dabs his mouth and regains his composure.

Niles   That's preposterous. I refuse to dignify that question with an answer.

Niles proceeds to stir his coffee while Frasier stares at him. Finally:

Niles (*snaps*) I don't know! There. I've said it. Are you happy? Oh, why couldn't you have just hired some beefy, Eastern European scrub woman who reeked of ammonia instead of Venus herself.

Frasier I asked, but it was an Olympic year. The agency was fresh out.

Niles I can't get her out of my mind. You probably haven't noticed, but sometimes, just to be near her, I make up silly excuses to come over to your house.

Frasier Yes, I began to suspect that when you dropped by yesterday to remind us to always buckle our seatbelts.

Niles When I look at Daphne, she stirs up a passion in me I've never known before.

Frasier You're not considering leaving Maris?

Niles Certainly not.

Frasier Well, if I may summarize this situation, it sounds like you want to stay with Maris, but have an affair with Daphne.

Niles Yes! Can I do that?

Frasier No, you can't.

Niles I didn't think so, but you got my hopes up there for a minute. Ah, but it's easier for you. You're free. You're happy. Though I may be getting ahead of myself. You still haven't answered that question. *Are you happy?*

Frasier I haven't answered that yet, have I? Well, let's see, I guess I could best describe my feelings by saying…

Roz (*o.c.*) (*pissed off*) This sucks.

They turn to see Roz approaching their table.

Frasier What happened?

Roz You think you're going to sit down and have coffee with someone who might, just might, lead you to something like, oh I don't know, a *life*. Then all of a sudden that old trap door opens again and you find yourself back in Roz's World.

Niles How could it go so wrong so fast?

Roz Oh, I've got it down to a science. He didn't want to date me, he wanted to convert me. He's a Jehovah's Witness! Here, anyone need a copy of the "Watchtower?"

She throws a pamphlet on the table.

Frasier	Aw, Roz, I'm sorry. Why don't you join us?
Roz	No thanks. I think I'll stroll over to the park, watch the children play on the swings and try to remember the last time I was happy.
Frasier	*(heartbreaking)* Roz…
Roz	Oh, I'm kidding. I'm going to get a half-gallon of Heath Bar Crunch and rent that Richard Gere movie where he shows his butt. That always does the trick.

Roz exits. Frasier picks up the "Watchtower," opens it and looks at it for a moment.

Frasier	It's a shame, isn't it?
Niles	She'll find somebody.
Frasier	Oh, I know she will. What I meant was how she reacted to that young man.
Niles	People seem to be so uncomfortable with religion these days.
Frasier	Yes, why is that? He was sincere in his beliefs.
Niles	I think It's something to be admired.
Frasier	Yeah, we could all use a little more spirituality in our lives. It's a shame that not everyone is as enlightened as we are.

Andy Winslow gets up and starts to cross toward them.

Frasier	*(alarmed)* Oh geez, here he comes.

Niles quickly turns his head and uses his hand to shield his face while Frasier bends over as if to tie his shoe while Andy exits.

Frasier	Is he gone?
Niles	*(looking)* Yes. I think I pulled a muscle in my neck.
Frasier	Believe me, it was worth it.

Niles sips his coffee.

Frasier	I look at Roz and I start to wonder about my own life. I haven't exactly been burning things up on the social scene. Who's to say this isn't how I'm going to spend the rest of my life… *(losing it)* sitting here waiting for a stupid cup of coffee!
Niles	Calm down. And don't be such a pessimist. You'll find somebody.
Frasier	But what if I don't? What if I do end up old and alone? I might have to buy a funny little dog and move in with Frederick. Will our relationship be any better than mine is with Dad?
Niles	Frasier, it'll never get to that. You're doing everything humanly possible to form a strong bond with your son. You call him on the

	phone every day, you fly back as often as you can. You even tried to teach him how to throw a football. How's it going, by the way?
Frasier	Pretty good. I've got it down to one-handed. Nonetheless, it doesn't keep me from feeling guilty.
Niles	Well I guess that brings me to my evermore tedious original question. Are you happy?
Frasier	Well, I guess I'd have to say…
	Martin enters with Eddie.
Martin	Hello, boys.
	Niles throws up his hands in frustration.
Frasier	Dad, what are you doing back here?
Martin	I don't know. I've been acting like a jerk the last couple of days, taking it out on you and Daphne. So, you know, all that stuff I said earlier, just forget it.
Frasier	Okay by me.
	Martin turns to go.
Frasier	Dad, has something been bothering you?
Martin	Naw, nothing, really.
Frasier	What is it?
Martin	It's stupid.
Frasier	Dad…
Martin	Okay. Last Sunday was my birthday.
	Niles and Frasier look at each other, realizing they've forgotten.
Niles	Of course it was. Frasier and I were planning a big surprise party. But it wouldn't have been a surprise if we did it on your actual birthday, so we waited a week. So… Surprise! *(Then)* If you could see the look on your face.
Frasier	Oh, give it up, Niles. Dad, I'm sorry.
Martin	Ah, that's okay. I shouldn't have let it bother me. Hey, all those years on the force I missed enough of your birthdays, I figure you're entitled to miss one of mine.
Frasier	Well, we can still celebrate. We're taking you out to dinner tonight. Wherever you want.
Martin	No, it's all right.
Niles	We insist. You name the place, okay?

Martin   Okay… How about Hoppy's Old Heidelberg?

Niles and Frasier exchange looks of horror.

Frasier/Niles   *(fake enthusiasm)* Oh, great.

Martin   They were voted the best bratwurst in town for three years in a row.

Frasier   Ach du Lieber.

Daphne enters.

Daphne   *(to Martin)* There you are. I was looking for you all up and down Third Street.

Martin   I was on Fourth Street. Eddie had already smelled everything on Third.

Daphne   Well, it's a good thing I got one of my psychic flashes. Bang. There you were, walking in the front door of Café Nervosa.

Martin   Well, we better get home. We're all going out to dinner at Hoppy's Old Heidelberg.

Daphne   Oh, good. German food. We whip their tail twice a century and they still have the last laugh.

Frasier   I have to stop by the radio station first.

Niles   That's all right, I'll give them a lift home.

Martin, Daphne and Eddie start for the door. Niles and Frasier stand.

Niles   As always, Frasier, I've enjoyed getting together with you for coffee.

Martin   What do you guys talk about all the time?

Niles   Oh you know, sports, baseball, monster truck rallies…

Martin   Okay, don't tell me.

Martin, Daphne, Niles and Eddie exit. The waitress comes over with a coffee and sets it on the table in front of him. She's really had it with him.

Waitress   Zimbabwe. Decaf. Non-fat milk. No cinnamon. I even threw in a few biscotti. Now… are you happy?

Frasier ponders this.

Frasier   You know, in the grand scheme of things, yes, I'd say I am.

He sits down and contentedly sips his coffee as we:

FADE OUT.

END OF ACT TWO

THE CANDIDATE

Written by
Chuck Ranberg & Anne Flett-Giordano

Created and Developed by
David Angell, Peter Casey, David Lee

Directed by
James Burrows

ACT ONE

SCENE A

> *FADE IN:*

INT. FRASIER'S LIVING ROOM — NIGHT — NIGHT 1

> *Frasier and Niles are seated at the table, playing chess. Martin is turning on the television.*

Martin   (*calling*) Frasier, Daphne, get in here. Come on, come on, come on!

> *Daphne enters from the kitchen.*

Daphne   All right, I'm coming.

Martin   Sit down, sit down.

> *Daphne sits on the opposite end of the sofa from Niles.*

Frasier   What is this all about?

Martin   Sit down. You'll see in a second.

> *Frasier goes to sit between Niles and Daphne, but Niles scoots over quickly to be near her. Frasier almost sits in his lap.*

Frasier   Oh, for heaven's sake.

Martin   Quiet, quiet, it's starting.

> *Frasier sits next to Niles. Coming from the television we hear:*

Announcer   (*v.o.*) The following is a paid political announcement for Holden Thorpe.

> *SFX: "The Star Spangled Banner".*

Niles   You dragged me over here to watch a commercial for Holden Thorpe?

Martin   Shh!

Frasier   The man is a Fascist. He's like Himmler without the whimsy.

Martin   Shh!

Announcer   (*v.o.*) "Now another American for Holden Thorpe…"

> *Angle on the television broadcasting this commercial. We see Martin on TV. This segment is shot informally with a hand-held camera on the streets.*

Martin   Hi, I'm Marty Crane.

> *Angle on the group's reaction.*

Frasier   Dear God.

Angle on the television.

Martin   For thirty years I was a cop walking a beat in Seattle. Then my hip was shattered by an assassin's bullet. An assassin who wouldn't have been on the streets if it weren't for those bleeding hearts we sent to Congress. I used to carry a gun. Now I carry a cane. I'm voting to elect Holden Thorpe. He's running because I can't.

Martin turns off the television. Frasier and Niles sit in shock.

Martin   *(proudly)* Well… ?

Daphne   *(delighted)* Oh, Mr. Crane, I don't know what to say. I'm in a state of shock.

Niles   Aren't we all?

Daphne   I mean you were wonderful. This calls for a celebration.

Martin   You're right, Daphne. I'm gonna have a beer.

Daphne   But it's a special occasion. You ought to be able to think of something better than that.

Martin   I'll have it in a glass.

She exits to the kitchen.

Frasier   Dad, how did this happen?

Martin   I stopped at the mall last week and they were holding a rally for Thorpe. I started talking to one of his people. Told him I was an ex-cop. Next thing I know, they were shoving a camera in my face.

Frasier   This is appalling.

Martin   They don't think so. They're running it six times a day until the election. Channel eight is showing the sixty second version where I actually limp and an old lady has to help me step off a curb. And channel fourteen is showing…

Frasier   Those people are exploiting you.

Martin   No, they're not. I like Thorpe.

Niles   How could you possibly support that odious, little hose-head? I once heard him say, "Cancer aside, tobacco is good for the economy."

Martin   He's gonna put more cops on the street.

Daphne enters from the kitchen.

Daphne   It couldn't hurt, now that everyone and his brother is walking around armed. Makes me glad we don't have so many guns in England.

SFX: The phone rings. Frasier crosses to answer it.

Frasier   You don't need guns, you've got kidney pie. *(Answering phone)* Hello… *(To Martin)* It's Duke.

Niles   *(to Frasier)* Sherry?

Frasier   I couldn't possibly. I'm too upset.

Martin   *(into phone)* Hey, Duke! Glad you liked it. I thought I was better in the second take, but the director said you can't say that on TV. I got a lot of show biz stories to tell you. Did you know you can make yourself cry on cue by pulling a hair out of your nose? Huh? Really? *(To Niles and Frasier)* Guys, quick! Turn on channel fourteen. Duke says they're showing my other spot.

Frasier turns on the television.

Martin   This one was my idea. Remember how Lyndon Johnson lifted up his shirt to show his scar?

Frasier   Oh, Dad, you didn't…

They cluster around the screen. This time we only hear Martin's voice coming from the television:

Martin   *(v.o.)* Hi, I'm Marty Crane. Crime isn't pretty and if you don't believe me, look at this.

Frasier, Niles and Daphne react. Martin beams and we:

FADE OUT.

SCENE B

INT. CAFÉ NERVOSA — A FEW DAYS LATER — DAY 2

Frasier is sitting at a table. A waitress approaches to take his order.

Waitress   Can I help you, sir?

Frasier   What's your special today?

Waitress   Kenyan blend.

Frasier   Sounds perfect. *(Then)* No, no, no. They're still poaching elephants over there. I don't like to support that. What else do you have?

Waitress   Dark roast Brazilian.

Frasier   I'd like to, but not until something's done about the loss of our rainforests. Sorry, but I'm feeling a little politically sensitive these days.

Waitress Salvadoran?

Frasier I've never forgiven them for their human rights violations.

Waitress Well then, we're down to the Hawaiian Kona blend — or have they slaughtered too many macadamia nuts?

Frasier The Kona will be fine.

The waitress moves to the counter. Niles enters and joins Frasier at the table.

Frasier Hello, Niles.

Niles Frasier. I can't stand it. I just walked past an electronics store, and there in the window were twenty-two television sets and on every screen was Dad's butt.

Frasier I saw it, Niles. I don't know what's worse — seeing his butt or what it stands for. When I think of our father supporting that self-serving fear monger…

Niles I've been giving this a lot of thought and I've realized Dad is not the problem. He's only supporting the candidate of his choice. The problem lies with us.

Frasier Us? We're not doing anything.

Niles Exactly. "The only thing necessary for the triumph of evil is for good men to do nothing."

Frasier Ah, yes, Edmund Burke.

Niles I have that quotation in a frame. I keep meaning to put it up in my office, but I never seem to get around to it.

The waitress approaches, sets down Frasier's coffee and turns to Niles.

Waitress Get you something?

He looks at the selections listed on the blackboard.

Niles I'll have the Kenyan.

Frasier Elephants.

Niles Oh, yes. Brazilian?

Frasier Rainforests.

Niles Hawaiian?

Frasier nods.

Waitress I haven't seen you guys here in a while.

She crosses back to the counter.

Niles	Anyway, Frasier, the time has come for you and I to get involved.
Frasier	What are you suggesting?
Niles	I propose we throw our support behind Thorpe's opponent, Phillip Patterson.
Frasier	Of course I intend to vote for Patterson.
Niles	I had something a little more ambitious in mind. I spoke to some people down at Patterson's headquarters this morning and your name came up. They'd like you to film a TV spot endorsing their candidate — something along the lines of Dad's, only without the cheesecake.
Frasier	I can't do that, Niles.
Niles	Frasier, he's smart, he's hard-working, he volunteers weekends to work in a soup kitchen. Finally, a politician who believes in the things we believe in.

A ten-year-old boy crosses by. He carries several boxes of chocolates in a larger cardboard box.

Boy	*(to Niles and Frasier)* Buy a box of chocolates, send a kid to camp?
Niles	Excuse me. Can't you see we're talking here?

He crosses off.

Frasier	I'd really love to help, Niles, but you must realize, as a psychiatrist I can't take the chance of alienating my listeners. People who need my help might be hesitant to call in because they disagree with me politically.
Niles	But a candidate like this doesn't come along that often. He shares our political sensibilities exactly.

The waitress sets down Niles' coffee.

Waitress	*(sarcastically)* He won't be joining you will he?

On their reactions, we:

FADE OUT.

SCENE C

FADE IN:

INT. RADIO STUDIO — DAY — DAY 2

Frasier is on the air finishing a call.

Susan	*(v.o.)* Thank you, Dr. Crane. I feel so much calmer now.

Frasier   That's what I'm here for, Susan.

Roz signals him.

Frasier   We'll be right back after these messages with more of the Dr. Frasier Crane show. Your port in the storm in this turbulent world — an oasis of peace and tranquility…

He pops in a cart and removes his headphones. Roz enters with some new carts as we hear the following commercial begin: SFX: Glass breaking, gunshots, and a siren howling.

Holden Thorpe   *(v.o.)* Crime. It's epidemic. It strikes fast, and it can strike you. I'm Holden Thorpe, and you should send me to Washington because…

Frasier turns down the sound, annoyed.

Frasier   …It beats having you here.

Roz   Piece of work, isn't he? He makes it sound like it's either vote for him or be murdered in your bed.

Frasier   Well you needn't worry, Roz. What are the chances of anyone finding you there alone?

Roz   You know, Frasier, there was this great expression we used to use in my college French class. What was it again…? Oh, yeah, I remember — bite me.

Bulldog enters Frasier's booth with his accoutrements for the Gonzo Sports Show.

Bulldog   Hey sports fan, how they hanging?

Frasier   I'm fine, Bulldog.

Bulldog   I was talking to Roz.

Roz   This is where the five-day waiting period really hurts. *(To Frasier)* Ten seconds.

Frasier turns up the commercial.

Thorpe   *(v.o.)* I'm Holden Thorpe and I get very angry when I think about the punks terrorizing this city. What about you? If you're mad, vote for me.

SFX: A police siren. Frasier is back on the air.

Frasier   You'd pretty much have to be, wouldn't you? This is Dr. Frasier Crane and we'll be back for one last call right after this newsbreak. Then stay tuned for Bulldog Brisco…

Bulldog bangs his gong in Frasier's ear.

Frasier   …and the Gonzo Sports Show.

The "on air" light goes off.

Frasier *(to Bulldog)* I've asked you not to do that.

Bulldog Way to be impartial, Doc. I happen to think Thorpe's a good man. He's tough on crime and he's gonna send those homeless people back where they came from.

Roz And some people think you're insensitive.

Bulldog Oh, let me guess. You're gonna vote for that pretty boy, Phil Patterson.

Roz Patterson's great. He sort of reminds me of one of the Kennedys.

Frasier Forget it, Roz, he's happily married.

Roz shrugs and exits back into her booth.

Bulldog So's Thorpe. Go figure. His wife's a cow and he still loves her.

Frasier Well, there's a bumper sticker.

Bulldog Hey, where's my LaSorda tape? Somebody took my tape of Tommy LaSorda belching. I need that tape to open my show. This is ticking me off! I'm going ballistic! Heads are gonna roll! Oh, here it is. No, this is Johnny Mathis belching. Don't ask me how I got this.

Bulldog exits to the hallway.

Roz Hey, I liked that little shot you took at Thorpe. It took guts.

Frasier Thank you. I do try, as a rule, to remain impartial, but I'm not afraid to stand up to a bullying demagogue.

They're on the air.

Frasier Welcome back, Seattle. So, Roz, who's our next caller?

Roz Well, on line one we have Holden Thorpe.

Frasier signals to Roz, waving the call off.

Roz Apparently he's running for Congress and he has a problem. Go ahead, caller. You're on the air.

Thorpe *(v.o.)* Crane? Thorpe. I believe we have something in this country called equal time so I'd like to answer that crack of yours in the spirit in which it was offered.

Frasier Please. I welcome contrasting viewpoints.

Thorpe *(v.o.)* Let me ask you something, Crane. Are you married?

Frasier Divorced.

Thorpe *(v.o.)* Ever serve in the military?

Frasier	Unfortunately, I have congenitally weak ankles. It's a family problem.
Thorpe	*(v.o.)* I see. So a guy like you, unmarried, didn't serve his country, sees fit to criticize a patriotic family man who fought in the battle of Grenada — I went in on the first wave, incidentally. Tell me, Crane, what have you ever done for Seattle besides listen to crybabies and pry into people's sex lives?
Frasier	I perform a needed, therapeutic service, sir. Many of my listeners are deeply disturbed people.
Thorpe	*(v.o.)* Well, they'd pretty much have to be, wouldn't they?
	He hangs up.
Frasier	You may think you've gotten the last word, but I've got something to say to you…
	Roz signals to him that time is up.
Frasier	…but we're out of time.
	FADE OUT.

SCENE D

A black screen. In white letters appears, "Citizen Crane."

FADE IN:

INT. FRASIER'S LIVING ROOM — NIGHT — NIGHT 3

Frasier is sitting in his Eames Classic looking out his window. After a beat, he turns and speaks to the camera.

Frasier	Oh, hello there. I'm Dr. Frasier Crane. Many of you know me from my radio show, but today I'm speaking to you as a private citizen… a concerned citizen. As a mental health expert, I've been listening to what my good friend Phil Patterson has to say. I like the way his mind works. He's a visionary, and he cares about the little people. That's why I'm proud to say that I'm behind Phil Patterson for Congress.
	The camera pulls back to reveal that Frasier is filming a commercial and reading from cue cards. Several people including the director — Jimmy, Patterson's advisors, etc., and Niles are there. Phil Patterson walks into frame.
Phil	Thanks, Frasier. Together we can live the dream.
	Frasier puts his arm around Phil and shakes his hand.

Frasier   Phil Patterson. The sane choice.

Jimmy   Okay, guys, give us five minutes to adjust the lights and we'll shoot it.

Phil   Thanks, Frasier.

Frasier   It's my pleasure, Phil. You deserve to be our next Congressman.

Niles   Of course he does. He's a man of the people, just like us! By the way, my wife, Maris, has all our servants down at your campaign headquarters licking envelopes, so I have to do the marketing. Do you know where one goes to purchase food in this town?

Phil   Well, there's a supermarket on just about every corner.

Niles   Well noted. You really know this town, don't you?

Daphne enters with Eddie through the front door.

Frasier   Daphne, I thought our agreement was that you'd keep him out of here for two hours.

Daphne   Well, I walked him around the park, but you know how he gets. He starts whining and whimpering until you can't stand it any longer.

Phil   *(to Eddie)* Don't let her talk about you like that little fella…

Martin enters through the front door.

Martin   She was talking about me. Hi, Marty Crane.

Phil   Phil Patterson. You look familiar, Mr. Crane, but I can't quite place you.

Martin starts to pull down his pants near his hip to expose his scar.

Martin   Maybe this'll help.

Frasier   Dad… *(To Phil)* My father made a commercial for your opponent.

Phil   Oh yes, the retired policeman.

Martin   I did it because me and Thorpe are tough, "take no prisoners" kind of men. None of that namby-pamby, sensitive guy stuff.

Phil   Well you made a very effective spot.

Martin   Really? You don't think I looked jowly?

Daphne   *(to Phil)* If you get elected, I hope you'll do something about that little pothole in front of our building. Mr. Crane swears a bloody blue streak every time he drives over it.

Phil   That is a problem. Unfortunately in this era of budget cutbacks, it's getting increasingly more difficult to allocate money for road work, especially in the face of big issues like homelessness, crime in the streets, and unemployment.

Daphne   Well, whenever you get to it….

Frasier   It's getting awfully hot in here with all the lights. Why don't we go out on the balcony and get some fresh air?

Frasier leads Phil out to the balcony.

Phil   Beautiful view.

Frasier   Thank you, I feel very lucky living here. I must say, I also feel quite lucky to be a part of your campaign.

Phil   Hey, it's me who's lucky. It's quite a boost for an underdog to be getting an endorsement from Frasier Crane.

Frasier   Oh, I don't know that my name carries that much weight.

Phil   Oh come on, people love you. I've listened to your show. To tell you the truth, I've even thought of calling in.

Frasier   Oh, you're just saying that.

Phil   No, really.

Frasier   About what?

Phil   Ah… It's kind of sensitive.

Frasier   Phil, speaking as a psychiatrist, anything you tell me will be kept in the strictest confidence. *(A beat, Phil's on the fence)* You know, when you keep things bottled up they often seem much bigger than they really are.

Phil   Well, I've never told anyone this before but okay, here goes. Six years ago I was abducted by aliens.

Pause.

Frasier   Aliens…?

Phil   They transported me up to their spaceship for a kind of conference. They're very concerned about what we're doing to our planet. *(Then)* Hey, you were right. Now that I've said it out loud, it doesn't seem like that big a deal.

Frasier   No…

They are interrupted by Niles.

Niles   They're ready for you, gentlemen. Come on in here and let's elect a Congressman.

Off Frasier's look, we:

FADE OUT.

END OF ACT ONE

ACT TWO
SCENE E

    FADE IN:

INT. FRASIER'S LIVING ROOM — A SHORT WHILE LATER — NIGHT 3

    As before, Frasier is sitting in his Eames at the window, looking out at the skyline. After a beat, he turns — this time he's startled, looking at the camera like a deer caught in headlights.

Frasier   Oh, hello there. I'm *(puts hand in front of mouth muffling words)* Dr. Frasier Crane…

Jimmy   Cut! Frasier, your hand's in front of your mouth — and you're really sweating. What's wrong?

Frasier   Must be the lights.

Jimmy   Okay, let's try it again. Roll it.

    Frasier stands at the window. After a beat he turns toward the camera. As before, he reads from the cue cards, his new knowledge making it increasingly difficult to get through the lines. Martin, Daphne and Niles watch from off-camera.

Frasier   Oh, hello there. I'm *(sorry to admit it)* Dr. Frasier Crane. Many of you know me from my radio show, but today I'm speaking to you as a private citizen… a concerned citizen… a *deeply* concerned citizen. As a mental health expert, I've been listening to what my good friend Phil Patterson has to say. I like the way his mind works. He's a visionary, and he cares about the little people. That's why I'm proud to say that I'm behind Phil Patterson for Congress.

    Phil Patterson walks into frame.

Phil   Thanks, Frasier. Together we can live the dream.

    Instead of a hearty hug, Frasier awkwardly pats Phil on the shoulder.

Frasier   Phil Patterson. The sane choice.

Jimmy   Okay, cut!

Frasier   God, I'm just burning up.

Daphne   Oh, you were wonderful, Dr. Crane. Very natural.

    She turns away, making a face to Martin that indicates she didn't think it was very good.

Jimmy	Frasier, you seemed a little nervous that time. Why don't you take a couple of minutes and we'll try it again.
Martin	I got mine on the first take.
Niles	Frasier, may I see you in the kitchen for a moment?
	Frasier follows Niles into the kitchen.
Niles	What's going on? You looked like a zombie out there.
Frasier	Oh God, Niles, something awful has happened. I'm dying to get it off my chest, but if I tell you, I'll be violating a doctor/patient confidence.
Niles	Ohhh, I see. Nothing is more sacrosanct than our professional ethics. Fortunately, I know a trick to get around them. For the next ten minutes, *I'll* be *your* psychiatrist, then you can spill your guts with impunity.
Frasier	It's borderline, but I'm desperate.
Niles	Okay — I'm the doctor, you're the patient, make it juicy.
Frasier	Just now on the balcony Phil Patterson told me he'd been abducted by aliens.
	Niles' face registers his incredible shock and dismay.
Frasier	He claims he was beamed up to the mother ship for a little interplanetary chit chat.
Niles	*(a beat)* This is bad, isn't it? *(Then hopeful)* He was kidding.
Frasier	No.
Niles	You're kidding?
Frasier	No.
Niles	You're kidding…
Frasier	If this gets out, we're going to look like idiots.
Niles	We? This was your idea. I knew I shouldn't have let you drag me into politics.
	They go into one of their rapid-fire exchanges, with lines like… "I didn't drag you." "You're so manipulative." "It'll be like Camelot again." "Oh, you had to be on all the A party lists." "You always placed the blame on me as a child." "That's how I got stuck with Dad…" etc.
Frasier	Stop it, Niles. This isn't getting us anywhere.
Niles	You're right, you're right. What are we going to do?
Frasier	Obviously we're going to have to convince Phil to drop out of the

race and seek professional help.

Niles   But if Phil drops out, Thorpe will win.

Frasier   Forget it, Niles.

Niles   Then you can also forget about the environment, education, funding for the arts…

Frasier   So you're still suggesting that we back this man?

Niles   Well, answer me this. Can you tell me with any certainty that in such a vast universe there *isn't* intelligent life on other planets?

Frasier   At the moment, I'm not sure there's intelligent life in this kitchen.

Niles   Okay, let's assume it was all in his imagination. How often does he see these aliens?

Frasier   Only the one time. *(Encouraged)* Which might suggest an isolated incident brought on by overwork rather than a pattern of paranoid delusion.

Niles   My diagnosis exactly.

Frasier   Phil's worked hard. He deserves his chance. Of course, we still have to see that he gets counseling.

Niles   The very best there is. But we're not going to turn our backs on him three weeks before the election.

Frasier   No, dammit, we're not.

Daphne enters the kitchen.

Daphne   Dr. Crane, you seem to be having a little attack of stage fright and I just remembered a tip my uncle told me. Whenever you feel threatened by your audience just imagine everyone in the room is stark naked.

Frasier   Thank you, Daphne. But I'm not nervous any longer.

Frasier starts out. Niles stares transfixed at Daphne.

Frasier   Niles, are you "ready to live the dream?"

Niles   *(longing)* Oh, yes.

As Frasier grabs Niles and they exit out of the kitchen, we:

FADE OUT.

SCENE H

> *A black screen. In white letters appears, "The Fault Lies Not in Our Stars, But in Ourselves."*

> *FADE IN:*

INT. RADIO STUDIO — A FEW WEEKS LATER — DAY 4

> *Frasier is on the air with a caller, Madman Martinez.*

Madman Martinez *(v.o.)* I don't understand it, Doc. I'm a successful guy. I have my own car dealership. But still I'm depressed. You've probably heard of me, Madman Martinez.

Frasier What seems to be the source of your depression, Madman?

Madman Martinez *(v.o.)* I guess it's just that business is down. I don't know why. I slashed prices this week. Right now I got an '88 Olds Cutlass on the lot in rare turquoise metallic, Cordova roof, leather, factory air...

Frasier *(getting dubious)* Madman...

Madman Martinez *(v.o.)* And that's nothing compared to the six brand new Supras I got in. They're priced to sell with a twenty percent discount to all your listeners. People say to me, "Madman, you're crazy," but I say, "Hey, I deal in volume so..."

Frasier So do I.

> *Frasier slides the volume down and Madman Martinez fades out.*

Frasier This is Dr. Frasier Crane. We'll be back after these *paid* commercial messages.

> *Frasier crosses into Roz's booth.*

Frasier Roz, could you be a scoche more discriminating in screening the calls?

> *Roz stares at herself in a compact mirror and doesn't answer.*

Frasier Roz...

Roz I think it's time to get my eyebrows waxed. I'm starting to get that Romanian peasant look again. Of course, it also doesn't help that I didn't sleep much last night.

Frasier Dating a snorer?

Roz You know, I'm getting a little tired of your constant insinuation that I sleep around. I didn't sleep because of that idiot Chopper Dave. When he gets bored doing traffic reports, he likes to buzz people's apartments.

Frasier   I can see how that would be annoying.

Roz   Well, it didn't bother me so much, but the guy I was with is a Vietnam vet and he started having flashbacks.

Bulldog bounds into the booth.

Bulldog   Greetings, losers. Have you heard the great news?

Frasier   Let me guess. One of your over-paid idols passed his urine test.

Bulldog   Laugh while you can. Word's out about your pal Patterson and those aliens of his.

Frasier   Oh dear God.

Roz   What aliens?

Bulldog   It's all over the TV.

Frasier   But how did they find out?

Bulldog   Are you kidding? You can't keep something like this quiet. Every station in town's serving his bleeding heart up on a platter.

Frasier   Isn't that always the way. They're like a pack of jackals sensing a fresh kill. They'll destroy a man's career just to feed the public curiosity. Well I have my own conduit to the public ear and I'm not letting Phil go down without a fight!

Frasier marches back into his booth.

Roz   What aliens?

Bulldog   Turns out Patterson's got a couple of illegals from Uruguay working in his house. No green cards, no documents, no chance.

Bulldog exits. Angle on Frasier, back on the air.

Frasier   I'm back, Seattle, and while we were in commercial, I learned it's now public knowledge that Phil Patterson, candidate for Congress, believes in aliens from outer space. He not only believes in them, he believes he's met them, that he was beamed aboard their spaceship where he engaged in an intergalactic tête à tête! Shocked?

We see Roz. She's shocked. During the following, she gestures to Frasier to stop. Her gestures grow increasingly more and more frantic.

Frasier   Well, all right, but let's ask ourselves these questions: Has this harmless delusion, most likely the result of over-work and sleep deprivation, adversely affected his voting record? I say, "No!"

Roz makes one final gesture to stop Frasier. Frasier waves her off. Roz realizes this is hopeless and gives up. She goes back to looking at herself in her compact.

Frasier   Don't all great leaders have their quirks? Reagan saw astrologers, General Patton believed in reincarnation, even J. Edgar Hoover let his slip show once in a while. People, we're talking about a great leader here. We shouldn't concern ourselves with a minor eccentricity. What's important is what's in here. I'm pointing to my chest now…

And as Frasier continues to hang himself, we:

FADE OUT.

SCENE J

A black screen. In white letters appears, "The Party's Over."

FADE IN:

INT. FRASIER'S LIVING ROOM — THE NEXT EVENING — DAY 5

Martin and Daphne are watching the election results on TV. Frasier is sitting alone at the table with his head in his hands.

TV Announcer   *(v.o.)* …The results from the last precinct are in. Holden Thorpe has been elected to Congress garnering a whopping ninety-two percent of the vote.

Martin turns off the TV.

Daphne   Well at least Mr. Patterson got eight percent.

Martin   They must be counting absentee ballots from the planet Xenon.

Frasier groans.

Daphne   Now, Dr. Crane, it wasn't all your fault. I'm sure having those Uruguayans in his home would have cost him some votes anyway.

Frasier   Those Uruguayans were on a student exchange program. Phil was giving them free room and board as a goodwill gesture between countries.

Daphne exits to her bedroom.

Martin   Well I'd like to stay here and gloat, but me and Daphne have to get dressed for the big victory party down at Thorpe headquarters. I'm sure you're welcome to tag along. You're kind of a hero down there.

Frasier   No, thank you.

Martin exits down the hall.

Frasier   *(slapping his forehead)* Stupid! Stupid! Stupid! *(Stops)* When will I learn it hurts when I do that?

   SFX: The doorbell rings. Frasier crosses and opens the door to Phil Patterson, who is holding a necktie.

Frasier   Phil! I, uh…

Phil   Hello, Frasier. I just came by to return this good luck tie you loaned me.

Frasier   Yes, I saw you wearing it on television when you delivered your concession speech.

Phil   A little embarrassing having to do it before lunch. On the other hand it gave me time to run some errands and pick up my dry cleaning.

Frasier   Phil, I'm so sorry about the misunderstanding.

Phil   Hey, it's okay. I know you didn't do it on purpose. You thought you were defending me.

Frasier   Still, I'm going to be reminded of this every day for the next two years. The people of Seattle deserve better than Holden Thorpe.

Phil   That's politics. It's just one election. I'll be back.

Frasier   Do you really think you can?

Phil   Maybe I'm a dreamer, but I like to believe anything's possible. Who knows, we might even work together again.

Frasier   I'd like that.

Phil   Maybe I'll run in California. A thing like this could actually help me there.

   Phil exits. Frasier closes the door and walks out to the balcony. He looks up at the stars.

Frasier   Anything's possible.

   A beat, then suddenly a light comes into view accompanied by a loud whooping sound. As it approaches, the light grows brighter and the sound louder. Frasier's eyes widen a little terrified. Then:

Frasier   Very funny, Chopper Dave!

   And we:

   CUT TO BLACK.

END OF ACT TWO

SEAT OF POWER

Written by
Steven Levitan

Created and Developed by
David Angell, Peter Casey, David Lee

Directed by
James Burrows

ACT ONE

SCENE A

> *FADE IN:*

INT. RADIO STUDIO — DAY — DAY 1

> *Frasier is on the air. Roz is in her booth.*

Frasier	I think we have time for one more call. Roz, who's up next?
Roz	Elliott is on line three.

> *Frasier hits line three and we hear Elliott, an adolescent boy who's trying to sound like an adult.*

Frasier	Hello, Elliott, I'm listening.
Elliott	*(v.o.)* Well, you see, Dr. Crane, I have this problem. I'm a salesman and…
Frasier	A salesman. How old are you?
Elliott	*(v.o.)* Forty-three.
Frasier	Forty-three?
Elliott	*(v.o.)* Yeah.
Frasier	Let's be truthful now.
Elliott	*(v.o.) (adamant)* I'm forty-three.
Frasier	Elliott, I wasn't born yesterday. Clearly, you are an adolescent trying to prove to your little friends how clever you are by getting on the radio, but what you're really doing is taking time away from people with real problems.
Elliott	*(v.o.) (angry)* Hey, I'm forty-three and I was going to say my problem is I have a very young-sounding voice that people make fun of all the time.
Frasier	*(embarrassed)* Elliott, I'm so sorry. That was terribly insensitive.
Elliott	*(v.o.)* Hah! Gotcha, Doctor Doofus!

> *We hear howls of laughter from Elliott's young friends.*

Frasier	Yes, you did "get us," Elliott. But, we're not so stuffy on this program that we can't enjoy a good laugh at ourselves every once in a while.

> *Frasier hits a button, taking him off the air momentarily.*

Frasier	*(furious)* Roz, can't you keep these pimply-faced little maggots off the air?

> *Roz doesn't react and Frasier hits another button and goes back*

on the air.

Frasier   Well, that's our show for today. This is Dr. Crane, wishing you good mental health.

He hits a button and they're off the air.

Frasier   Have a nice weekend, Roz.

Frasier exits into her booth.

Roz   Frasier, I'm going to ask you a question and I'd like an honest answer.

Frasier   No, that outfit does not make you look fat.

Roz   That wasn't the question. *(A little annoyed)* Why would you think it was?

Frasier   Because whenever a woman prefaces a question with "I'd like an honest answer," that's usually the question.

Roz   Well, I'm not that insecure.

Frasier   Of course you're not. I'm sorry. What is your question…?

Roz   Would you say the back of my head is unattractive?

Frasier   Have you completely lost your mind?

Roz   I'm serious. You know how I have season tickets to the Seahawks games? Well, there's this really cute guy who sits right behind me. A few weeks ago, he smiled at me and we said hi, but so far he hasn't asked me out. So, I started to think that maybe the back of my head is, you know, weird.

Frasier   But there could be hundreds of reasons why he hasn't asked you out.

Roz   Thanks, I feel much better now.

Frasier   Maybe he's married or in a relationship. Maybe he's gay. Or maybe, just maybe, he's there to watch a football game, not cruise chicks.

Frasier grabs his briefcase and starts for the door.

Roz   You're right, I'm being ridiculous.

Frasier   Of course you are. See you Monday.

Frasier detours to check out the back of Roz's head.

Roz   I saw that. *(Beat)* So what do you think? Is it too flat?

On Frasier's reaction, we:

FADE OUT.

SCENE B

> *A black screen. In white letters appears, "Heir to the Throne."*

> *FADE IN:*

INT. FRASIER'S LIVING ROOM — SATURDAY MORNING — DAY 2

> *Frasier is dressed casually, drinking a cup of coffee and eating a scone while reading the morning newspaper. Eddie just stares at him. Frasier won't look at Eddie.*

Frasier   *(without looking at Eddie)* You're not getting any of my scone, so just forget it. *(Beat)* And it's really good too. *(Beat)* Look, you may think you can wear me down, but as far as I'm concerned, you're not even here. *(Eddie keeps staring)* Oh, for God's sake, here. Get fat.

> *Frasier gives him the rest of the scone. Eddie retreats to enjoy it in peace, passing Martin as he enters.*

Martin   He got you again, huh? You're such a soft touch.

Frasier   I am not.

Martin   He never begs when *I'm* eating.

Frasier   Maybe he doesn't like what you eat.

Martin   Trust me, he's not picky. I've seen him eat a beetle.

> *Daphne enters with a leash.*

Daphne   *(calling)* Eddie... Let's go for a walk.

Martin   *(to Daphne)* I thought you already walked him this morning.

Daphne   I did, twice. Eddie...

Martin   He has to go again?

> *She hooks the leash onto Eddie's collar.*

Daphne   No, actually, I do. *(Beat)* That didn't sound right. There's a very nice-looking gentleman who plays frisbee with his Labrador in the park. Eddie and I are hoping to run into them. *(To Eddie)* C'mon.

> *She takes a few steps but Eddie doesn't.*

Daphne   C'mon, Eddie. He's just playing hard to get.

Frasier   I'm glad somebody is.

> *Daphne and Eddie exit.*

Martin   Would you please do me a favor and take care of that toilet of yours? It's running and the noise is driving me crazy.

Frasier   Sure, Dad, I'll call the plumber.

Martin   Plumber? You got two hands, fix it yourself.

SFX: The doorbell rings. Frasier goes to the door.

Frasier   Dad, I am a doctor. I've got more important things to do than fix a toilet.

Frasier opens the door.

Frasier   Hello Niles.

Niles enters.

Niles   Good news, Frasier. I pulled some strings at the spa and they're squeezing us in for a salt-glow with our Swedish massage.

Martin   Forget the plumber, I'll do it myself. My manicurist cancelled on me.

Frasier   No, you won't, Dad.

Martin   I'll bet you don't even have any tools around here.

Frasier   As a matter of fact, yes, I do. Here… *(Produces a ridiculous little gadget)* Every tool you ever need all in one. *(To Niles)* Hammacher-Schlemmer.

Niles   Is that turquoise inlay?

Frasier   They also have ebony and onyx.

Niles   Oh, onyx is so showy.

They both go on in this vein ad-libbing things like: "You think so?", "That's how I feel about ivory.", "But I gave you those onyx cufflinks.", "Yes, I know." etc.

Martin   This is why I never took home movies. *(Beat)* Do you realize what a couple of delicate doilies the two of you are? You don't know the meaning of the word self-sufficient. God forbid there should ever be a national disaster. You'd be helpless.

Martin exits toward his bedroom.

Niles   *(re: tool)* Oh, a garlic press.

Frasier   You know, I'm not usually one for this kind of challenge, but I'd like to fix that toilet just to prove Dad wrong.

Niles   Frasier, when a man is born with superior genes, the last challenge he should face involving a toilet is learning how to use one.

Frasier   Come on, Niles, we've conquered the intellectual world, but in the nuts-and-bolts world, we're at the mercy of tradesmen.

Niles   You're serious?

Frasier   Yes, we'll borrow some tools and fix it ourselves. It'll be good practical experience and, more importantly, it'll shut Dad up.

Niles   Well that's certainly appealing. We'll show him we're made of tougher stuff than he thinks.

Frasier   Exactly.

Niles   And it's still early. We can let the eucalyptus wrap be our reward.

And we:

FADE OUT.

SCENE C

A black screen. In white letters appears, "If You Want It Done Right."

FADE IN:

INT. FRASIER'S BATHROOM — AN HOUR OR SO LATER — DAY 2

Frasier and Niles have been working diligently on the toilet. Each has a grease stain or two. While Frasier assembles a few parts, Niles sits on the toilet lid, speaking to Maris on the wall phone.

Niles   *(into phone)* Maris, I'm afraid I'll be delayed a few hours. *(Beat)* Frasier and I have taken it upon ourselves to tackle a home repair. *(Beat)* Yes, I'm working with my hands. *(Beat)* Yes, I've worked up a bit of a sweat. *(Beat)* I suppose I could take my shirt off.

Frasier   What are you doing?

Niles   *(covering phone)* She seems to be getting aroused by my attempt at manual labor. *(Into phone)* Maris, I'm holding some sort of wrench.

Frasier   *(grabbing the phone)* Give me that! *(Into phone)* Maris, Niles is busy right now. *(Beat)* Never mind what I'm wearing.

Frasier hangs up, then takes up his position under the toilet.

Frasier   May we continue?

Niles   Fine. *(Referring to a book)* Take the ball-cock assembly and thread it through the tank hole and fasten it to a... *(Handing it to him)* locknut under the tank.

Frasier   See, before today you didn't even know what a locknut was.

Niles   That Niles is dead. Call me Dutch.

Frasier   *(as he works)* You know, working with our hands like this, I'm reminded of the glorious tradition of the Amish barn-raising. The men of the village coming together, the minds, the muscle, working as one toward that simple, yet extraordinary goal. *(Then)* All right, we're ready to flush!

Frasier turns the water back on.

Niles   Well, here's to what the Crane brothers can accomplish when they put their minds to it. Flush away.

They clink their tools in a toast. Frasier flushes the toilet. They watch intently.

Frasier   It's working. It's actually working! The water's rushing out of the tank into the bowl.

Niles   *(suddenly into it, referring to the book)* Now the bowl is refilling… Then the tank… I've seen it a million times but never has it meant so much. *(Beat, suddenly concerned)* Frasier, shouldn't the water be stopping now?

Frasier   One would think so.

The toilet overflows.

Niles   It's overflowing.

Frasier   I can see that! What does the book say about this?

Niles   *(furiously flipping through the book)* It doesn't! Where are all your Amish friends now?!!!

Frasier starts bailing water into the tub, and we:

FADE OUT.

SCENE D

A black screen. In white letters appears, "The Circle of Life."

FADE IN:

INT. FRASIER'S LIVING ROOM — A SHORT TIME LATER — DAY 2

Frasier is almost dried off. Niles enters with two glasses of wine.

Niles   The plumber's on the way, the wine's properly chilled, suddenly my world makes sense again.

Frasier   Yes, we put in a tough day, tangled with a little pipe and porcelain, now "It's Montrachet time."

Niles	You know, when you think about it, our only mistake today was trying to fix that toilet ourselves.
Frasier	Yes, we were tampering with the natural order of things.
Niles	But now order has been restored. By hiring a plumber, that plumber can afford, say, a Dolly Parton album. Which means that Dolly can then finance a national tour, which will stop in Seattle, allowing a local promoter to make enough money to send his cross-dressing teenage son to us for one-hundred-and-fifty-dollar-an-hour therapy.
Frasier	To the circle of life.
	They clink their glasses. Martin enters from the bedroom. SFX: The doorbell rings.
Frasier	That must be the plumber.
Martin	Well, are you gonna answer it or are you gonna hire someone to do that for you too?
Frasier	Dad, we tried, okay?
	SFX: The doorbell rings again.
	Daphne enters from the bathroom with a wet mop.
Daphne	Oh, please, I wasn't doing anything, let me get it.
	She answers the door. Danny Kriezel, the plumber, stands on the other side with all his tools.
Danny	Somebody call a plumber?
Daphne	*(glaring at Frasier and Niles)* Not nearly soon enough.
Martin	Just follow me.
	Martin leads him toward the bathroom.
Daphne	*(re: mop)* What a lovely way to spend an afternoon.
Frasier	Sorry, Daphne, we're not plumbers. We're psychiatrists.
Daphne	Well, there are some heads you shouldn't tamper with.
	Daphne exits down the hall. Niles freezes. A horrified expression comes to his face.
Niles	Frasier, you've got to get him out of here.
Frasier	Why?
Niles	The man isn't fit to touch your toilet.
Frasier	Niles, are you self-medicating again?
Niles	That was Danny Kriezel.

Frasier	Kriezel the weasel?
Niles	Yes!
Frasier	Are you sure? It's been twenty-five years.
Niles	I'd recognize him anywhere. He bullied me throughout my childhood. You could pluck my eyes out — by the way he tried to do that — and I would be one-hundred-percent sure that was him.
Frasier	Well, he certainly didn't recognize you just now.
Niles	*(snapping)* That's because he wasn't flushing my head in a toilet! That was his trademark. He called it a swirly!!
Frasier	Niles, I don't need to be reminded of the Kriezels reign of terror. I'm confident my fear of confined spaces can be traced back to when his brother Billy shoved me in a locker wearing a girl's field hockey uniform.
Niles	I'm sorry. I didn't mean to deny you your pain.
Frasier	Thank you.
Niles	I can still hear the laughter, and Kriezel's mocking voice as he'd hoist me over the bowl: "Hold your breath, jocko." Then the crowd would begin its awful chant, "There goes Crane, down the drain. There goes Crane, down the drain. There…"
Frasier	*(interrupting)* Niles, get hold of yourself. You're not an awkward teenager anymore. You're a renowned psychiatrist. Danny Kriezel may have won a battle or two in junior high, but that's where his life peaked. You won the war. You know the expression: "Living well is the best revenge."
Niles	It's a wonderful expression, but I don't know how true it is. You don't see that turning up in a lot of opera plots: Ludvig, maddened by the poisoning of his entire family, wreaks vengeance on Gunther in the third act by living well.
Frasier	All right, Niles…
	They cross to the kitchen. As they go:
Niles	Whereupon, Woton, discovering his deception, avenges his betrayal by living even better than the duke.
Frasier	Oh, all right. It's just an expression.
	As they exit into the kitchen, we:
	CUT TO:

SCENE E

INT. FRASIER'S BATHROOM — TEN MINUTES LATER — DAY 2

> *Martin is watching Danny work on the toilet. Danny is in the process of putting in a new part.*

Martin   That's a new part, right?

Danny   Yeah.

Martin   Because I'm sure you're charging me for a new part and I wouldn't want you using a used part.

Danny   Who are you, the plumbing police? It's not bad enough I have to drive around town with a giant, inflatable toilet on top of my truck, but now I gotta take your abuse too.

Martin   I'll be back.

> *Martin exits. Danny continues to work. After a beat Niles enters carrying a glass of wine and crosses to the medicine cabinet.*

Niles   Don't mind me. I just came in for a few aspirin. Tannic acid gives me the tiniest headache, but that's the price I pay for drinking nothing but expensive wines.

> *Danny doesn't respond. He keeps working on the toilet.*

Danny   You've got a mess here. I'm going to have to call the shop and have my partner bring over some parts. We're looking at two men on golden time, okay?

Niles   It's only money.

Danny   Has somebody been trying to fix this thing?

Niles   Not me. I don't even try to set the clock in my Mercedes E320.

Danny   Hey, that's a nice car.

Niles   Yes, I should say it is.

Danny   I had one for a while, but it was too small for the family so I traded up to an S-Class.

Niles   You have the big Mercedes?

Danny   Yeah, and I'll tell you, my thirteen-year-old already has his eye on it. What a great kid. Except for the other day, he got into a fight at school.

Niles   Oh, with some small-boned child with superior language skills?

Danny   No, with some big jerk on the football team who took his lunch money.

Niles   Yes, there's nothing worse than a bully.

Danny   I'd rather my kid be a bully than one of those wussy kids who always get picked on. You know the kind I'm talking about, the ones who are too gutless to fight back.

Danny kneels down and reaches deep into the tank to remove some part. His head is perched precariously over the bowl. Niles takes this in.

Niles   So, you admire someone who fights back?

Danny   Sure. If you don't fight back, what are you? You're a wimp, a wuss...

There's a beat, then Niles drops a coin into the toilet bowl.

Niles   Oops!

Danny   Nice going, jocko!

Danny reaches into the bowl to get the coin and Niles moves in for the kill. As he's about to dunk Danny's head, Frasier enters.

Frasier   Stop!

He rushes in and restrains Niles.

Danny   Stop what?

Frasier   *(covering)* Stop bothering this man while he's trying to work.

And as Frasier pulls Niles out, still enraged and trying to get at Danny, we:

FADE OUT.

END OF ACT ONE

ACT TWO

SCENE H

FADE IN:

INT. FRASIER'S LIVING ROOM — MOMENTS LATER — DAY 2

Eddie is there. Niles paces out on the balcony. At every turn he swats at the leaves of a plant. Daphne enters and notices Niles.

Daphne   What's Dr. Crane doing?

Frasier   He's just a little frustrated because I wouldn't let him do something. He's taking his anger out on my ficus.

Niles begins swatting wildly.

Daphne   My, I've never seen him so angry. He's like a mad man.

Niles runs in still swatting wildly.

Niles   Good Lord, there's a bee out there the size of a wood finch.

Frasier   Niles, you've had some time to cool off. Can we talk about this now?

Niles   I'm not ready yet.

Niles moves off to the kitchen. Daphne has gone to the telescope and is peering out.

Daphne   Oh, my, is that…? Yes! It's Frisbee Boy and his Labrador. Eddie, ready for another walk?

Eddie pretends to fall asleep.

Daphne   Oh, please, like I never did anything for you. I know you're not really sleeping. Let's go.

Eddie gets up and goes to the door.

Daphne   And this time, there will be none of that embarrassing sniffing. Well, at least from you.

Daphne and Eddie exit. Frasier joins Niles in the kitchen where Niles is pouring a glass of wine.

Frasier   I have to be honest, Niles, I'm a little disappointed in you. Were you really going to stick another human being's head in a toilet?

Niles   Yes, and if you hadn't stopped me, right now I would be savoring my revenge.

Frasier   No, right now you'd be at the emergency room having a pipe wrench-ectomy.

Niles   It would have been worth it. *(Beat)* You don't seem to understand. I feel this rage. It's as if this beast has been awakened in me.

He hands Frasier a bottle.

Niles   Could you help me with this?

Frasier   Niles, please, we all have a beast inside of us, but part of being a healthy adult is knowing how to control it. That's what separates us from the Kriezels of the world.

Niles   That and their tendency to squat on their haunches and groom each other.

Frasier   Yes, but you have the opportunity to do something with Danny Kriezel that I never had the chance to do with Billy — to confront him as a calm, rational adult and achieve closure.

Niles   Easier said than done. The minute you look into that blank, oafish face, those dead Kriezel eyes — you realize there's no hope for communication.

Frasier   Yes, there is, Niles. There has to be.

Niles   *(thinks, then)* I can't go back in there. The minute that coward turns his back, I'll attack him again.

Frasier   No, you won't. You're not a child anymore. Now come with me. I'm taking you to the bathroom.

As they go, we:

CUT TO:

SCENE J

INT. FRASIER'S BATHROOM — CONTINUOUS — DAY 2

Frasier and Niles enter the bathroom. Danny Kriezel is working near the toilet, another workman lies beneath the toilet tank. Frasier gives Niles a sign of encouragement. Niles clears his throat, then:

Niles   *(to Danny)* Excuse me, sir. May I have a word with you?

Danny   *(sighs)* Yeah, sure. Go ahead.

Danny puts down what he's doing and faces Niles.

Niles   I'd like to take you back in time to the nineteen seventies. There was an intellectually-gifted young student who went to John Adams Jr. High School…

Danny   Hey, I think I went there.

Niles   You did, Danny. *(Beat)* You took it upon yourself to terrorize that student only because he was different than you. I was that student.

Danny   No kidding?

Niles   I was hoping that we could step into the living room and try to come to some understanding.

Frasier gives Niles an approving glance.

Danny   Okay with me. Whatever room I'm in it's fifty-nine an hour. *(To the other plumber)* I'll be right back, Billy.

Niles exits and Danny follows.

Frasier   *(taken aback)* Billy?

Billy   That's my brother for you, always getting into stuff. But, you ask me, your friend there's getting all worked up over nothing.

Frasier   You think so, Billy…?

Billy   Kids pick on other kids. It's all just a part of growing up. If anything, it made those weak kids tougher.

Frasier   Really?

Billy   Come on, you're a big guy. I'm sure you were involved in some of this stuff.

Frasier   Oh, I was involved. In fact, I'd like to take you back in time to...

Billy   No, let me take you back first. I remember once we jammed this poindexter into a locker wearing a girl's field hockey uniform. Half the school saw the janitor cut off the lock and pull him out wearing a white blouse and a little plaid skirt.

Frasier   *(controlled rage)* I'm sure he made it work.

CUT TO:

SCENE K

INT. FRASIER'S LIVING ROOM — SAME TIME — DAY 2

Danny is staring at Niles from several different angles obviously trying to place him, then:

Danny   Nope. Sorry. I just don't remember you.

Niles   Well, maybe you remember third period gym class. You used to make me wear my jock strap like a tiara.

Danny   Wait a minute. Are you the guy who used to carry your gym shorts in an attaché case?

Niles   It was a valise.

Danny   Oh, yeah, now I remember you. Those were some crazy times, huh. You ever see any of the old gang?

Niles   You're missing the point. I was severely scarred by those experiences.

Danny   Hey, look, I can't defend everything I did in junior high. Who can? But let's face it. When you show up at school wearing a tweed blazer with elbow patches and carrying a "valise"... I mean, I think the guilt here is fifty-fifty.

CUT TO:

SCENE L

INT. FRASIER'S BATHROOM — SAME TIME — DAY 2

Billy laughs as he recounts another of his pranks.

Billy	… he's yelling something at us about "repressed tendencies," so we stuck a fire extinguisher down his pants. We called it…
Frasier	A jet pack!
Billy	*(howling with laughter)* That's it! Man, you know 'em all!
Frasier	But, you know, on the subject of repressed tendencies…
Billy	Hey, did you ever pack a guy's nose with cottage cheese?

As the rage builds in Frasier, he tenses up and squeezes a toothpaste tube. As a stream of toothpaste squirts out, we:

CUT TO:

SCENE N

INT. FRASIER'S LIVING ROOM — SAME TIME — DAY 2

Niles and Danny are now both seated.

Niles	*(very much the psychiatrist)* Well, then my next question to you would be, why did you behave that way?
Danny	*(contrite)* I don't know. I guess because people thought it was funny.
Niles	I see. So, to get this validation, you would, say, squeeze my head between your ankles and hop around the lunchroom.
Danny	I did that to you?
Niles	Yes. How does that make you feel?
Danny	Kinda bad.
Niles	Go on.
Danny	I mean I was a real jerk.
Niles	*(with a self-satisfied smile)* Good. Good. The healing has begun.

CUT TO:

SCENE P

INT. FRASIER'S BATHROOM — SAME TIME — DAY 2

Billy resumes working as he talks. Now he reaches around to the tank with his head perched above the bowl.

Billy	*(laughing as he recalls)* So in front of the whole bus we pantsed him.

Frasier gets the same crazed look Niles had before.

Billy	He's yelling at me to give him his pants back but, oops, they fell out the window.
Frasier	*(incensed, but laughing along)* Oh, that's rich.
Billy	*(with delight)* Then we made him dance the hula in his underwear in front of all the girls.

Frasier moves closer, his hands reaching for Billy's head.

Billy	*(singing)* A-lo-ha oy…

Billy snickers derisively.

Billy	You shoulda been there.
Frasier	I was there!

As Frasier closes in, we:

CUT TO:

SCENE R

INT. FRASIER'S LIVING ROOM — SAME TIME — DAY 2

The "session" continues:

Niles	…then, it's possible these acts of aggression were actually misdirected outbursts aimed at your father?
Danny	*(teary)* Yes.
Niles	He was the real bully, wasn't he?
Danny	*(emotional)* Yes!
Niles	Let it out, Danny. Let it out.
Danny	Nothing I ever did was good enough for him. I'm so sorry I picked on you, man. I just wanted to be good at something, and I was good at that.
Niles	You were the best.
Danny	Thank you. Man, this has been terrific for me.
Niles	I can't take all the credit. Half of the thanks belongs to my brother. He convinced me that a civilized adult can work anything out as long as he approaches it in a calm, rational manner.

SFX: Toilet flushing. Suddenly Frasier runs screaming through the room.

Frasier	Run, Niles, run! The beast is loose!!!

Billy Kriezel runs in with wet hair. As he chases Frasier out the door, we:

DISSOLVE TO:

SCENE S

INT. FRASIER'S BATHROOM — A FEW HOURS LATER — DAY 2

> *Martin and Frasier are working on the toilet together. Eddie is staring.*

Martin   So, you really shoved his head right in here?

Frasier   I think so, Dad. The whole thing's a blur. I just lost all control.

Martin   It felt good, though, didn't it?

Frasier   No… It felt damn good.

Martin   If you'd listened to me twenty years ago, you could've given him a much better swirly. These low-flow toilets don't give you the same velocity as the old ones did. *(They share a laugh, then)* So, what'd he do to you?

Frasier   Nothing. He didn't dare touch me.

Martin   You paid him off, huh?

Frasier   I've never written a check so fast in my life.

> *Martin flushes the toilet. It's working once again.*

Martin   Well, she's good as new.

Frasier   Thanks a lot, Dad. Let me buy you a beer.

> *They head out. Over his shoulder, Martin notices Eddie lapping water out of the toilet bowl.*

Martin   Oh for God's sake, Eddie, don't drink out of the toilet. Some guy had his head in there.

> *As we:*

> *FADE OUT.*

END OF ACT TWO

SCENE T

END CREDITS

INT. FRASIER'S LIVING ROOM — DAY — DAY 2

> *Daphne repeatedly throws a frisbee, trying to teach Eddie. He never moves.*

> *FADE OUT.*

END OF SHOW

THE INNKEEPERS

Written by
David Lloyd

Created and Developed by
David Angell, Peter Casey, David Lee

Directed by
James Burrows

ACT ONE

SCENE A

> *FADE IN:*

INT. RADIO STUDIO — DAY — DAY 1

> *Gil Chesterton is on the air. Roz is in her booth listening to the show. Frasier enters.*

Frasier Hi, Roz.

Roz Hi. Gil's just finishing.

> *They listen to Gil.*

Gil …so, in the opinion of this critic, Mickey's Good Time Tavern is anything but. Dismal décor, perfunctory service and cuisine that's only marginally preferable to hunger. *(Then)* And finally: on a sadder note. Orsini's, the grande dame of Seattle restaurants, is putting up its shutters.

Roz I thought he was the grande dame of Seattle restaurants.

Gil Yes, after fifty-three years at the same location, Orsini's is closing its doors. And so tonight a sad adieu to an old friend. Until next time, this is Gil Chesterton saying "bon appetit, buon appetito, and nifty noshing."

Frasier I can't believe Orsini's is closing.

Roz I know — it's an institution.

Frasier When I brought Lilith home to meet the family, Dad took us there to celebrate — for want of a better word.

> *They enter Frasier's booth.*

Roz Gil, why is Orsini's closing?

Gil The owner's getting old; he wants to sell. And just between us, I'm afraid Orsini's is a bit like wine that's stayed too long in the cellar. It retains only memories of its former glory.

Frasier Not comping your check any more?

Gil Not for months now.

> *Gil exits.*

Frasier *(to Roz)* Have you ever been to Orsini's?

Roz Are you kidding? My typical date's idea of a gourmet evening is take-out, make out and home by "Letterman."

> *Niles appears at the door of the booth.*

Niles Knock, knock.

Frasier   Niles, this is not a good time for a visit. My show starts in two minutes.

Niles   Just enough time to show you the John Steinbeck first edition I bought at the rare book fair.

He takes a small, very thin book from the bag.

Niles   *St. Katy The Virgin* — in "Like-New" condition.

Frasier   Yes, well, she'd have to be, wouldn't she?

Niles   Quite a charming book, really. It's a shame more people haven't read it.

Roz   *(reaching)* Let's see.

Niles   *(snatching it back)* Don't touch. The smallest smudge decreases its value.

Frasier   So Niles — you'll never believe what thriving Seattle night spot is closing its doors.

Niles   Roz, you're moving?

Roz gives him a look, snatches up his book and bops him on the head with it, then hands it back to him.

Frasier   Orsini's is closing.

Niles   It can't be. It's part of Crane history. Grandfather took me there for my eighth birthday. *(Reflecting)* Childhood memories are so vivid: wearing paper hats — singing "Happy Birthday" — sending back the veal Prince Orloff.

Roz   What was wrong with your veal?

Niles   Nothing — but like all eight-year-olds I was full of the dickens. Still, that elegant room, that incomparable cuisine, gone?

Roz   *(interrupting them)* Thirty seconds, Frasier.

Frasier   You know what we should do? Tonight let's go to Orsini's for one glorious farewell dinner.

Niles   Why not? I'll make the reservations. It's still probably the most exquisite dining experience anyone could ask for. We'll take Dad. And Daphne.

Frasier   And Maris.

Niles   She wouldn't like it. She had a bad experience there once. It was one Christmas Eve long ago. An Italian soccer team was at the next table. Maris announced that she was in the mood for a goose, and, perhaps inevitably, tragedy ensued.

And we:

FADE OUT.

SCENE B

FADE IN:

INT. ORSINI'S RESTAURANT — THAT EVENING — NIGHT 1

It is old, ornate, faded — maybe potted palms that have seen better days, paintings on the walls so dark you can barely determine the subject, one very elderly waiter (Otto) fiddling with the silverware. The only customers are an older couple sharing a table. The owner is standing off to one side as Frasier, Niles, Martin and Daphne enter. Frasier and Niles are aghast at what they see.

Frasier (*sotto*) My God! What has happened to this place?

Niles I know. It's like running into a movie star you worshipped as a child, only time has left her hair brittle, her eyes sunken and dull, her skin waxy and sallow…

Martin Well, I've got quite an appetite. How 'bout you, Daph?

The owner approaches.

Owner Yes, sir. Did you have a reservation?

Frasier The name is Crane. For four…

Owner makes a show of checking his book.

Owner Ah yes. Let's see… Crane, Crane, Crane… (*A beat*) Was that smoking or non-smoking?

Frasier (*looking around*) Surprise us.

Owner Table nine is free. Right this way…

As he leads them to their table:

Owner Your waiter will be right with you.

Frasier Thank you.

The owner walks away. Niles spots the elderly waiter.

Niles Oh, look. It's Otto.

Frasier You know, I think it is. (*Explaining to Daphne*) Otto is legendary. He's been with them forever. Never writes an order down — keeps it all in his head. (*Calling*) Otto!

Startled, Otto looks around, then realizes they're calling him.

Otto Oh. Coming up…

He dodders toward them.

Otto (handing check) Your check, sir.

Frasier No, no, wrong table. We want menus.

Otto Oh, sorry.

As Otto crosses to the other table:

Otto I hate it when we're crowded.

Martin rises.

Martin I'm going to the men's room. Order me a beer.

Frasier Dad, in an Italian restaurant, it's customary to drink wine.

Martin It's also customary to get machine gunned in the middle of your pasta. We can bend the rules.

He exits.

Niles Well, the owner's going to have his hands full finding a buyer for this place. Perhaps it's not worth saving.

Frasier Yes. I know one old relic that is overdue for the wrecking ball.

Otto arrives with the menus and gives Frasier a look.

Frasier No, not you, Otto.

Otto places the menus in front of Daphne, Frasier and Niles. He looks at the place Martin just vacated and is confused.

Niles It's okay. He's in the men's room.

A puzzled Otto takes the menu and starts for the men's room.

Frasier (re: menu) No, no. Leave it here.

Otto leaves the menu and crosses off.

Daphne I think this is a grand old place. Why are Americans always in such an almighty rush to tear things down? At home we treasure our antiquities. But you people just can't wait to bring in the bulldozers. You never consider preserving anything.

Niles You know — I'm inclined to agree with Daphne.

Frasier I'll try to contain my amazement.

Daphne It would be a crime to lose a landmark like this after fifty-three years. I mean, look at it: It's well-built — good structure.

Niles It does have good bones, and it's in a very good location.

Frasier Excellent location. If they had valet parking…

Niles If they just took down those awful curtains.

Frasier	And knocked out the partitions.
	Martin crosses back to the table.
Frasier	You know, I've always dreamed of owning a four-star restaurant.
Niles	What growing boy hasn't?
Frasier	It would need a new chef—
Niles	I happen to know the chef at L'Etoile is very unhappy—
Frasier	Everyone knows that; the man's tete d'veaut is a cry for help—
Niles	Frasier, are you thinking what I'm thinking?
Frasier	I'm even laying tile and sandblasting the wine cave.
Martin	Wait a minute. You guys aren't seriously considering doing a dumb-ass idiotic thing like buying the place, are you?
Frasier	Well, Dad's on board. What do you think, Daphne?
Martin	Owning a restaurant is hard work.
Daphne	I can tell you a bit about that. If you don't scald yourself or lop off a finger with the cleaver you spend your whole time gagging at grease fires, killing rats and brawling with labor racketeers. (*Off their questioning look*) My aunt had a little tea room.
Frasier	With all due respect, Dad. We're not exactly neophytes in this realm. We know about food, we know about wine.
Niles	Lord knows we have style, taste and refinement.
Frasier	And social connections up the wazoo.
Martin	See, that's the way you guys always are. It's not about the hard work or the long hours. To you, owning a restaurant is nothing but wearing fancy clothes, hobnobbing with your friends and turning your enemies away at the door.
Niles	(*enjoying it*) I hadn't even thought about that.
Frasier	We should be writing these things down.
Martin	Look, all I can tell you is when I was a cop walking the beat, there was this one restaurant on the corner. In ten years it must've changed hands twenty times. First it was Ling Fung's Leechy Palace. Then it was Tony's Meatball Hutch. Then it was A Little Taste of Yorkshire. English food. Big surprise, that lasted about five minutes.
Daphne	Excuse me. You never seem to have trouble sucking down a second helping of my bangers and mash.
Martin	Everybody thinks they know how to run a restaurant and they all

lose their shirts. Do you see my point?

Niles   Yes, Dad. A lot of people lost a lot of money for one reason. A terrible name can kill you in this business.

Frasier   True, Niles, but I've got something special. I was working on this while Dad was talking — Maison Crane.

Niles wrinkles his nose.

Frasier   You're right. Too obvious.

Niles   We want our name to be inviting and welcoming. What's the word for "light-hearted" in French?

Frasier   There isn't one. *(A beat)* I've got it — Les Frères Heureux.

Niles   The Happy Brothers. Brilliant. It's homey and just hard enough to pronounce to intimidate the riffraff.

Frasier   And anyone who mispronounces it can't get in. Oh yes, we'll keep it very exclusive. No sign on the outside, no advertising and an unlisted phone number.

Martin   Here's an idea. Why open at all? You'll really clean up.

Frasier   I believe, Niles! Do you believe?!

Niles   I believe!

Otto steps up with his pad.

Otto   Have you decided what you'd like?

Frasier   Yes! I'd like the whole thing from the wine cellar to the rafters!

Otto writes it down.

Otto   And for the lady?

And we:

FADE OUT.

END OF ACT ONE

ACT TWO

SCENE C

FADE IN:

INT. LES FRERES HEUREUX — TWO MONTHS LATER — NIGHT 2

It's a split set: we see both the kitchen and the front, with the wall between containing double doors, one for "in" and one for "out." In addition, the kitchen has at least one door leading to the outside and the dining room has a main entrance as well as a small bar with a bartender.

In the kitchen are a chef, two assistants and a dishwasher. There are two waiters out front. It's an hour or so into the evening and most of the tables are filled with happy diners, including Martin and Daphne at one table.

Frasier and Niles make a grand entrance and stop to speak by a large dessert tray near the main entrance.

Niles We're a hit — a palpable hit. Every table in the house is filled except for that tiny one wedged in that horrible, dank, little corner next to the men's room.

Frasier Remember, Niles, that's not a corner. That's the grotto.

Niles I've been getting nothing but compliments.

Frasier Chef Maurice's really outdone himself. This menu couldn't be improved upon.

Niles I agree. *(Tasting)* Unless it would be to add just a soupcon of brandy to these cherries jubilee.

Frasier Yes. That's the difference between success and failure, those who don't skimp. I want those cherries to be jubilant! Speaking of jubilance, it's opening night. Where's Maris?

Niles You know her better than that, Frasier. Maris has been arriving fashionably late since the day she was born. She was three weeks overdue and still barely weighed five pounds.

Frasier crosses to speak to Daphne and Martin, smiling and adlibbing greetings to other tables. Left alone Niles pauses to add a generous dollop of brandy to the cherries, then crosses and exits into the kitchen.

Frasier *(picking up bottle of wine)* More wine?

Martin It's empty.

Daphne giggles.

Frasier So I take it everything is fine here?

Daphne Oh yes, Dr. Crane. Whatever this anguilla is, it's perfectly smashing.

Frasier It's our chef's specialty. The man does things with eels you wouldn't believe.

Martin I arrested a guy for that, once.

Frasier And Dad, the truffle atop your tournedo was flown in this morning from Tuscany.

Martin   Yeah? Well once I scraped all that crap off, there was a perfectly decent steak underneath.

Daphne   You and your brother really pulled it off, Dr. Crane.

Frasier   Yes, just look around. This is exactly how I pictured it — dignitaries and taste-makers reveling in our cuisine. Tomorrow we'll be the toast of Seattle.

He crosses away smiling and stops to speak to a waiter.

Frasier   These lights are too bright. Give me atmosphere.

Waiter does so. Frasier starts to the kitchen, then notes the cherries. Stops long enough to add a healthy jolt of brandy. Angle on Niles in the kitchen. He stands next to a large tank and speaks to the sous-chef.

Niles   What's in here?

Sous-chef   Anguilla.

The sous-chef takes a wriggling eel out of the tank and shows it to Niles, who recoils.

Niles   Dear God.

Sous-chef   Maurice prefers to kill them to order. That's his specialty.

Niles   I'm glad his specialty isn't prime-rib.

Chef Maurice is preparing a tray of souffle cups to go in the oven.

Niles   Are these soufflés for table nine, Maurice?

Maurice   I'm just about to bake them.

Niles   I know it's not my place to second guess your presentation, but would you be averse to trying something radical?

Maurice   What?

Niles   Instead of individual soufflés, bake one large one and dish out portions at the table. It would make me very happy.

Maurice   Then it is done.

Maurice starts scooping the soufflé mix out of the individual cups into one large dish. Niles exits the kitchen. We follow him out. A waiter stops him.

Waiter   There's a party at the door without a tie or a reservation.

Niles   Leave them to me. And turn these lights up, will you? We're not developing photographs in here.

Waiter goes to do so and Niles confronts a badly-dressed Bulldog Brisco and his trashy date at the door.

Bulldog   Hey, Miles, baby!

Niles   Good evening, Mr. Brisco. May I help you?

Bulldog   *(snickers, re: his date)* Does it look like I need help tonight?

Niles   Do you have a reservation?

Bulldog   Hey, the Bulldog doesn't need a reservation. I'm a celebrity. Treat me right and I'll give you an eight-by-ten to hang in the can. I want the best table you got.

Niles   I'm afraid we're all booked.

Bulldog   Okay, okay. I know what you're sniffing around for. *(To date)* These guys are all alike. *(Pulls a bill from his pocket, then to Niles)* Mr. Lincoln wonders if you've got a table for Bulldog and his lady.

He hands the bill to Niles.

Niles   Well, Mr. Lincoln's in luck. *(To waiter)* Seat these people in The Grotto.

Bulldog   *(to date)* You see that? A little flash of green and you can get whatever you want. But look who I'm telling.

They follow a waiter to the grotto. Niles starts to cross away, then notes the cherries and stops long enough to add a slug of brandy. Angle on Frasier in the kitchen, scolding Maurice.

Frasier   Maurice, not to second guess your creativity, but I thought we agreed that the soufflé mix would be poured into individual cups ten minutes ago?

Maurice   But, I was asked to change…

Frasier   Opening night is no time for change. You'll have years to experiment. Now let's get those egg whites flying.

Muttering darkly, Maurice starts pouring the mix back into the individual cups as we follow Frasier out of the kitchen. He crosses to Martin and Daphne's table. They're having coffee.

Frasier   If you're almost finished I'll send for your car.

He takes out a walkie-talkie.

Daphne   You know — your valet looked familiar, Dr. Crane.

Frasier   It's Otto, the old waiter. I didn't have the heart to let him go. *(Into radio)* Otto?

Otto   *(v.o.) (startled)* Who is this?

Frasier   *(into radio, patiently)* It's Dr. Crane, Otto.

Otto   *(v.o.)* Hi, Dr. Crane. How's tricks?

Frasier   *(into radio)* It isn't necessary to have a conversation each time, Otto. Just bring up *(consulting Martin's ticket)* car number forty-four. *(To them)* One of my innovations. This way it will be waiting for you.

He starts away, encounters a waiter.

Frasier   Will you dim the damned lights? We're not performing surgery in here…

Frasier turns and — as an afterthought — pauses to add a jolt of brandy to the cherries. Angle on Niles, entering the kitchen. He discovers the individual soufflé cups just about to go into the oven.

Niles   Now I asked you politely the first time, Maurice. One big bowl for the soufflé.

Maurice   Wait a minute. This is crazy. This is my kitchen.

Niles   Which happens to be in my restaurant. Now one big bowl and chop-chop.

As a now homicidally-glowering Maurice starts virtually hurling the contents of the soufflé cups back into the larger bowl, Niles turns to a waiter in the kitchen.

Niles   Table twelve is still waiting for their entrée. Don't force me to send them complimentary zucchini.

Niles turns and starts to hurry out what happens to be the "in" door. Hits something solid and rebounds from the impact.

Waiter   That's the "in" door, sir.

Niles   Good lord. I wonder what I hit.

Angle outside on Frasier discovering the other waiter stretched full-length on the floor outside the "in" door. Scandalized, he looks around for help. Bartender hastens to his aid.

Bartender   What happened?

Frasier   This man seems to have fainted. Help me get him in the kitchen.

Frasier picks up one end, the bartender takes the other, and Frasier backs hard into the "out" door and rebounds from the impact, just as Niles did.

Bartender   That's the "out" door.

Frasier   Oops. Well — no harm done.

Angle on kitchen where Niles and sous-chef are ministering to other waiter who is flat on his back.

Niles   He's unconscious.

Sous-chef   What shall we do?

Niles   Well, for one thing start ladling out zucchini.

          Frasier and the bartender haul the other waiter into the kitchen.

Sous-chef   That one's out cold, too.

Bartender   Give me a hand; I'll drive them both to the emergency room.

          *He and the sous-chef take one; sous-chef's assistant and the
          dishwasher take the other. They carry them out. Niles is starting
          to lose it but struggling to keep calm.*

Niles   Does it strike you as the tiniest drawback that we're suddenly left
          with neither waiters nor a bartender?

Frasier   First rule of the kitchen: keep calm.

          *He turns over to see Maurice about to put the large soufflé dish
          in the oven and loses it.*

Frasier   (*screaming*) No! No! No! — individual cups, you oaf!

Niles   I told him one large dish.

          They now do one of their overlaps.

Frasier   I gave him specific instructions, you went behind my back, I'm in
          charge, I'm the owner, this was my idea, etc.

Niles   I countermanded them, I went over your head, I took some
          initiative, I own a larger share, I provide the knowhow, etc.

          *While they do this, behind them Maurice simply takes off his
          apron, throws his toque on the floor, takes his coat off a rack.
          They notice just in time to see him head for the door.*

Niles   No, Maurice, wait, he didn't mean anything—

Frasier   I was using "oaf" in the complimentary sense—

Niles   Too late. Now what?

Frasier   Very simple. We award a battlefield promotion.

          *The sous-chef, his assistant and the dishwasher come back in.
          Frasier turns to the sous-chef.*

Frasier   Congratulations: You're the new head chef.

Sous-chef   Thank you.

Frasier   Now make us proud. We've got some very important clientele
          out there.

Niles   I'll say. At the governor's table alone we have two state senators and the head of the Immigration Bureau.

At those magic words all the remaining employees melt out the back door.

Frasier Any other names you'd like to drop?

Frasier picks up the chef's toque and hands it to Niles.

Frasier Now you're the chef.

Niles Don't be absurd. I can't possibly—

Frasier Of course you can. Most of the dishes are already started. And Daphne and Dad can help. *(Takes out walkie-talkie)* Never mind car forty-four, Otto.

Otto *(v.o.) (startled)* Who is this?

Frasier *(frantic)* It's Dr. Crane, it's always Dr. Crane, I'm the only one on here!

As Niles dons toque and apron and starts peering under lids, we follow Frasier out to dining room. He at once switches to his "reassuring the customers" face until he reaches Martin and Daphne.

Frasier *(sotto)* I need both your help. We've had a small disaster.

Martin *(loud)* What kind of disaster?

Frasier Shhh. *(Beams at room, then sotto)* We've lost all our staff. It's a long story but right now *(To Daphne)* I need you in the kitchen. And, Dad, I need you tending bar. You can gloat later.

Martin I'll pencil it in.

Martin crosses to the bar.

Daphne Well it won't be the first time I had to wash dishes for my supper. But who's going to wait on all these tables?

Roz enters with Brad, her date. Roz is dressed in the most gorgeous and "dressy"-looking outfit we can manage. Frasier spots her and rushes to her, arms outstretched, beaming like a fool as Martin crosses to the bar and Daphne to the kitchen.

Roz Oh, Frasier…

Frasier Roz, Roz, Roz. *(Hugs her)* Roz, Roz, Roz, Roz…

Roz *(breaking free)* Hey, I'm glad to see you, too. *(Meaningfully)* This is my date, Brad.

Frasier *(extending hand)* Pleased to meet you, Brad.

They shake.

Roz	So, have you got our special table?
Frasier	Oh indeed I do. A fine, fine table.
	He leads them to a table near the bar.
Frasier	But before you actually sit at it, Roz, may I have a word with you?
Roz	*(to Brad)* Probably some kind of surprise.
Frasier	*(leading her off)* Try to fool you…
	As Frasier leads Roz to the kitchen:
Roz	Boy, this place is great.
Frasier	Yes, just a little family restaurant where we all know secrets about each other which we wouldn't dream of telling unless we needed a really big favor.
	Frasier and Roz exit to the kitchen, Brad sits. From the bar, Martin addresses him.
Martin	Hey, buddy, you from around here? How about those Supersonics? Name your poison.
Brad	Oh I don't know. Maybe I'll wait for Roz.
Martin	Have it now.
Brad	All right, but I'm not much of a drinker. What do you recommend?
Martin	Have a boilermaker.
Brad	You really think?
Martin	You'll thank me.
	As Martin pours, Roz slams out of the kitchen wearing an apron and crosses to Brad.
Roz	*(calling into kitchen)* Blackmailer! *(Then, quickly changing)* Honey, I'm really, really sorry but Frasier's a dear friend and his waiter's had an accident and it's his grand opening and he really, really needs help and I just hope you'll try to understand.
Brad	No problem. *(Beat)* Listen, could I get a menu? And what about some bread and butter?
Roz	*(through her teeth)* Coming up…
	She starts to move off, then turns back, downs the boilermaker and then crosses away. Frasier crosses to bar to speak to Martin.
Martin	*(to Frasier)* Hey, buddy, you from around here? How about those Supersonics?
Frasier	Niles is starting to panic back there. I don't know if we can pull

this off.

Martin   Why don't you just level with people and tell 'em what happened?

Frasier   You know, you may be right. Maybe honesty is the best policy.

Frasier crosses to a spot by the front door and holds up his hands.

Frasier   *(to the crowd)* Excuse me, ladies and gentlemen—

As he does so, Gil Chesterton enters with four friends.

Gil   Good evening, Frasier.

Frasier   Gil. You — you said you weren't coming.

Gil   I knew it would only make you fret. Especially if you knew I was bringing *(indicating friends)* an entire table of restaurant critics.

Frasier   Oh, well, I — gosh, I'm sorry but all our tables are booked.

Gil spots table vacated by Martin and Daphne and heads for it.

Gil   We'll take this one. We don't mind squeezing in — we're simply salivating to try the anguilla. We hear your chef is an absolute wizard with eels.

Frasier   Yes, but his real tour de force is scrambled eggs. *(Off their looks)* Eels it is.

He heads for the kitchen. Angle on kitchen. Roz is giving an order to Niles and Daphne. Daphne is now wearing a hairnet and white smock. As Roz requests substitutions the two of them do a series of moves (choreographed by the director) shifting items back and forth between plates with tongs, spatulas, etc.

Roz   …This one wants the sole veronique but without the grapes… spinach instead of broccoli, risotto instead of pilaf… and this one wants the swordfish, hold the capers, potatoes instead of pasta, extra broccoli.

Frasier enters and crosses to Niles.

Frasier   Quick, Niles: Kill five eels.

Niles neither looks up nor stops what he's doing. After a beat he speaks.

Niles   …I'm going to pretend I didn't hear that.

Frasier   I'm serious. Every major food critic in Seattle is out there and they all want anguilla so start wasting eels.

Niles   How do you suggest I do that?

Frasier   How do I know? You're the chef. Throw a toaster in the tank for all I care.

Frasier exits. We follow him out as he crosses to Gil's table.

Gil   Our mouths are watering, Frasier.

Frasier   Have no fear, Gil. The anguillas are on the way. Our chef is in the process of…

At that moment, all the lights in the restaurant dim almost to darkness, then gradually flicker back to normal.

Frasier   …frying them now.

Gil   Splendid.

Frasier crosses off. Behind him we see Roz virtually hurling plates onto a table. Frasier pauses by the dessert cart long enough to add just a dash more brandy to the cherries. A woman (Joan) calls to him.

Joan   Excuse me. This is veal piccata — I ordered veal marsala.

Frasier   A thousand pardons, madam. I'll rectify it at once.

He takes her plate and rushes to the kitchen. We follow him in.

Frasier   (to Niles) This veal piccata should be veal marsala.

Niles snatches it from the plate with tongs and tosses it to Daphne, who catches it with one rubber glove. With the other hand she grabs spray attachment from the sink and hoses the veal down then tosses it back to Niles who catches it with the tongs, slaps it back on the plate and, with the other hand, ladles sauce onto it.

Niles   And now it is.

Roz enters.

Roz   The mayor's party all want cherries jubilee for dessert.

Frasier   Fine. (Tosses her matches) You flame them and I'll be out to serve them.

Roz exits, Frasier turns back to Niles.

Frasier   What about the eels?

Niles   I'm just trimming them.

Niles picks up a cleaver and begins energetically whacking it directly into the water in the tank.

Frasier   Take them out first.

Niles   (still whacking) Not until I'm sure they're dead.

Daphne   Oh, for heaven's sake.

She reaches into the tank, takes an eel by the tail, whacks its head on the counter, then matter-of-factly hands it to Niles.

Niles   My God, you're brave.

Daphne   Oh, well, I think you stunned him.

We hear a loud "whoosh!" — almost like an explosion — and the kitchen door swings inward from the force, followed by a cloud of smoke.

Frasier   What was that?

Roz enters in shock. She still holds the stub of a match in her hand and her eyes are very wide. Maybe her face is smudged.

Roz   ...Big blue flash... all the way to the ceiling...

Daphne   Lucky it didn't set off the sprinkler system.

Frasier   Fortunately, there's a built-in safety delay for just that sort of thing. You have fifteen seconds to turn it off before the sprinklers—

The sprinklers come on, showering down in the kitchen.

Frasier   —Kick in.

Daphne   Where do I turn that off?

Frasier   Right there.

He indicates. Daphne rushes to turn it off and does after a beat or two.

Niles   Well I hope you're satisfied. You've thinned my brown sauce.

Frasier dashes out of the kitchen. We follow him. In the dining room the guests are dripping. Many are standing, trying to dry hair, faces, clothing, with napkins. They are not happy. Frasier tries to be jovial.

Frasier   Good news: that was just a test.

Joan stands and thrusts her parking check at him.

Joan   I want my car. *Now.*

Frasier   At once, ma'am. *(On walkie-talkie)* Otto, bring car twenty-three and hurry.

Otto   *(v.o.)* Who is this?

Frasier   *(screaming)* It's the voice of God.

Bulldog and his date approach from the back, equally soaked.

Bulldog   Nice touch with the sprinklers, Doc. My date's dress is clinging to her like Saran Wrap.

Other diners rise, some start waving their car checks, adlibbing requests.

Frasier   Ladies and gentlemen, every restaurant goes through a period of adjustment.

A lot of them move toward the door, grabbing coats and hats, muttering angrily. Frasier pursues them, still trying.

Frasier   Some day you'll remember this as an adventure.

Gil   And if they don't remember it I'll remind them.

Frasier   Those of you who are leaving, I hope you'll keep us in mind for your next special occasion… We plan a lot of exciting innovations in the weeks ahead—

With a horrendous crash the front end of a car driven by Otto (big tag saying "23" on windshield) comes through one wall. Everyone stops in his tracks, staring in horror. After a beat Frasier recovers.

Frasier   —Starting with our new drive-through window…

At which the remaining customers stampede for the exit and we:
FADE OUT.

SCENE D

FADE IN:

INT. LES FRERES HEUREUX — LATER THAT NIGHT — NIGHT 2

The place is empty now. Frasier sits forlornly at a table eating a cherries jubilee. Niles is looking up at the ceiling. The charred remains of the dessert cart stands to the side.

Niles   What do you suppose is the minimum firepower necessary to embed a cherry into an accoustic ceiling tile?

Frasier   Yet another question we should have asked ourselves before we entered the exciting world of food service.

Martin enters through the front door.

Martin   Man, those eels are starting to stink.

Frasier   Oh no, and just when things were going so perfectly.

Niles   Dad, for the last hour you've been circling us like a shark so why don't you just give your little speech and be done with it.

Martin   Hey, come on, that's not me. I don't need to give you some big "I told you so" speech to make you feel bad.

Frasier   Because you're not that kind of guy, right Dad?

Martin   No, cause Maris is here and she'll do it for me.

Niles   Frasier, if I pick up the tab, will you take the blame for all this?

Frasier   Oh, what's a happy brother for?

               And we:

               FADE OUT.

END OF ACT TWO

SCENE E
END CREDITS

               FADE IN:

INT. LES FRERES HEUREUX — DAY — DAY 3

               There are several "For Sale" signs visible. Frasier and Niles are escorting a party of Japanese businessmen around, pointing out advantages as the prospective buyers nod, murmur to each other and jot down notes.

               Perhaps one notes the hole in the wall and clearly queries Frasier about it. Frasier pantomimes cars pulling up, orders being dispensed, cars driving away, a model of efficiency. The others nod approvingly and smile.

               FADE OUT.

END OF SHOW

BREAKING THE ICE

Written by
Steven Levitan

Created and Developed by
David Angell, Peter Casey, David Lee

Directed by
Philip Charles MacKenzie

ACT ONE

SCENE A

> *FADE IN:*

INT. RADIO STUDIO — DAY — DAY 1

> *Frasier is on a commercial break. Roz is in her booth. Frasier takes a call from Jake, a spacy twenty-year-old man. (Think Keanu Reeves in "Parenthood.")*

Roz	Ten seconds, Frasier, and we've only got time for one more call.
Frasier	Well then, let's make it a good one.
Roz	Oh, okay, as opposed to the dullards I've been putting through all day?
Frasier	Someone got up on the wrong side of the trampoline this morning.

> *Roz points to Frasier.*

Frasier	We're back, Seattle, with time for one more call. Who do we have, Roz?
Roz	We have Jake on line three.

> *Frasier hits a button.*

Frasier	Hello, Jake. This is Dr. Crane, I'm listening.
Jake	*(v.o.)* Yeah, Doctor… uh… My girlfriend gets mad at me because she says I have, uh, trouble… uh…
Frasier	Communicating?
Jake	*(v.o.)* No… uh…
Frasier	Concentrating?
Jake	*(v.o.)* Hmmmm… well…
Frasier	Functioning in the real world?
Jake	*(v.o.)* Yeah, that's it.
Frasier	Let me ask you a question, Jake: Do you have a job?
Jake	*(v.o.)* Why? Are you looking for someone?
Frasier	God, no! What I meant…
Jake	*(v.o.)* 'Cause that would really get her off my back. Should I come down for an interview?
Frasier	No, you're not getting my…
Jake	*(v.o.)* I'm busy tomorrow… uh… how's Monday? *(Yelling to his girlfriend in the background)* Would you shut up?! I'm getting a

	job! (*After a beat, to Frasier*) She wants to know what it pays.
Frasier	Nothing! There is no job! It pays nothing!
Jake	(*v.o.*) Then I don't think I'd be interested. But thanks for calling.
	Jake hangs up and we hear a dial tone.
Frasier	Well, as we all try to imagine what callers Roz passed over in favor of Jake, this is Dr. Frasier Crane signing off.
	Frasier takes off his headphones and goes into Roz's booth.
Frasier	A little off our game today, aren't we, Roz? Is something wrong?
Roz	Yes. I told a guy I love him.
Frasier	Somebody you know this time?
Roz	Oh, forget it, I know you don't like to hear about my love life.
Frasier	Don't be ridiculous. I care about you. If you have a problem, I want to help. Just keep the details on a need-to-know basis.
Roz	Okay. We've been dating a couple of weeks, and last night he was licking behind my ear. See I've got this little spot—
Frasier	(*interrupting*) Do I…?
Roz	Yes, you need to know this. So anyway, I wanted to say, "Oh, I love that." But I got so caught up, I yelled out, "Oh, I love you." And, all of a sudden, he gets this look on his face — like Indiana Jones running from that big ball.
Frasier	Well, do you love him?
Roz	I don't know yet. The point is, whether I meant it or not, I said it, but he didn't say it back. And he should have — whether he meant it or not. It's just polite.
Frasier	There's no phrase in the human language more emotionally charged than "I love you." Some people are just incapable of saying it. It makes them too vulnerable. My father, for example, is incapable of saying "I love you" to anyone. But, deep down, I know he loves me.
Roz	Your father's never told you he loves you? God, that explains so much.
Frasier	What's that supposed to mean?
Roz	Well, maybe if he had, you wouldn't be so emotionally needy that when a close friend is pouring out her heart to you, you have to steer the conversation back to your own problems. (*Then*) Anyway, now that I've told this guy I love him, how do I take it back?

Frasier   It's very simple, Roz. Remember when I said I cared about your problem and I wanted to help you? I take it back.

As Frasier exits, we:

FADE OUT.

SCENE B

A black screen. In white letters appears, "I Only Have Ice For You."

INT. FRASIER'S LIVING ROOM — DAY 1

Martin is at the table, organizing his tackle box. Eddie is nosing around in it. Martin shoos him away

Martin   Get away from there, Eddie. You'll get a fish hook up your nose.

Daphne enters from the kitchen spraying air freshener.

Daphne   Don't you ever clean that thing out?

Martin   Nah, it's bad luck, everybody knows that. You show up on a fishing trip with a bait box that doesn't smell like the most disgusting, rancid thing on the face of the earth and nobody'll sit near you.

Frasier and Niles enter from outside.

Niles   What an odd combination of odors. It smells like a fish died and all the other fish sent flowers.

Frasier   *(to Niles, noticing Martin's tackle box)* Dad's taking his annual ice fishing trip to Lake Nomahegan.

Martin   Just getting my gear ready. Duke rented a cabin right on the lake and I'm bringing the bait and the porkrinds. *(Playfully)* Now I don't want you boys throwing any wild parties just because your old man's out of town.

Frasier   How can we, Dad, if you're taking all the porkrinds?

SFX: The telephone rings. Daphne answers it.

Daphne   *(into phone)* Hello. *(Pause)* Oh, hello. Yes, he's right here. *(Handing it to Martin)* It's Duke.

Martin   *(into phone)* Hey, Duke! *(Pause, Martin stops smiling)* Is she okay? *(Pause)* Yeah, I understand. No problem. *(Pause)* Hey, don't worry. We'll do it next year. We've had too many good times up there to let this tradition die. Yeah, yeah, I love ya, you big lug.

This registers on Frasier.

Martin   Yeah, take care, Duke. Bye.

Martin hangs up.

Daphne   Your trip's been cancelled?

Martin   Yeah, Duke's wife has the flu. He can't leave her alone.

Daphne   Oh, what a shame. You were so looking forward to it.

Martin   Well I still got the cabin, but I can't go alone...

Martin looks to Frasier, who doesn't respond.

Martin   *(to Frasier, prompting)* I would need to go with someone else...

Frasier   Dad, I'd love to do something with you this weekend, but I just don't think ice fishing is it. Wait, what about this? There's a revival of "The Ice Man Cometh" playing downtown. We could catch a matinee, go out for sushi and still stay well within the theme.

Martin   Thanks, anyway.

Daphne   Well, I'd go, but, to me, ice fishing is strictly a man's sport. I remember the cold winter mornings when my brother and his friends would return from the Lake District with their catch. Their hearty muscles strained, their chiseled faces wind-burnt... it made me feel so feminine and flushed.

Niles   *(interrupts)* I'll go ice fishing, Dad.

Frasier   You, ice fishing?

Niles   Why not? I like to think of myself as a man of the great al fresco.

Frasier   You get a runny nose watching figure skating on TV.

Martin   *(excited)* Thanks, Niles, but are you sure?

Niles   It's the very least I can do if it'll save your trip for you.

Martin   Great.

Frasier   That's very noble of you, but we're talking ice fishing, Niles — in an arctic tundra where large men spit and it freezes in their beards.

Niles   After you've seen Maris's interpretive dance group perform "Afternoon of a Faun" in the east garden, the wilderness holds no terror.

And we:

FADE OUT.

SCENE C

> *A black screen. In white letters appears, "Who Loves Ya?"*

INT. FRASIER'S KITCHEN/LIVING ROOM — A COUPLE OF DAYS LATER — DAY 2

> *Frasier enters to find Daphne making lunches for the trip. She's in a great mood. Eddie stands beside her, waiting for scraps.*

Frasier   Morning, Daphne.

Daphne   *(very chipper)* Good morning. Lovely day, isn't it?

Frasier   You're in a good mood.

Daphne   Yes, well, as much as I love your father, with him gone it's going to be a wonderful weekend… Care to make it perfect?

Frasier   Sorry to disappoint you, but I'm staying.

Daphne   In that case, are you planning to use your bathroom today?

Frasier   Well, I wasn't actually planning, but if history proves correct…

Daphne   I was hoping to use your tub this afternoon for a nice, long hot soak.

Frasier   Be my guest. But please just don't use all those salts and scents you women always do that end up clogging the drain. You can use my bath beads.

> *Martin enters, dressed for fishing and carrying a thermos.*

Martin   *(in a great mood)* Found the Thermos. Make sure the coffee's extra strong. I'll need it for Niles.

Daphne   Oh, he'll be driving?

Martin   No, talking.

> *Eddie crosses over to Martin and whimpers. Martin pets him affectionately.*

Martin   *(to Eddie)* Hey, champ, I know you'd like to go with me, but we're going to be on the ice and it'll be too cold for you. *(Petting Eddie)* Ohhhhh, yessssss, I love ya, you little mutt.

> *Again this registers on Frasier.*

Martin   *(as he goes)* Well, I better go make sure I have everything.

> *Martin exits.*

Frasier   Did he just say "I love you" to the dog?

Daphne   Oh that's nothing. I had an aunt who used to say "Goodnight, Mr.

Vanderpump" to a hat rack.

A beat.

Frasier Does he say that to Eddie a lot?

Daphne I try to give them their privacy.

Frasier Sorry, Daphne, it's just curious to me. Without sounding too maudlin, I don't remember Dad ever saying that to me.

Daphne Oh, you know what a crusty old git your father is.

Frasier Yes, I do. But he can say it to the dog. He even said it to Duke the other day.

Daphne Well, Duke and your father go way back. He's his chum.

Frasier And I'm not?

Daphne Well, think of it this way. When your father wants to go ice fishing, at least Duke will go with him.

Frasier So, you're saying I should go along, pretend I'm enjoying myself, do something that gives me absolutely no satisfaction, just to hear the words "I love you?"

Daphne Why not? Women have been doing it for centuries.

SFX: The doorbell rings. Frasier answers the door to find Niles decked out like the Orvis poster child, complete with all the latest in camping and fishing gadgetry.

Niles *(proudly)* Call me Ishmael.

Frasier You have got to be kidding.

Martin enters.

Martin Hey, Niles, you look great!

Niles Thanks, Dad.

Martin And I was worried you wouldn't be warm enough.

Niles No problem there, I dressed in layers: Polo, Eddie Bauer and Timberland.

Frasier You look like a skinny Elmer Fudd.

Martin *(to Frasier)* Lay off, at least he's trying.

Niles Dad, I can't wait to show you everything I got. I never knew how much I liked fishing until I realized all the shopping involved. Look: *(showing him)* Graphite poles, battery operated ear muffs, electric socks, and "Hot Buns." They're seat cushions. You microwave them and they stay toasty warm and plump for hours.

Martin They sound good enough to eat.

Frasier	You know, Dad, maybe I was a little hasty the other day when I…

Daphne enters with more food.

Daphne All right, here we are, some snacks for the trip up. *(Noticing Niles)* Ooh, Dr. Crane, look at you in your new togs.

Martin Some outfit, huh? The fish will see him coming.

Daphne Well the salesman certainly did.

Frasier Listen, Dad, I feel kind of bad that I turned you down when you invited me.

Martin Hey, no problem.

Niles *(to Martin)* And just wait 'til you taste the freshly-smoked Turkey Jerky.

Martin takes some. Daphne pulls Frasier aside

Daphne Oh, for heaven's sake. You know you want to go, so why don't you just ask him?

Frasier I can't. I already said I didn't want to. It'll sound so whiny.

Martin *(re: Turkey Jerky)* That's delicious!

He puts the uneaten portion back into the bag.

Niles No, no don't put it…

Martin does anyway.

Martin Well, Niles, it's getting late.

Niles Yes, let's hit the road.

Frasier You know, it's a pretty long trip, are you sure you two can handle the drive?

Martin Frasier, I'm getting some mixed signals here. You don't want to go with us, do you?

Frasier *(pretending to be put-out)* Oh, all right! It's better than having to listen to you nag, nag, nag. Fine, I'll go.

As Frasier heads to get his things, the camera pans to the kitchen where we see Daphne and Eddie airpumping and celebrating a weekend to themselves, and we:

FADE OUT.

END OF ACT ONE

ACT TWO
SCENE D

> A black screen. In white letters appears, "Fishing Cheek to Cheek."

> FADE IN:

INT. ICE FISHING SHELTER — AFTERNOON — DAY 2

> *Typical sparse ice fishing shelter — roughly ten feet by eight feet. Among the cheesy decorations are fishing advertising posters featuring women in bikinis. Frasier and Martin enter. Frasier walks gingerly on the ice; he is obviously horrified by the surroundings, but tries not to show it.*

Martin   C'mon, it's not gonna break. This lake's been frozen solid for three months.

Frasier   I'm sorry this isn't exactly how I pictured it when you mentioned Duke had a cabin on the lake.

Martin   It's a cabin, it's *on* the lake.

Frasier   Yes, and if it warms up a few degrees, it'll be *in* the lake.

> *Niles enters.*

Niles   That was amazing! I've never felt so in touch with nature.

Martin   What happened?

Niles   For the first time in my life, I just urinated outdoors. Another cup of coffee and I'll go back to dot the "i."

> *Martin laughs and slaps Niles on the back.*

Niles   *(looking around)* Oh, this is great, Dad.

Martin   Frasier doesn't think so.

Frasier   Well, I'm not complaining, I just expected, I don't know, something lake-adjacent. Something rustic with hand-made quilts, knotty pine furniture, maybe a floor… Are we actually going to sleep here?

Niles   *(sotto to Martin)* Who is this rube? Maybe we can trick him into touching his tongue to the bait bucket.

> *Martin and Niles share a laugh.*

Martin   *(to Frasier)* We're fishing here, we're sleeping someplace else. Remember when we turned off the highway? *(Frasier nods)* Well, just down the road from there is the Bed 'N Bass Motel.

Frasier	Bed 'N Bass. Oh yes, one of the finer of the fish-themed hotels. I understand they drove the Pike 'N Pillow right out of business. *(Then)* So, we just drill a hole in the ice with that corkscrew thingy and start fishing?
Niles	It's called an auger.
Frasier	Well, imagine my embarrassment.
Niles	*(handing it to him)* Here's your "Hot Buns," Dad.
Martin	Thanks.

Martin and Niles sit on their "Hot Buns."

Frasier	What am *I* supposed to sit on?
Niles	The auger's free.

Frasier shoots him a look; Niles begrudgingly moves over and offers half of his "Hot Buns" to Frasier. Frasier walks over, rolls his eyes and sits next to Niles on the "Hot Buns." As they scrunch together, we:

FADE OUT.

SCENE E

FADE IN:

INT. ICE FISHING SHELTER — AN HOUR OR SO LATER — DAY 2

Frasier, Niles and Martin sit motionless, their lines dropped in the water. Frasier and Niles are still scrunched together, but in opposite places. Martin and Niles look perfectly warm and content, contrasted to Frasier who looks freezing and ready to jump out of his skin. He checks his watch.

Martin	I saw that.
Frasier	I'm not bored. I was just wondering how long we've been sitting here enjoying ourselves.
Niles	If the fish don't feel peckish just yet then fine, we'll pass the time in good conversation. *(To Martin)* Dad, did you know that Lake Nomahegan was formed by the retreat of several glaciers during the Cenozoic Era?
Frasier	Which, coincidentally, was the last time anyone caught a fish in it.
Martin	How do you know all this stuff, Niles?
Niles	Well, last night I just happened to be browsing through a copy of *Fielding's Geological History of Western Canada*. It's fascinating. For example, this very lake at its deepest is eighty-nine meters

and it boasts fifty varieties of fish.

Frasier   Oh, Alex, I'll take bodies of water for five hundred!

Niles   There's Lake trout, Rainbow trout, German Brown, Wall eyed Pike…

Frasier   How'd you like to be sleeping with them?

Martin   *(to Frasier)* You know, you could learn a thing or two from your brother about getting into the spirit of things.

Frasier   I'm sorry. It's just that my back hurts, I'm hungry and I'm tired of sitting here in twenty degree weather. *(To Niles)* That's minus two degrees Celsius — a system named after Anders Celsius the noted Swedish astronomer and compulsive temperature taker. *(Then)* Switch, Niles.

Niles nods. They both stand and circle each other in order to switch places to warm the opposite bun.

Niles   I believe you're on my side.

Frasier   I am not.

Niles   Yes, you are. You crossed the border.

Frasier   Oh, this is insane. Why am I even here?

Niles   I was just thinking the same thing.

Martin   Guys…

Niles   If you're having such a terrible time, why don't you just head back to the Bed 'N Bass?

Frasier   Oh, there's an idea Niles. Just what I need — a brisk, five-mile hike in sub-freezing conditions.

Niles   Oh for God's sake, here. Take the car and go. *(Reaching into pants pocket)* Oh, no. There's a hole in my pocket!

Martin   You lost the keys?

Frasier   Where?

Niles   If I knew where, they wouldn't be lost. They could be anywhere between here and the car.

Martin   Well, good luck finding them. It's been snowing all day.

Niles   Great! We'll have to stay here all night.

Frasier   We'll never make it through the night. By morning we'll be Stouffers' Frozen Entrees for wolves!

Martin   Wait a minute. *(Points)* Is that them down there?

Niles   Oh, thank God.

MY COFFEE WITH NILES

Martin If my hip is in good enough shape to walk down here, maybe it's time I found a place of my own.

Frasier Oh, no, not this again.

MY COFFEE WITH NILES

Niles Well I guess that brings me to my evermore tedious original question. Are you happy?

THE CANDIDATE

Niles Can you tell me with any certainty that in such a vast universe there isn't intelligent life on other planets?

Frasier At the moment, I'm not sure there's intelligent life in this kitchen.

SEAT OF POWER

Niles Now the bowl is refilling… Then the tank… I've seen it a million times but never has it meant so much. *(Beat, suddenly concerned)* Frasier, shouldn't the water be stopping now?

SEAT OF POWER
Danny Wait a minute. Are you the guy who used to carry your gym shorts in an attaché case?
Niles It was a valise.

SEAT OF POWER
Billy Hey, did you ever pack a guy's nose with cottage cheese?

THE INNKEEPERS
Bulldog Hey, the Bulldog doesn't need a reservation. I'm a celebrity.

BREAKING THE ICE
Martin You show up on a fishing trip with a bait box that doesn't smell like the most disgusting, rancid thing on the face of the earth and nobody'll sit near you.

BREAKING THE ICE

Frasier You look like a skinny Elmer Fudd.

DEATH AND THE DOG
Daphne You know, I've heard they have therapists for dogs. Do you suppose calling a dog psychiatrist could be the answer?

DEATH AND THE DOG
Niles Come on, Girl. Do your stuff. That's it. I can see her magic working already.

TO KILL A TALKING BIRD
Niles Frasier, the bird seems to be holding on to my scalp. I can't pull it off.

TO KILL A TALKING BIRD
Niles I know! Get the lighter. Fire frightened her onto my head, maybe fire will frighten her off.

FRASIER'S IMAGINARY FRIEND

Niles Oh, Frasier, whatever it is that makes you feel the need to perpetuate this fantasy woman, you don't have to on our account.

FRASIER'S IMAGINARY FRIEND

Kelly What's that noise?
Frasier I don't hear anything.
Kelly It sounds like a camera…
Under your pillow.

Niles rushes to the keys and picks them up.

Frasier   I don't trust you. Give them to me now.

Niles   Fine, Mr. Big Brother.

Niles tosses the keys to Frasier, but he throws them short and the keys drop down the hole. Frasier, Niles and Martin all just stand around and stare after them for a beat stunned. Then:

Niles   *(to Frasier)* Nice catch.

Frasier   Me? You throw like a girl!

Martin   I was always saying to you guys, "Come on, let's go out to the backyard and throw the old ball around…" But no… *(mimicking)* "We've got homework to do."

Niles   Let's all stay calm. There's still a chance the keys got caught in the tackle.

One by one they lift their hooks from the hole.

Martin   Nothing.

Frasier   Nope.

Niles   Oh please, please, please…

Niles pulls up a big, flopping fish, which scares the hell out of him.

Niles   Aaaaaaah!

The fish escapes the hook and falls back into the hole.

Martin   Let's not panic. We should be fine out here 'til morning. Actually, the same thing happened to me and Duke about ten years ago.

Niles   You dropped your keys into the hole too?

Martin   No, we weren't idiots. The car battery went dead, but the three of us got through the night just fine.

Niles   You, Duke and who?

Martin   Mr. James Beam. *(Pulling out a bottle)* You're not the only one who got some fishing supplies.

Frasier   Who would've thought by the end of this day I'd be yearning for a night at the Bed 'N Bass?

And we:

DISSOLVE TO:

SCENE H

INT. ICE FISHING SHELTER — AN HOUR OR SO LATER — DAY 2

> *Still passing the now-half-empty bottle, on their way to drunk, but not quite there. Suddenly they hear a large ice groan.*

Frasier   What was that?

Niles   What?

Frasier   That groaning sound. It was like an enormous hungry animal.

Martin   Will you stop scaring everyone. It's just the ice cracking underneath us.

> *Frasier and Niles immediately lift their feet off the ice.*

Martin   Relax. It happens all the time.

Niles   You know, if we should happen to fall in, we have ninety seconds before hypothermia sets in.

Frasier   One more fact and you're going in that hole.

Martin   Hey, would you two stop going at each other already? I know… we're going to lighten the mood out here. We're drinkin', this calls for a drinkin' song.

Frasier   Oh, there's a great drinking song from "La Traviata" called "Libiamo Brindisi."

Niles   That's from "Rigoletto."

Frasier   No, it's from "La Traviata." *(Singing)* Li-bia-mo, li-bia-mo ne' lie amo-re…

Niles   No, it starts *(singing)* li-bia-mo, libia-mone' lie-ti ca-li-ci che la…

Martin   Well, at least it'll keep the bears away.

> *And we:*
>
> DISSOLVE TO:

SCENE J

INT. ICE FISHING SHELTER — AN HOUR OR SO LATER — DAY 2

> *Frasier, Niles and Martin are now completely smashed, all three belting out the big finish of "Libiamo Brindisi."*

All   *(singing)*…ne sco-prail nuo-vo, il nuo-vo di, si, ne sco-pra, ne scopra il nu-ovo di!

> *They congratulate themselves on a fine performance: "Well done," "Bravo," etc.*

Martin   Well, I gotta step outside for a minute. I'll be right back. Leave a light on in the window for me.

As Martin exits Niles and Frasier ad-lib "goodbye's."

Niles   He's a great guy, isn't he?

Frasier   The best. *(Then)* Niles, can I ask you a personal question? What the hell are you doing here?

Niles   Whatever do you mean?

Frasier   Oh, this whole Sergeant Niles of the Yukon. It can't all be about impressing Daphne.

Niles   All right. I suppose it's going to make me out to be a bit of a pitiful weenie, but I wanted to do something to feel closer to Dad. He is great.

Frasier   Yeah, the best.

Niles   *(shouting)* You're great, Dad!

Martin   *(o.s.) (shouting back)* Thanks!

Niles   Look at you two guys — how close you've gotten over the last couple of years. I wanted to experience that for myself.

Frasier   Ha!

Niles   What do you mean, "ha"?

Frasier   *(loudly)* Ha!

Martin   *(o.s.) (shouting back)* Ha!

Frasier   If we're so close then why did I come all the way up to this stinking, God forsaken beer cooler—

Niles   *(interrupting)* It's called a shanty.

Frasier   Shut up. *(Continues)* —Just to get Dad to say "I love you?"

Niles   What?

Frasier   He's said it to everyone, but he's never said it to me.

Niles   You are so competitive, Frasier. If I'm pathetic, you have to be more pathetic.

Frasier   Oh good, I win! *(Putting out hand)* Give me three, Niles! That's all I can feel.

Niles gives Frasier a high-five as Martin enters.

Martin   Whoa, boy. I did it. I had to borrow an "N" from Niles, but I did it.

Frasier   Well, we seem to be leaving quite the urological crossword puzzle out there.

Martin	What were you guys laughing about? What'd I miss?
Niles	Oh, we were just laughing because two renowned psychiatrists, highly respected in their field, drove three hundred miles acoss the frozen Northern wasteland to be in a clapboard igloo just so our father could kiss us on the forehead and tuck us into bed.
Martin	I don't get it.
Frasier	I was telling Niles that the whole idiotic reason I came out here was because in my whole life I've never heard you say "I love you" to me.
Martin	I've said it.
Frasier	No, you haven't. No, no, no, no, no…
Martin	Yes, I have. I've said it.
Niles	I never heard it.
Martin	What, you too? *(Then)* Well, you know I feel it. That's the same as saying it.
Frasier	Nope. No, no, no, no, no…
	They stare at him expectantly.
Martin	What? You expect me to say it now? In a shanty?
Frasier	Well where would you like to do it — strolling arm in arm in a clover patch?
Martin	All right. You think I can't do it, but I can do it. *(Then)* Don't stare at me.
	A beat.
Niles	*(prompting)* "I…"
Martin	All right, I love you. Now shut the hell up.
Frasier	I just don't think you've captured the spirit of the phrase, Dad.
Martin	All right, I love you. Now leave me alone.
Frasier	Better, but still a little run-on.
Martin	All right, you both want to hear it so bad? Fine. *(Takes a beat to prepare, works a kink out of his neck, then)* Frasier, I love you. Niles, I love you.
Frasier	Thanks, Dad. I love you too.
Niles	And I love you too. But I hate ice fishing.
Martin	*(gently)* Well, neither of you ever have to come again.
Frasier	In that case, I really love you.

Niles   Me too, Dad. I love you. I love, love, love, love, love you.

As they do a group hug a ranger enters. A beat, then:

Ranger   I'm afraid you guys will have to come off the ice for the night.

Martin   Yes, sir, we would but we lost our car keys down our ice hole.

Martin, Frasier, Niles crack up.

Ranger   Why don't I take you to your motel and you can call a locksmith for your car in the morning.

Frasier   Thank you, officer, you're a very nice man.

Martin   We love you.

Frasier   Love you.

Niles   Love, love, love you.

As Frasier, Niles and Martin continue to profess their love for the ranger, and as they all head off the lake, we:

FADE OUT.

END OF ACT TWO

SCENE K

END CREDITS

INT. APARTMENT — THE FOLLOWING NIGHT — DAY 3

Frasier and Martin enter with their catch from the trip. Martin presents Daphne with five big fish. Frasier proudly gives her three big fish. Niles enters, gives Daphne one teeny fish and all his new fishing equipment, then exits, and we:

FADE OUT.

END OF SHOW

DEATH AND THE DOG

Written by
Suzanne Martin

Created and Developed by
David Angell, Peter Casey, David Lee

Directed by
James Burrows

ACT ONE

SCENE A

FADE IN:

INT. RADIO STUDIO — AFTERNOON — DAY 1

Frasier is at his console flipping through a magazine. A plate of cookies is nearby. Roz is in her booth. She has her headphones on.

Roz	Fifteen seconds, Frasier.
Frasier	Roz, I can't help noticing there are no blinking red lights.
Roz	I know.
Frasier	Who am I supposed to talk to?
Roz	Seattle.

She points to him to begin the show. He puts on his headphones.

Frasier	Hello, Seattle. This is Dr. Frasier Crane. I have some good news for you all. Perhaps because this is the first sunny day we've had in weeks, all of our lines are open. So call in. No waiting.

He glances over at the phone panel. Nothing.

Frasier	C'mon now, somebody's marriage must be on the skids, somebody's career must be going badly… other than mine. Hey, how about all you Agoraphobics? I know you're not outside.

A light goes on on the panel.

Frasier	There's a call. I'll get it.

He hits the button.

Frasier	Hello, I'm listening.
Alice	(v.o.) Hi, Dr. Crane. My name is Alice and I'm usually a happy person, but today, well, I just started thinking about all kinds of sad things. My job isn't that exciting, my kids don't call as often as I'd like… pretty soon I was in a full-blown funk.
Frasier	You know, Alice, seeing as things are a bit slow today, I'd like to tell you a little story I think might help you. Do you have some time?
Alice	(v.o.) It's three o'clock and I'm still in my bathrobe.
Frasier	Perfect. It all started three days ago. My father was very concerned about his beloved dog, Eddie, so he'd taken him to the vet.

FLASHBACK TO:

SCENE B

INT. CAFÉ NERVOSA — THREE DAYS EARLIER — DAY 2

> *Frasier, Martin, Daphne and Roz are seated together. Eddie is with them, ignoring the cup and saucer placed before him.*

Roz So, what did the doctor say?

Martin He's stumped. I told him he's not sleeping, he's not eating, he's not even sniffing stuff.

Frasier Welcome news to Mrs. Frobisher in thirteen-B.

Martin He said he couldn't find anything wrong with him physically. He thinks it might be an emotional problem.

Daphne You know, I've heard they have therapists for dogs. Do you suppose calling a dog psychiatrist could be the answer?

Frasier Only if the question is, "What is the most asinine thing we could do?"

Martin I don't know about a psychiatrist. Maybe Eddie's just lonely. I was even thinking maybe we could get another—

Frasier Stop right there. We're not getting another dog.

Martin Come on! What could be more fun than having a little brother or sister around the house to play with?

Frasier I fell for that little trick once, Dad, don't push your luck.

Martin All right, I'm gonna get this little guy home.

> *He heads for the door with Eddie.*

Daphne I'll meet you outside. I want to get some beans before I go.

> *They ad-lib goodbyes. Martin and Eddie exit. Daphne crosses to the counter. Roz notices a man across the room.*

Roz That guy over there's checking me out. Now, he's coming over. Quick, get out of here. Too late. Pretend you're not with me.

> *The man, Dr. Stephen Kagen, stops at their table.*

Dr. Kagen Hello, Dr. Crane.

Frasier Oh, Dr. Kagen.

Dr. Kagen I hope I'm not interrupting.

Frasier Not at all. I don't even know who she is.

Roz Oh, Frasier. *(To Dr. Kagen)* Roz Doyle.

Dr. Kagen Dr. Stephen Kagen.

Frasier Dr. Kagen moved into my building a few months ago from…

Chicago as I recall.

Dr. Kagen Yes, that's right. I love what I've seen of Seattle so far, but I'm still finding my way around.

Frasier Well, Roz is an excellent tour guide.

Dr. Kagen If you have a free afternoon sometime, maybe you could show me all the hot spots.

Frasier Something tells me that could be arranged.

Roz I'd be happy to. I'm free tomorrow. *(Takes a card from her pocket)* Here's my number.

Dr. Kagen *(takes it)* Great. I'll give you a call. Nice meeting you, Roz. Dr. Crane.

Frasier Dr. Kagen.

  He exits.

Roz Thanks, Frasier. A gorgeous doctor, and I didn't get you anything. So what kind of doctor is he?

Frasier A gynecologist.

Roz *(hits Frasier)* That's not funny.

Frasier What's the matter?

Roz He really *is*? I can't go out with a gynecologist. Do you know what they do all day?

Frasier I have a general idea, yes.

  Daphne crosses by. Roz stops her.

Roz Would you ever date a gynecologist?

Daphne Oh, God, no.

Roz *(to Frasier)* See?

Daphne I wouldn't even date a dentist. Hands in people's mouths all day. And after watching Eddie's complete physical I'm not anxious to date a vet anytime soon either.

  We hear the sound of tapping on glass, and we:

  CUT TO:

SCENE C

INT. RADIO STUDIO — AFTERNOON — DAY 1

  Roz is tapping on the glass. She's holding up a sign that reads "Why are you telling her this?"

Frasier   But that's really more of a side trip. Getting back to our main story, by the time I got home that day Eddie was no better.

And we:

CUT TO:

SCENE D

INT. FRASIER'S LIVING ROOM — THAT AFTERNOON — DAY 2

Eddie is on the couch, still depressed. Martin is on the floor next to him with a variety of doggie toys. Frasier is coming through the front door.

Frasier   Dad, what are you doing?

Martin   I went out and got these new toys for Eddie. I thought they might cheer him up. *(Picks one up)* Look, Eddie, it's a hamburger. Juicy, meaty. You want a bite, don't you?

He offers it to Eddie. Eddie doesn't go for it.

Martin   Okay, but that just means more for me.

Martin bites into the toy.

Martin   *(the toy muffling his speech)* I sure hope you don't bite the other side!

Eddie still ignores him. Deflated, Martin removes the hamburger from his mouth.

Martin   No reaction. Did you ever see anything sadder than that?

Frasier   No, I can't say that I have.

SFX: The doorbell rings. Daphne enters from the kitchen and crosses to the door.

Daphne   That'll be Dr. Crane. He said he was going to bring his dog over.

Martin   You mean that Maris dog?

Frasier   Don't call it that in front of him.

Martin   Why not? It acts like Maris, it barks like Maris. Aside from the fact that it eats now and then, they're dead ringers.

Daphne opens the door to Niles and his whippet, Girl. They enter.

Niles   Hello, all. I heard Eddie was down and I thought a playmate might cheer him up. So voila.

Martin   I appreciate the thought, Niles, but I already tried it in the park with real dogs and it didn't work.

Niles   You'll change your tune when you see my Girl turn on the charm. Go to Eddie, Girl. Go to Eddie. *(She doesn't)* Okay.

He moves the whippet face to face with Eddie. The two dogs look at each other with total disinterest.

Niles   Come on, Girl. Do your stuff. That's it. I can see her magic working already.

Eddie yawns and the whippet bolts out of the room.

Niles   Girl! Come back here, Girl! Come back this instant.

She doesn't.

Niles   Okay.

Niles follows her out. Martin and Daphne hover over Eddie.

Martin   Geez, Eddie, it's breaking my heart seeing you like this.

Daphne   How would a nice big batch of Grammy Moon's sugar biscuits sound?

Frasier   Do you honestly believe he can understand what you're saying?

Martin   I read that some dogs can recognize up to four hundred words. A supersmart dog like Eddie probably knows a thousand.

Frasier   Oh really, Dad?

They continue debating this, and we:

CUT TO:

EDDIE'S POV.

Martin, Daphne and Frasier's faces loom large above him and all he hears is a low, pompous voice, a high British voice and a regular guy voice all saying, "blah, blah, blah, Eddie, blah, blah, Eddie."

CUT TO:

HUMAN POV.

Niles re-enters.

Niles   Well, the crisis has passed. She just needed a rest. Fortunately, I remembered to bring her sleep mask. How's Eddie?

Martin   Worse. I think it's time we call one of those dog psychiatrists.

Frasier   You can't be serious.

Martin   I'm desperate here. We've tried everything else.

Niles   A dog psychiatrist?

Frasier   Honestly, Dad, it's the very definition of charlatanism.

Niles   I must agree. The principles of human psychology simply cannot be applied to animal behavior.

Frasier   Precisely. Animals operate on instinct, whereas human beings have the ability to reason, to cogitate, to…

CUT TO:

MARTIN'S POV.

He hears the same voices Eddie did, only saying, "blah, blah, blah, Dad, blah, blah, blah, Dad," and we:

FADE OUT.

SCENE E

FADE IN:

INT. RADIO STUDIO — DAY — DAY 1

Frasier   Thank you for staying with us through the commercial break. We're talking to Alice who's found herself with a case of the blues today. I've been relating a story of my own life to help her through it. Any questions so far, Alice?

Alice   I was wondering, what happened to Roz and the gynecologist?

Roz   Well, seeing as Frasier has told the most embarrassing part of the story, something kind of funny did happen…

FLASHBACK TO:

SCENE H

INT. CAFÉ NERVOSA — DAY — DAY 3

Roz is sitting with Dr. Stephen Kagen, enjoying coffee.

Roz   You're kidding? I went to Camp Lakeridge too. What years were you there?

Frasier   *(v.o.)* Roz. Roz…

CUT TO:

SCENE J

INT. RADIO STUDIO — DAY — DAY 1

Frasier   We're trying to help this woman. We don't have time for your pointless tangents. Anyway, Alice, my father got his way and made an appointment with the dog psychiatrist who insisted the entire household be present for the first session.

And we:

FLASHBACK TO:

SCENE K

INT. FRASIER'S LIVING ROOM — THAT AFTERNOON — DAY 3

    Martin, Frasier, Niles, Daphne and Eddie are there.

Martin   What's keeping this guy? He should have been here by now.

Frasier   Perhaps he's been detained by his "fear of fetching" group.

    Frasier and Niles share a laugh. SFX: The doorbell rings.

Martin   You two cut it out.

    Martin heads for the door and opens it to reveal a well-dressed, dignified-looking gentleman carrying a briefcase.

Dr. Shaw   Hello, I'm Dr. Arnold Shaw.

Martin   *(extending hand)* Marty Crane. Come on in.

    Dr. Shaw enters. Martin leads him in to the couch area.

Martin   This is Daphne Moon and these are my sons Frasier and Niles.

    Handshakes all around.

Martin   *(re: Eddie)* And that's the patient, of course.

Frasier   I don't know if my father mentioned it, but Niles and I are psychiatrists.

Dr. Shaw   How nice. I always enjoy being in the company of colleagues.

Niles   I'm sorry, did you say "colleagues" or "collies?"

    He and Frasier laugh to indicate it was a joke.

Dr. Shaw   *(smiles politely)* Ah, very clever.

    He sets his briefcase down and sits down next to Eddie.

Dr. Shaw   Hello, Eddie. I'm Dr. Shaw and I'm here to get to know you and help you get better. You're very sad aren't you? It's okay to be sad. Sometimes I'm sad, too. We're going to spend the next hour trying to figure out why you're sad.

Frasier   *(sotto, to Niles)* And when you give a dog an hour, you can bill him for seven.

He and Niles stifle their giggles.

Dr. Shaw I'm sorry, but I'm getting the feeling that some of us aren't taking this seriously.

Frasier I apologize, but the truth is I can't help thinking this all seems a little… well, silly.

Dr. Shaw Oh, really? I'll have you know I just attended the funeral of one Buttons McFarland whose owners felt the same way.

Frasier and Niles try not to crack up.

Martin Hey, knock it off.

Frasier Okay.

Niles Sorry.

Dr. Shaw Now, Martin, when we spoke on the phone, I asked you to think if anything has changed in Eddie's routine.

Martin Well, I thought about that, but I couldn't come up with anything.

Dr. Shaw *(opening briefcase)* Well then, let's proceed. First I'd like to administer a dog personality profile quiz I developed. My first questions are based on how you think Eddie might behave if he were a human being.

Frasier *(sotto)* Oh, boy.

Daphne Shh! This is serious.

Dr. Shaw Question One: If human Eddie were planning a dinner party, what might he serve? *(To Frasier)* Feel free to say the first thing that pops into your head.

Frasier Oh, I think we better skip over that.

Martin I say meatloaf. But not just plain, maybe with that fancy tomato soup glaze on top.

Niles It might be a bit underdone, though. He has trouble reaching the knobs on the stove.

Daphne Poached salmon. I don't know why.

Dr. Shaw Interesting. *(To Frasier)* Dr. Crane?

Frasier Could we move on to the next question?

Dr. Shaw Question two. What would you imagine human Eddie's first words to be?

Frasier Well, I hope, "Give me a breath mint." I'm sorry, I'm sorry. Next one.

Dr. Shaw What do you imagine would be human Eddie's favorite cologne?

Martin   Aqua Velva. It's a little strong, but I think he could pull it off.

Daphne   Grey Flannel. I don't know why.

Frasier   Cologne? Actually I think he would prefer toilette water.

Niles   And by the way same answer for favorite beverage.

Dr. Shaw   I'm sensing a lot of hostility here.

Frasier   I'm sorry, but I don't see the point. What is any of this telling you about Eddie?

Dr. Shaw   The point was not to learn about Eddie, but to learn about all of you. And might I say, mission accomplished. Perhaps now is a good time to examine Eddie one-on-one. Is there a room I can use?

Martin   Yeah, my room. Second door on the right.

Dr. Shaw   Come with me, Eddie.

Eddie gets up and follows him. They exit.

Daphne   If Eddie were one of the Beatles, I think he'd be George. I don't know why.

She exits to the kitchen.

Frasier   And yet she's never been committed. I don't know why.

FADE OUT.

END OF ACT ONE

ACT TWO

SCENE L

FADE IN:

INT. FRASIER'S LIVING ROOM — AN HOUR LATER — DAY 3

Niles and Frasier are on the couch bored out of their minds. Daphne is playing solitaire. Martin is pacing nervously.

Frasier   Okay, I'll say it. What the hell have they been doing in there for an hour?

Martin   He's probably just talking to him. Eddie happens to be very complex and interesting.

Frasier   Oh, yes. I must remember to sit next to him at his next dinner party.

Niles   Be prepared. He'll be up and down checking on his meatloaf.

Dr. Shaw enters from the back room with Eddie in tow.

Dr. Shaw   I have my diagnosis.

Frasier   Finally, the white smoke.

Dr. Shaw   Eddie is indeed depressed. If, as you say, there has been no change in his routine, I can only surmise that he's reacting to someone else's unhappiness. Is any one of you suffering from depression?

Frasier   Not me.

Daphne   I'm not depressed.

Martin   Me neither.

Niles   I'm cheer personified.

Dr. Shaw   Well he's picking it up somewhere. To be on the safe side, you should all be conscious of how you appear when you're in front of him. Try to speak in pleasant, happy tones. Call me in a few days and let me know how he's doing.

Martin   Thanks for all your help, Dr. Shaw.

Dr. Shaw heads for the door. Frasier follows.

Dr. Shaw   Sorry to rush off, but I have a four o'clock appointment at the zoo. There's a hyena there that won't even crack a smile. *(Beat)* See, I can joke too.

Dr. Shaw exits. As Frasier closes the door he hears:

Roz   Hold it.

Frasier   *(opening door)* Roz! What are you doing here?

Roz enters.

Roz   I want to kill myself.

Martin   Shh! Not in front of Eddie.

Roz   What?

Daphne   *(happy)* That gentleman that just left was a dog psychiatrist.

Martin   *(happy)* He thinks it's a good idea we speak in happy tones when we're around Eddie.

Niles   *(having no trouble being happy)* So please tell us why you want to kill yourself.

Roz   *(strained happy)* Well, I went out with Dr. Kagen and everything was going so great I almost forgot what he was.

Martin   *(happy)* What is he?

Frasier   *(happy)* A gynecologist.

Martin	*(happy)* Aw, geez. Maybe I don't want to hear this. C'mon Eddie.

Martin picks up Eddie and they exit to Martin's bedroom.

Frasier	So what happened?
Roz	We came back here to his place, he poured a glass of wine and — do you know what a speculum is?

We hear the sound of pounding on glass.

CUT TO:

SCENE N

INT. RADIO STUDIO — DAY — DAY 1

We see an infuriated Roz finish pounding the glass, then cross and enter Frasier's booth with a cup of water.

Frasier	Apparently, he was an avid collector of antique gynecological equipment.

Roz pours the water on his head.

Frasier	I've just gotten the signal from Roz that I'm running out of time, so I'll skip ahead in our story.

FLASHBACK TO:

SCENE P

INT. FRASIER'S LIVING ROOM — LATER — DAY 3

They are all in the living room, except Eddie.

Frasier	I don't know why we're still talking about it. If you ask me his entire theory was a lot of mumbo jumbo. Who here has any reason to be unhappy?
Daphne	Well… Mind you, I'd never say this if it weren't for Eddie's sake, but… comparatively speaking *(to Niles)* Dr. Crane, you have the most to be depressed about. What with your separation from Mrs. Crane and all.
Niles	I'm not unhappy. And besides, I don't even live here.
Daphne	Oh, please, you're here more than I am.
Frasier	If anyone is giving off unhappiness, I'm sorry, Dad, but I'm afraid it's you. What with your hip and—
Martin	Me? You're the one who hasn't had a date in a year.
Frasier	Thanks for the recap.

Martin	Not to mention two failed marriages.
Frasier	And yet you did. Okay, maybe there is a grain of truth in what you're saying. Maybe I'm not entirely happy. Why should I be? My son lives across the country, there's no woman in my life. Maybe I am the one who is making Eddie sad.
Daphne	Now, now, don't you take all the blame. If I give my life a good once over I realize it's not all jam. I just lost the only boyfriend I've had in years and the biggest thing in my life is I got my hair all cut off months ago and no one's even mentioned it.
	They all ad lib compliments. She waves them off.
Niles	Daphne, maybe you were right before. I'm not really so happy. It does look like my marriage is over, and I'll probably never have a child.
Martin	It could be me. My life hasn't been a picnic since Hester died.
Roz	And now that I think about it, what have I got to be happy about? Of course, how would that affect Eddie? Unless Frasier picked up something from contact with me.
Niles	Well, he wouldn't be the first one who… *(Losing steam)* Oh, I'm too depressed.
	They're all quiet for a beat.
Frasier	How loosely woven is the fabric of our happiness. A tug or two and it unravels to reveal how empty our everyday lives really are.
Niles	And then there are the empty nights… accompanied by thoughts of loneliness and… death.
Martin	You think about that, too? I thought it was just me.
Frasier	Everybody thinks about it.
Martin	Do you lie still and hold your breath and pretend you're in the ground?
Frasier	No, that's just you.
Roz	When I die, I want it to be on my hundredth birthday, in my house on the beach in Maui, and my husband is so upset he has to drop out of college.
Daphne	I once had a psychic tell me the strangest thing. That one day I'd go off my rocker, take up a kitchen knife, kill the entire household and then kill myself. Silly old woman. Though she was right about my moving to Seattle.
Martin	I don't know how I want to go, but my years in the police morgue taught me a few things. First off, you don't want to swallow

either Drano or rat poison. And if you're gonna kill yourself with an axe, get it right the first time.

Frasier   We can think about it, talk about it, none of us will ever know how or when.

Roz   One second we're as alive as anyone else and then… What?

Frasier   Darkness, nothingness… Afterlife?

Niles   I've always liked the notion of meeting great figures from history. But then I wonder, what if it's like high school and all the cool dead people don't want to hang out with me? Mozart will tell me he's too busy and then later I'll see him out with Shakespeare and Lincoln.

Martin   This whole thing is depressing the hell out of me. Remember, my number's coming up sooner than you guys.

They all ad-lib agreement.

Niles   None of us knows when our time is up.

Roz   And it's never long enough. My great grandmother was ninety-two when she died and her last words to me from her deathbed were, "It's so short." *(Beat)* Of course it was the seventies. She could've been talking about my skirt.

Niles   "Must not all things at the last be swallowed up in death."

Frasier   Plato.

Niles   Even deader.

Niles shifts in his seat and absentmindedly pulls a doll from under his cushion. He tosses it behind the couch. Unnoticed by others, Eddie enters and walks behind the couch. As Frasier speaks, Eddie finds the doll and starts jumping up and down with glee.

Frasier   Perhaps Dr. Shaw was right. Eddie, the simple beast, has peered beneath the masks of happiness we all wear and seen what lurks below. Despair. No wonder he's depressed. *(Noticing Eddie)* Though he seems to be rallying.

Martin   Look at that. He's happy again. Do you suppose that's all it was? He was missing his favorite doll.

Eddie runs off with the doll.

Frasier   Apparently he wasn't taking his cue from us.

Niles   Well, we've certainly taken a cue from him. I've never been so depressed.

Roz   Tell me about it.

Daphne	I wish I was a dog. All it takes is a little toy to make him happy again.
Frasier	I'm afraid we're a little more complex than that, Daphne. We know for whom the bell tolls.

They all sit quietly for a long, depressing beat. SFX: A kitchen timer goes off.

Daphne	Oh, my biscuits. *(Sighs)* I guess they're done.

She gets up slowly. They're quiet for another beat, then...

Frasier	By biscuits you mean cookies?
Daphne	Yes, that's right.

One by one they begin to perk up a bit.

Martin	They smell good.
Niles	Fresh from the oven.
Roz	All nice and warm.
Daphne	And I've got a fresh pitcher of milk for dipping.
Frasier	I believe there's ice cream, too.
Niles	Oooh.

As the human animals happily scamper off to the kitchen, we:
CUT TO:

SCENE R

INT. RADIO STUDIO — DAY — DAY 1

Frasier	... And so Alice, no matter who we are and how we live, even the happiest of us can find reasons to be unhappy if only we look for them. So don't look for them. Take a tip from our dog friends and treat yourself to your favorite toy, whatever that might be.
Alice	*(v.o.)* I'll do that right now. Thank you, Dr. Crane, I really do feel better.
Frasier	This is Dr. Frasier Crane, reminding everyone life is too short to dwell on every bump in the road. Try to give thanks for the simple pleasures. In short, eat a cookie.

Frasier pushes a button and goes off the air. He happily takes a big bite and immediately winces with pain.

Frasier	Ow, walnut. I broke a tooth. Now I have to go to the dentist. He'll tell me I haven't flossed. My lip will be all fat. My life sucks.

FADE OUT.

END OF ACT TWO

SCENE S

END CREDITS

INT. CAFÉ NERVOSA — DAY — DAY 4

> *A woman sits alone at a table and sips coffee. Dr. Kagen enters, notices her, and asks if the empty seat at her table is taken. The woman says no and eagerly invites him to sit with her. He places his jacket on the back of the empty chair and says he'll be right back. They exchange a smile and he crosses to the bar to order some coffee. None of this has escaped the attention of Roz, who crosses over to the woman, whispers to her and exits. The woman's eyes widen at the news. She quickly gathers her things and sprints from the café like a rhesus monkey through an open laboratory window. As Dr. Kagen returns with his coffee to an empty table, we:*

> *FADE OUT.*

END OF SHOW

TO KILL A TALKING BIRD

Written by
Jeffrey Richman

Created and Developed by
David Angell, Peter Casey, David Lee

Directed by
David Lee

ACT ONE

SCENE A

> *FADE IN:*

INT. FRASIER'S LIVING ROOM — NIGHT — NIGHT 1

> *Martin is in his chair, eating from a small white ramekin. Daphne is on the couch. They are watching television. Daphne looks over at Martin.*

Daphne   Oh dear, your chair's got another big rip at the bottom.

Martin   *(looking down)* Aw geez. Hand me my re-upholstery kit, would you?

> *Daphne reaches into a cabinet, pulls out a roll of duct tape and tosses it to Martin. He tears off a strip as Frasier enters from the bedroom.*

Daphne   Oh Dr. Crane, don't you look smart.

Frasier   I don't feel smart. I've let Roz set me up on another blind date.

Daphne   Oh? Who's the lucky woman?

Frasier   A friend from her aerobics class. Perhaps it won't be so bad. She's thirty-two, remarkably fit and apparently thinks I'm God's gift to broadcasting.

Martin   At least you have one thing in common.

> *Martin finishes repairing the chair.*

Frasier   Dad, at what point do you think we can stop blighting our environment with that atrocity?

> *SFX: The doorbell rings.*

Frasier   Can't you see it wants to die? Let it go.

Martin   I keep having a dream where you're saying those same words — only I'm in a hospital bed and you're slipping the nurse a twenty.

Frasier   Oh, Dad, that will never happen. I have medical power of attorney. It won't cost me a thing.

> *Frasier opens the door. Niles and his whippet enter.*

Niles   Hello, Frasier. We were in the neighborhood getting a pedicure and a seaweed wrap and thought we'd stop by. Of course the pedicure was for—

Martin   Stop right there. There's no way to finish that sentence that'll make me proud.

Niles   I have some wonderful news. I just signed a lease for an apartment in the most prestigious building in Seattle.

Frasier   You don't mean…?

Niles   *(handing him the lease)* I do. As of next week I will be a resident of… The Montana.

Frasier   Why would you want to live in a stodgy building like that? When I tried to get an apartment there they treated me like riff-raff.

Niles   If you're going to ask and answer your own questions, what do you need me for? The best part is, I'll never have to say my address again. From now on, I will simply be: Dr. Niles Crane — The Montana.

Daphne   That's a lovely building. I've only been there once, applying for a job.

Niles   I can't imagine anyone passing up a chance to hire you.

Daphne   I hope you're right. I haven't heard yet. Well, good night.

Daphne exits.

Martin   *(concerned)* Hey, Fras, do you think she really…?

Frasier   Relax, Dad. She's just angling for more vacation time.

Martin   What if she's not?

Frasier   They'd still have to call me for a reference. Either way, she's not going anywhere.

Niles notices that his whippet is glancing in Martin's general direction.

Niles   My gosh, that's uncanny.

Martin   What is?

Niles   The way she's taken to you, Dad! She's simply mesmerized by you. Come on, Girl. Go to Grandpa. Go on. *(Nothing)* Okay!

Niles picks up the whippet and deposits it near Martin. Martin pets the aloof whippet.

Martin   Hey Niles, is your dog always this cold? It's shivering.

Niles   Not shivering, Dad, shaking with joy. That's a full-body wag. I can see I'm going to have a tough time tearing you two apart.

Frasier   I'm going to go out on a limb here… The Montana doesn't allow pets, does it Niles?

Niles   On the contrary, they welcome pets. Just not cats or dogs.

Martin   Then you're in luck. I don't know what this thing is.

Frasier   Niles, that dog is not moving in here with us.

Niles	Please? At least if she's here I can visit her. I can't just turn her over to strangers. She worships me.
Frasier	Oh, you must realize by now that dog feels no genuine affection for you. You only pretend it does because it's a canine substitute for Maris.
Niles	That is the most absurd piece of psycho-babble I've ever heard.
Frasier	She's high strung, cold to the touch and ignores you. Stand her upright and put a Chanel suit on her and what have you got?
Niles	That's ridiculous.
Frasier	Oh? Remember the pill-box hat Maris wore to the Duchamps wedding?

Frasier takes the small white ramekin, now empty, and places it upside down on the whippet's head.

Niles	Oh my God!

And as Niles reels from the shock of recognition, we:

FADE OUT.

SCENE B

INT. RADIO STUDIO — DAY — DAY 2

Roz is in Frasier's booth preparing the carts for the show. Frasier enters.

Frasier	Morning.
Roz	Hey, Frasier. So, how did it go with Rita last night?
Frasier	She didn't quite take to me.
Roz	Oh, you're probably just being hard on yourself like you always are.
Frasier	You tell me. Over appetizers, she suddenly remembered a very early morning meeting and suggested we skip the jazz club after dinner.
Roz	People have meetings.
Frasier	When the waiter suggested a soufflé for dessert that would take an extra thirty minutes, she replied, "Oh dear God, no."
Roz	She's probably on a diet.
Frasier	After I dropped her off, I discovered she'd left her suede jacket in my car. When I called and offered to swing by with it, she said, and I quote, "Just keep it."

Roz	Well, that could mean… suede, huh? *(Appalled)* What did you do to her?
Frasier	Nothing. I've had it, Roz. For the last six months I've done everything you're supposed to do to meet a woman: blind dates, singles' bars, lecture series at the museum. I've even spent long hours in the grocery store looking helpless in the produce section. I give up. I'm off the market. Frasier Crane has thumped his last melon.
Roz	You know, Frasier…
Frasier	No, no, I know what you're going to say. I've got to get right back on the horse, I'm too great a catch to give up.
Roz	No, I think you should give up.
Frasier	What? But I don't really want to give up. I only said that to get your sympathy.
Roz	Look, this happens sometimes. When you're on a really bad streak you start to get desperate. Women can sense that. They can smell it.
Frasier	Smell it?
Roz	Yeah, the way an animal can smell fear. And trust me, once a guy starts acting overeager — you know, complimenting you too much, laughing too hard at your jokes — you just want to turn and run.
Frasier	I don't do that.
Roz	Frasier, wake up and smell… well, yourself. You just need some time to air out. And in my experience, the minute you stop looking is when the perfect person just falls in your lap.
Frasier	Roz, not that I don't appreciate your comparing me to a dead squirrel in a heating duct, but I happen to think you're wrong.
	Just then, gorgeous Christine walks in, carrying some papers.
Christine	Hi, Roz, I have that research you asked for. Hi, Dr. Crane.
Frasier	Hello, you're looking lovely today Christine. It is Christine, isn't it?
Christine	That's what it says on my driver's license.
	Frasier laughs uncontrollably. As she moves into Roz's booth, Frasier leans in to Roz.
Frasier	Dear God, I reek, don't I?
	And we:
	FADE OUT.

SCENE C

INT. NILES' APARTMENT — DAY — DAY 2

>*The Montana. It's everything it's cracked up to be: high ceilings, oak panelling, french doors leading to terraces, etc. Niles enters the living room leading Martin and Daphne.*

Niles   …And we conclude our little tour back here in the living room.

Daphne   It's very posh.

>*SFX: The doorbell rings.*

Martin   Yeah, Niles. But why the bed in the living room?

Niles   It's not a bed, Dad. It's an antique fainting couch.

Daphne   My goodness, they had furniture for everything back then.

Martin   Speaking of which, after that big lunch, I'm looking forward to getting back to my burping chair.

>*Niles opens the door to Frasier who enters.*

Niles   Glad you made it.

Frasier   You know, this precious building of yours isn't as exclusive as you think. Your doorman waved me right through.

Niles   That's because he knows you.

Frasier   Oh? A fan of my show?

Niles   No, he lives in your building.

Martin   What did you do with your dog, anyway?

Niles   I found a family to adopt her. Of course it devastated the poor thing, though she put up quite a brave front for my sake. If you'd seen her — romping around, wagging her tail, licking the faces of their five children — you'd never have guessed how heartbroken she was.

>*Niles places a candy dish lid onto a nearby statue of a whippet, pill-box hat style, and sighs wistfully.*

Daphne   Well, I'm sure it won't take you long to adjust to being alone again.

Niles   Actually, I don't have to. Follow me. There's someone I'd like you to meet.

>*He heads toward the kitchen. Frasier, Martin and Daphne follow him.*

Niles   It was love at first sight. She's very exotic, only eats every other day and she's so white, she's almost blue.

He enters the kitchen. The rest lag behind for a moment.

Martin   I'm getting nervous. That's the same thing he said when he introduced us to Maris.

They follow Niles into the kitchen in time to see a white cockatoo leave its perch and land on Niles' shoulder.

Niles   Everyone, meet Baby.

Bird   I love you.

Frasier   You bought a bird?

Niles   Well, I started to think how quiet it would be around here and she is beautiful, isn't she? The best part is how affectionate she is.

Bird   I love you.

Niles   She says that all the time. *(To bird)* I love you too, Baby.

Bird   I love you, Grandma.

Niles   She's still in transition from her last owner.

SFX: The doorbell rings.

Bird   Squawk!

Niles flinches as the bird digs its claws into his shoulder.

Niles   Ow, ow! She's digging her claws into my shoulder. Don't like that noise, do you Baby?

Gently disentangling the bird's claws, he sets Baby down on the counter.

Niles   Go to your food.

The bird goes to its perch.

Niles   Excuse me.

He exits to the living room.

Daphne   I've always been fascinated by these birds that actually learn how to talk.

Martin   They can't really talk. They drill a few words into them at the pet store and that's the last thing they ever learn.

Frasier   It is attractive, though.

Martin   They're all like that. Cute, but stupid.

Bird   Cute but stupid.

Frasier   Daphne, perhaps we should give these two a moment. I'm sensing a real battle of wits shaping up here.

Frasier exits to the living room where Niles is closing the front door. Niles has a stack of mail.

Niles   *(closing door)* Thanks so much. Well, I'm off to an auspicious start in this building. My neighbor got my mail by mistake. Look at all these bills. What must she think of me?

Frasier   What are you talking about? Everyone gets bills.

Niles   Not at The Montana, they don't. They all have people. The bills go to their people. I want them to think I have people too. I used to have people, only they were Maris' people.

Frasier   Keep this up and you won't even have the people who don't care you don't have people.

Niles   This just proves how essential it is to make a good first impression when moving into a new building. Which is precisely why I'm throwing a dinner party Friday night for a select group of residents. I'll show them such a good time there won't be any question that I belong here.

Frasier   Am I invited?

Niles   Yes of course, but I'm afraid you won't be able to bring a date. You know how I hate a crowded table.

Frasier   Quite alright. I've decided to take myself off the dating circuit for the time being. I'm afraid I was getting a bit desperate.

Niles   I must say I was a little concerned when you called to ask if Gloria was our first or second cousin.

Martin pokes his head out the kitchen door.

Martin   Hey Niles, you gotta see this. Your bird's eating peanut butter. It's even funnier than when Eddie does it.

Niles   Oh dear God. Dad—

SFX: The doorbell rings.

Niles   Frasier, get that will you. And pretend you're my people.

Niles exits to the kitchen. Frasier opens the door. It's Stephanie Garrett, an attractive, up-scale woman holding several pieces of mail.

Frasier   Hello.

Stephanie   Hi, I found some more of your— Oh, I'm sorry. I was looking for Dr. Crane.

Frasier   Well, I'm a Dr. Crane.

Stephanie   Oh my gosh. You're Dr. Frasier Crane from the radio, aren't you? I love your show.

Frasier Thank you.

Stephanie Well, this is an unexpected pleasure.

Frasier For me too. Sometimes the greatest pleasures in life come when you least expect them.

Stephanie I'm Stephanie Garrett. *(They shake)* You know, you're not going to believe this, but when I was a freshman at Harvard, I saw you play the Pirate King in the production of Pirates of Penzance.

Frasier Oh dear God.

Stephanie No, no, you were great. In fact, I brought my husband back to see you the next night. Well, he wasn't my husband then. Actually, he's not my husband now.

Frasier Well, I'm glad to hear that. That you came to see me a second time, not that you have an ex-husband. I have one too. Not an ex-husband, a wife. Ex-wife. Is it warm in here?

Stephanie A bit. Well, it was nice meeting you.

She begins to leave, then notices she still has Niles' mail.

Stephanie Oh, I almost forgot. These are for your brother.

She begins to leave again. Niles enters from the kitchen.

Frasier Wait! *(Then)* Uh, Niles is having a few of his enchanting new neighbors over for dinner Friday — would you possibly be free to join us?

Stephanie Friday? Yes, I'm free. *(To Niles)* As long as you have room, Niles.

Niles Yes, the more the merrier.

Frasier Lovely. See you then.

Stephanie I'll look forward to it.

Frasier As will I.

She walks away. He closes the door.

Frasier Roz was right! The moment I stopped looking for Miss Right, she fell into my lap.

Niles Well, I hope you're comfortable with that arrangement, because that's where she's going to be seated Friday night. You knew I didn't have room for her.

Frasier Trust me, Niles, I was doing you a favor. *(Hands him mail)* Now she knows you get free detergent samples.

And we:

FADE OUT.

END OF ACT ONE

ACT TWO

SCENE D

    FADE IN:

INT. NILES' APARTMENT — EVENING — DAY 3

    Niles, the bird on his shoulder, puts place cards around the elegantly set dinner table as he tries to teach Baby a new phrase.

Niles   Bon Appetit. Bon Appetit. Now you say it, Baby. Bon Appetit.

Bird   Bon Appetit.

Niles   What a quick little study you are. "Bird-brained" indeed. You already know more French than my father.

    SFX: The doorbell rings. The bird squawks and digs into Niles' shoulder.

Niles   Ouch! If you don't start getting used to the bell, we're going to have to consider a very serious manicure.

    SFX: The doorbell rings.

Niles   Ow. Coming, coming! Stop ringing.

    He opens the door. Frasier enters.

Frasier   Evening, Niles. *(Off bird)* Or should I say, "Avast ye matey."

Niles   I've no time for your badinage, Frasier. I'm only just setting out my placecards.

    Niles crosses to the table, resumes placing his seating cards.

Frasier   Placecards, eh? Very elegant. Who's Peter Soutendeck?

Niles   He's sitting on your right and he's an investment banker from Amsterdam. Apparently, he handles a lot of Bill Gates' money, so don't say anything derogatory about the Netherlands or Microsoft.

Frasier   Well, there goes my opening joke about the Dutchman trying to install Windows '95.

Niles   And on your left is Carol Larkin, Seven D, *(points to chairs)* her husband Alfred — he's in publishing — and their niece Wella.

Frasier   But I'm over here. I'm not sitting next to Stephanie?

Niles   No, you see Peter's bringing a date so I thought I'd put

	Stephanie — *(sees Frasier changing the cards around)* What are you doing?
Frasier	I did not come here to make small talk with the Little Dutch Boy and Carol from Seven D.
Niles	So you're going to throw off my whole seating arrangement?
Frasier	Look, I've waited a long time to meet someone like Stephanie. She's sophisticated and intelligent and in case you hadn't noticed, has a body to die for. It would be nice if I had your blessing.
Bird	Bon Appetit.
Frasier	Thank you, Baby. *(Then)* Now, if you really want to impress these people, you should create some atmosphere. I'll light a fire and you dim those lights.
	Frasier crosses to the fireplace, picks up the lighter and starts to ignite the fire. The fire ignites with a whoosh, scaring Niles and Frasier who jump back. The bird squawks, terrified, and flies onto Niles' head.
Frasier	Sorry about that.
Niles	Ooh, digging in a little tight here, aren't we, Baby? Everything's okay. Go to your perch.
	He reaches up to lift the bird off his head. It won't budge.
Niles	Poor thing is petrified. *(Tries again to lift bird)* Go on, Baby. Go to your perch. Go to your perch.
	Nothing. The bird is frozen.
Niles	Frasier, the bird seems to be holding on to my scalp. I can't pull it off.
Frasier	If you can pull off that jaunty beret you wore to brunch last Sunday, you can pull off anything.
Niles	I'm serious.
	Frasier tries to lift the bird off Niles' head.
Niles	Ow!
Frasier	Hold still, it's caught.
Niles	*(a bit frantic)* It's not working. My guests are going to be here any minute. I know! Get the lighter. Fire frightened her onto my head, maybe fire will frighten her off.
	Frasier gets the lighter, flicks it on in front of Baby's face.
Niles	Ow ow ow!

Frasier   (*still flicking*) It's not scaring her.

Niles   Yes it is! Stop! Ow!

Frasier picks up a cordless phone.

Frasier   All right, here's a better idea.

Niles   Good thinking! (*Grabs phone, pulls out antenna, holds it up to Bird*) Hop on, Baby! Come on! Hop hop!

Frasier   I meant maybe we should call someone.

Niles   Whom did you have in mind, a fez rental? (*Throws phone down, frantically pulling at bird*) Go to your food! Go to your perch! Go to your bed!

Frasier   Niles, try to stay calm.

Niles   Calm? How can I stay calm? I have six people coming to dinner in—

SFX: The doorbell rings. The bird squawks.

Niles   Ow! God, she hates that bell like poison.

Frasier   Go call the vet. I'll take care of things out here.

Niles runs into the kitchen. Frasier answers the door. It's Stephanie. He instantly forgets everything else.

Frasier   Well, hello again. Please come in.

She enters.

Stephanie   I'm not early, am I?

Frasier   Not at all. May I get you a drink?

Stephanie   Yes, white wine, please. (*Looks around*) What a lovely table.

Frasier   (*as he pours*) Yes. I just happened to notice we've been seated next to one another.

Stephanie   Good. Then I won't have to change the placecards around.

She smiles flirtatiously at him. He smiles back as he hands her her drink.

Frasier   (*toasting*) To the girl next door.

Stephanie   Actually, it's a little farther down the hall.

Frasier   Well, if you need a ride home later, don't hesitate to ask.

They clink glasses. SFX: The doorbell rings.

Niles   (*o.s.*) Ow!

Stephanie   What was that?

Frasier   (*vamping*) Uh… Niles must have burnt himself cooking. He's all thumbs.

Frasier answers the door. It's Carol and Alfred Larkin, a well dressed couple in their fifties and their twenty-two year old niece Wella.

Frasier   Hello, welcome, won't you come in?

They enter.

Frasier   *(extends hand)* I'm Frasier Crane, Niles' brother.

Carol   Carol Larkin, my husband Alfred, our niece Wella.

Everyone shakes hands, ad-libs "how do you do," etc.

Frasier   Please make yourselves comfortable. I'm just going to run into the kitchen and… check on the bird.

He exits into the kitchen where Niles is on the phone.

Niles   *(into phone)* So you've seen this sort of thing before… I see. Well, all right. Thank you.

He hangs up.

Frasier   What did he say?

Niles   He thinks Baby was traumatized by the fire and went into a kind of shock. He says we shouldn't try to force her off. We need to relax her.

Frasier   Good. You take care of that. I've got the future Mrs. Frasier Crane waiting in the other room.

Niles   Wait! How am I supposed to relax this bird?

Frasier   I don't know. Sing to her. Rock her back and forth. If that doesn't work, try a rum-soaked cracker.

Frasier exits into living room.

Frasier   So, how's everyone doing?

Stephanie   We're fine. *(Smiles)* Why don't you come sit down?

Frasier   *(smiles back)* I'd love to.

Alfred   Will Dr. Crane be joining us soon?

Frasier   Yes, yes. Any minute.

Frasier is about to sit when: SFX: The doorbell rings.

Niles   *(o.s.)* Ow!

Carol   Oh dear. Is everything all right?

Frasier   I keep telling him, get yourself a decent oven mitt, but he never listens…

Frasier answers the door. It's Peter Soutendeck, a handsome man in his forties and his date, Elaine Hensley, tall, thin, a tad brittle.

Frasier   Hello, come right in.

They enter.

Frasier   I'm Frasier Crane.

Peter   *(slight accent)* Peter Soutendeck. And this is Elaine Hensley.

Everybody shakes hands.

Elaine   *(to Frasier)* Actually, your brother and I are well acquainted. Maris is a dear, dear friend of mine.

Frasier   Really.

Elaine   Yes. So where is Niles?

Frasier   Actually, he's in the midst of preparing dinner in the kitchen. He's favoring us with a lovely pheasant.

The bird squawks.

Frasier   As you know, he's a stickler for freshness.

Frasier exits into kitchen where Niles is sitting at the table with a towel on his head, covering the bird.

Frasier   Now what? You're gonna wash that bird right out of your hair?

Niles   Ssh. I'm trying to make it seem like night so she'll fall asleep.

Frasier   Well, you look very cute.

Bird   Cute but stupid.

Frasier   I can't stall them much longer. They're all asking about you. The Dutchman's date even knows Maris.

Niles   What!? Who did he bring?

Frasier   Elaine somebody.

Niles   Which Elaine? Maris knows three.

Frasier   I don't know. She's thin, exquisitely dressed, dripping with attitude.

Niles   Well, that narrows it down.

Niles runs to the door, opens it a crack and peeks out. Frasier looks out from above Niles and Baby, so they appear stacked up like a totem pole. They close the door.

Niles   Oh dear God, that's what I was afraid of: it's the bad Elaine. She's Maris' oldest friend. Nothing would delight her more than reporting back to Maris that I gave a soiree with a cockatoo on my head.

Bird	*(from under the towel)* Bon Appetit.
	Angle on: the living room.
Elaine	What was that?
	Frasier enters carrying the tray of hors d'oeuvres.
Frasier	*(covering)* Bon Appetit! Crab puffs everyone! Bon Appetit.

TIME DISSOLVE TO:

INT. LIVING ROOM — TWENTY MINUTES LATER

The hors d'oeuvres tray is empty. Everyone sits listening to Frasier.

Frasier	…At which point, the woman said to Churchill, "Sir, if you were my husband, I'd put poison in your coffee." To which he saucily replied, "Madam, if you were my wife, I'd drink it."
	Frasier laughs heartily. The guests sit in stony-faced silence.
Frasier	Perhaps you've heard that story.
Alfred	Yes. From Churchill.
	More silence.
Frasier	Well, may I freshen anyone's drink?
	Everyone immediately holds up their glass for a refill.
Frasier	I'll just come by with the bottle.
	He gets up, crosses to the bar. Stephanie follows him.
Stephanie	I didn't realize you were going to have to be the host tonight. We've hardly had a chance to talk and I'm afraid I'll have to make it an early night.
Frasier	Oh, no. Really?
Stephanie	Yes, I'm leaving for Paris first thing in the morning.
Frasier	Mon Dieu. Well, let's not waste any more time. I'm completely at your disposal.
	He sees Elaine crossing toward the kitchen.
Frasier	Right after this.
	Frasier dashes over and intercepts Elaine, placing his body between her and the kitchen door, striking a casual pose with his arm against the doorjam.
Frasier	Can I get something for you, Elaine?
Elaine	I was just going to see what Niles is up to in there — perhaps I

can be of some help.

Frasier   Actually, you could pour this wine.

Frasier hands her the bottle. Thwarted, Elaine turns back to the room as a hand reaches out from the kitchen, grabs Frasier's arm and pulls him through the door. Niles still has the towel over his head.

Frasier   What are you doing? You're ruining any chance I may have with Stephanie!

Niles   Yes, that was my first concern too. Look, you can't abandon me just because you're hoping Stephanie is as horny as you are. You've got to help me.

Frasier   Well, obviously you have to go to the vet and have that bird removed.

Niles   Are you mad? I can't walk out there! I'll be the laughing stock of the Montana!

Frasier   What're you going to do, stay in the kitchen all night?

Niles   Those people live for gossip. I've only been here three days and already I know Carol's a lush and Peter's a letch. God knows what they'll say about me!

Frasier   I've spent the last forty-five minutes with your guests and I happen to think they're nice, reasonable people who'll be quite sympathetic to your problem.

Niles   Really? You don't think they'll laugh at me?

Frasier   No, I don't. Although I might lose the towel. But more importantly, if you stay in here, they'll think you are rude, ill-mannered and — dare I say it — a bad host.

Niles   Very well. But if they ridicule me, let it be on your head.

Frasier exits to the living room.

Frasier   Excuse me, everyone. There's been a little mishap. Niles is going to require a brief trip to the doctor. It's nothing serious. He just… needs to have something removed.

Niles enters, sans towel, bird on head. Everyone gasps.

Frasier   Somehow, his bird had a trauma and attached itself to his scalp. He was hoping not to have to cancel dinner but unfortunately—

Niles   Frasier, it's not necessary. Can we just go? Evening, everyone. I'm terribly sorry about this.

He starts for the door. Elaine stops him.

Elaine	*(sympathetic)* Oh, Niles, you mean all this time you were hiding in there because of your bird? You poor dear.
Peter	You know, the same thing happened to my mother once, only with her cat. Now *that* was a sight!
Carol	Who hasn't had an embarrassing moment at a party? Look, I just spilled wine on my dress.
Stephanie	Listen, I saw crazier hats this spring at the runway shows in Milan.

Everyone laughs, including Niles.

Niles	This is such a relief. I must say, I feel a little silly now for staying in there so long.
Alfred	Are you in any pain?
Niles	No. So long as nobody rings the doorbell, I'm fine.
Frasier	You know, Niles, now that you've relaxed a little maybe the bird will relax. We could give this another minute or two.

Everyone ad libs "yes, you should stay," "it's a lovely party," etc. Niles forgets about the bird and begins to play host.

Niles	All right then, who needs more wine? Alfred? Cheese? Crackers?

The bird squawks.

Niles	Now, now, Baby. Guests first.

Everyone laughs.

Niles	That dress is absolutely smashing, Carol.
Carol	Thank you.
Bird	Carol's a lush.

Niles and Frasier freeze.

Carol	Did the bird just say something?
Wella	Yes, it sounded like it said—
Bird	Carol's a lush.
Alfred	Where did the bird learn a phrase like that?
Niles	Birds today. Who knows where they pick these things up? Well, shall we all join Peter at the table?
Bird	Peter's a letch.
Peter	What did you say?
Niles	I said, let's all join Peter at the table.
Bird	Peter's a letch.

Peter	Is this your idea of a joke?
Alfred	I've had quite enough of this. Come on Carol.
Bird	Carol's a lush.
Frasier	*(to Alfred)* That one was really your fault.

Everyone gets up, starts collecting their things, including Stephanie.

Niles	No, no, wait. Please don't go. I didn't teach the bird those things. I don't know where he picked them up.
Frasier	You'll stay, won't you Stephanie?
Bird	Stephanie's horny.
Stephanie	*(to Frasier)* Oh my God. Is that what you've been saying behind my back?
Frasier	No, I never said it about you, I said it about me. I'm the horny one. All I've been saying about you is how cute you are.
Bird	Cute but stupid.
Stephanie	*(sarcastic)* Well, thank you both for a wonderful evening. Goodnight.
Frasier	Please. I can explain.
Niles	I know we got off on the wrong foot, but we are neighbors now and I'd like to think that—

Stephanie turns and venomously rings the doorbell. SFX: The bird squawks.

Niles	Ow!

She slams the door closed. Frasier stares at Niles.

Frasier	Well. Thank you very much.
Niles	Oh, please. I lost far more than you did.
Frasier	Oh? I lost the most promising romantic prospect I've had in ages, whereas you lost the respect of a posh lush and a Dutch letch. *(To bird)* Let's see you repeat that!
Niles	All right. I apologize.
Frasier	Thank you. Now, if you'd like, I'll drive you to the vet. We could take the service elevator.
Niles	Why bother? My reputation can't suffer any more than it already has.
Frasier	I'm not sure about that. Wearing a white bird after Labor Day.

> *Niles gives him a look, and they go. And we:*
>
> *FADE OUT.*

END OF ACT TWO

SCENE E

END CREDITS

> *FADE IN:*

INT. NILES' APARTMENT — EVENING — DAY 3

> *Niles is on the telephone, frantically talking and gesturing in front of an empty perch. Pan over to reveal a glowering Frasier sitting at the table with a towel on his head. Frasier soaks a cracker in his brandy and offers it under the towel. After no response, Frasier eats the cracker himself.*

FRASIER'S IMAGINARY FRIEND

Written by
Rob Greenberg

Created and Developed by
David Angell, Peter Casey, David Lee

Directed by
David Lee

ACT ONE

SCENE A

> *FADE IN:*

INT. AIRPLANE — NIGHT — NIGHT 1

> *Frasier and Joanne, the pretty woman he followed onto the plane in our last episode, are taking seats side by side.*

Frasier   We're fortunate they were able to find us two seats together.

Joanne   Well, I should warn you, if we hit turbulence, I may hold on to you for dear life.

Frasier   Then I should warn you, I'm hoping for a bumpy ride.

> *Joanne is charmed.*

Joanne   So — why are you going to Acapulco?

Frasier   Actually, it's a rather amusing story. You see I came down to the airport on sort of a blind date with a cello player — well, she didn't know it was a date. That was all in my head. Anyway, that didn't pan out, but then I bumped into you, and when you said you were going to Acapulco, I thought why not tag along?

Joanne   So the only reason you're on this plane is because of me?

Frasier   Call it kismet.

Joanne   *(to passing stewardess)* Can I switch seats?

Stewardess   Sure.

> *Joanne, creeped out, stands and gathers her belongings.*

Stewardess   You're lucky. Normally this flight is jammed.

Frasier   See, kismet.

> *Joanne hurries to the back of the plane. Felicity, an attractive woman sitting in the row behind Frasier, taps him on the shoulder.*

Felicity   I didn't mean to eavesdrop, but I have to say, I'd be flattered if someone got on a plane to be with me.

Frasier   *(pleased)* Really?

Felicity   Yeah, you just dropped everything. What could be more romantic than that?

Frasier   You know, it's a little awkward talking this way. Is that seat taken?

Felicity   No, come sit here. Please.

> *Frasier moves to the row behind him. He squeezes past a large*

man on the aisle to get to the middle seat.

Frasier   *(to large man)* Excuse me. Sorry. *(To Felicity)* Ah, made it. *(Introducing himself)* Frasier Crane.

Felicity   Felicity Campbell.

Frasier   *(they shake)* A pleasure…

Felicity   *(re: large man)* And this is my husband, David.

Frasier   … An unexpected pleasure. *(They shake)* Oh darn. I forgot to order my kosher meal.

Frasier squeezes out past David.

Frasier   Nice meeting you.

Discouraged, he finds an empty row, takes the window seat, and buries himself in an issue of "Vanity Fair". A fabulous woman, Kelly Easterling, rushes on the plane at the last minute. The stewardess helps her put her bags in an overhead compartment near Frasier.

Kelly   *(to stewardess)* Thank God the flight is late. I was sure I'd missed it.

Kelly sits in Frasier's row. He sees her and smiles. He returns to his magazine and flips back a few pages to an ad featuring a stunning model. Is it Kelly? He glances back at her.

Kelly   Yes, it's me. It's amazing what they can do with make-up and lighting.

He looks at the picture again.

Frasier   Yes, it is amazing. Not that they didn't have plenty to work with. By plenty I wasn't referring to anything specific. *(Then)* You don't have to get up. I'll change my seat.

Kelly   No, wait. Don't go. Your voice sounds really familiar.

Frasier   Frasier Crane, from the radio. It's nice to meet you.

Kelly   Kelly Easterling, from the magazine. I'm a big fan.

They shake hands.

Kelly   So why are you flying to Acapulco?

Frasier   Well, actually, it's a rather amusing tale. You see… *(bails)* I'm on vacation. *(Then)* I guess it's not that funny.

Kelly   No, it probably is. You know models, we never get jokes…

Frasier   I'm assuming you're off to a photo shoot on the beaches of Mexico?

Kelly	No, actually, I only model part-time these days. I'm in a Ph.D. program at the University of Washington.
Frasier	Oh? What's your field?
Kelly	Zoology. That's why I'm going to Mexico, to observe the spiny-tailed iguana.
Frasier	A model and a scholar? This is the part where I normally wake up.
	And we:
	FADE OUT.

SCENE B

FADE IN:

INT. ACAPULCO HOTEL ROOM — MORNING — DAY 2

Clothes strewn recklessly. The warm Mexican sun streams through the curtains on Frasier and Kelly asleep in bed. Frasier stirs, momentarily confused, but then he gazes at the fabulous Kelly and remembers their glorious night of passion. She stirs and smiles at him.

Frasier	Good morning. I love it that you wake up smiling.
Kelly	It's easy when you go to sleep that way.
	There is a quiet beat as they lean back against their pillows with happy smiles.
Frasier	I bet I know what you're thinking about. Last night, when we walked down to the beach, kicked off our shoes and looked up at that amazing blanket of stars.
Kelly	Actually, I was remembering when that iguana ran across your foot and you jumped into my arms.
Frasier	Oh, yes, that. You're really quite strong.
Kelly	I am a supermodel. *(Then)* So, Frasier, is there any chance you'd be interested in seeing more of me?
Frasier	There's more?
	Kelly slaps him playfully.
Frasier	Of course. I was hoping we would.
Kelly	Oh that's great. Which brings me to kind of an awkward subject.
Frasier	What is it?
Kelly	Well, I'm in the process of breaking up with someone. He plays for the Seahawks, and with all of us in the public eye, these things

have a way of getting out. So I'd appreciate it if you didn't tell anyone about you and me.

Frasier   You have nothing to worry about, what happened between us will never leave this room.

Kelly kisses Frasier to thank him.

Frasier   And if there's a God in heaven, neither will we.

And we:

CUT TO:

SCENE C

INT. RADIO STUDIO — DAY — DAY 3

Roz, in Frasier's booth, gets ready for the show. Bulldog stands in front of the candy machine, feeding quarters into it. He keeps selecting the same item.

Roz   Hey, have you seen Frasier?

Bulldog   He's not back from the airport yet?

Roz   No.

Bulldog collects a handful of cheese and cracker packages from the candy machine.

Roz   That's a lot of cheese and crackers. Are you gonna eat all of those?

Bulldog   Don't be stupid. I'm having people over tonight.

Frasier saunters in from the other door. He wears a colorful Mexican shirt with his jacket casually slung over one shoulder.

Frasier   Buenos dias, compadres.

Roz   I was about to give up on you. So, Mr. Impulsive, I got your message. How was Mexico?

Frasier   *(barely stifling a grin)* Fine. Relaxing. Not much to report.

Roz   Hey, come on, I've been around a lot of guys. I know that grin. I've seen that grin. I've caused that grin.

Frasier   No, no, the truth is, I just caught up on my reading, swam, walked on the beach…

Roz   Oh, I'm sorry.

Frasier   Sorry?

Roz   Well, considering the slump you've been in lately, I'm sure you were hoping for a little, you know, action.

Frasier   Roz, just because the last time you went to Mexico you were hit on more often than a piñata, it doesn't mean that was the purpose of my visit as well.

Roz   Oh that's right, you wanted to hear the Acapulco Philharmonic.

Bulldog bursts in.

Bulldog   So Doc, you get any?

Frasier   That's none of your business.

Bulldog   I knew it! Swing and a miss!

Frasier   This is ludicrous. What I did or did not do on my vacation is none of your concern. Don't you people have lives?

Roz and Bulldog head into Roz's booth.

Bulldog   Hey, we're just making conversation.

Roz   Yeah, it's not like we sit around here all day talking about your sex life.

Roz and Bulldog exit into Roz's booth. They close the door.

Bulldog   (to Roz) You owe me twenty bucks.

Roz   (opening her wallet) I don't get it. You have a pulse you get lucky down there.

Frasier   (o.c.) (into mic) Roz, you might want to turn off your microphone.

As Roz reaches for the power switch, we:

CUT TO:

SCENE D

INT. FRASIER'S LIVING ROOM — DAY — DAY 3

Martin, on his back, is doing exercises with Daphne. Eddie sits in Martin's chair watching.

Daphne   All right, now flip over. Ten kicks on each side.

SFX: The doorbell rings. Daphne crosses to get it as Martin gets on all fours and starts swinging his bum leg back and forth.

Martin   Ah jeez, I hate this one. What's it do anyway?

Daphne   Nothing for you, but it does get a nice breeze going.

She opens the door. Niles enters and surveys the scene.

Niles   Hello, Eddie. Good boy, Dad.

Martin quits.

Martin   (*to Daphne*) That's it, I'm done.

Niles   So where's Frasier?

Daphne   He got in a while ago but jumped right in the shower.

Niles   So we still have no idea why he went to Mexico?

Martin   You heard the same message we did. He struck out with that cello player and jumped on a plane.

Niles   And this doesn't concern you? It's not exactly like him to impulsively board a plane without reservations, luggage, neck pillow…

Daphne   Well, we were all encouraging him to be spontaneous.

Niles   This is beyond spontaneous. It's even beyond madcap. I'd call it reckless.

Martin   Aw, he probably just went down there to try and meet women.

Niles   I've seen this with my patients. They become so distressed after a series of failures — in Frasier's case, romantic ones — that they act out in bizarre ways.

Daphne   What do you mean by bizarre ways—

Niles   Shh, shh.

Frasier enters from his bedroom. He wears a bathrobe and is drying his hair with a towel.

Frasier   Is there anything more refreshing after a long flight than a nice hot soak in eucalyptus salts and a snifter of warmed Poire William?

Niles   (*sotto to Martin and Daphne*) Nothing yet, but keep your ears open.

Daphne   You know, Dr. Crane, we're all awfully eager to hear about your trip. Did you have a nice time?

Frasier   Oh yes, lovely.

Martin   Did you meet any girls?

Frasier   No, no, I… can't say that I did.

Martin   Oh, don't worry, you'll meet a nice girl soon.

Frasier   Don't tell me you're harping on that too.

Martin   I'm just trying to make you feel better. I know what it's like, I went through a pretty bad dry spell myself. Just when I thought it couldn't get any worse, boom, it was over just like that. 'Course it

	didn't hurt that I got shipped off to Korea.
Frasier	So you're saying it would take an international conflict for me to attract a woman?
Martin	Hey, don't get huffy. We're just feeling sorry for you.
Frasier	I am sick of people pitying me. What would you say if I told you I did spend the weekend with a woman — and not just any woman, a gorgeous supermodel? Because that's exactly what happened.
Martin	Why didn't you just tell us that in the first place?
Niles	Yes, keeping something like that under wraps does seem a tad... *(for Martin and Daphne's benefit)* bizarre.
Frasier	Well, you see... I'm really not at liberty to discuss it.
Niles	Ah yes, that pesky Club Med oath of silence.
Frasier	I hesitated because she's in the process of ending a relationship with a rather well-known sports figure.
Martin	No kidding? Who?
Frasier	Some player on the Seahawks. It doesn't really matter now anyway, she likes me better. But, before I go on, I'm going to have to ask you not to repeat any of this.
Niles	I'd urge you to do the same.
Frasier	Her name is Kelly Easterling.
Daphne	The supermodel?
Frasier	Thank you.
Daphne	She's beautiful.
Frasier	I thought so. We were inseparable the entire weekend. Oh, wait, I have a picture, I'll be right back.
	Frasier dashes out of the room.
Niles	It's one thing to concoct a little white lie, but to come up with a supermodel...
Martin	Who just dumped a pro football player for Frasier.
Daphne	Oh, I think you two are being just awful. I've never known Dr. Crane to tell a lie. Besides, it's not so far-fetched.
	Frasier re-enters, with a picture ripped out from a magazine.
Frasier	Here she is.
Martin	This picture's from a magazine?

Frasier   Yes. She's in lots of magazines. And now she's my girlfriend.

Martin and Niles exchange a look.

Frasier   Well, I'm off to bed. I didn't get much sleep over the weekend, if you know what I mean.

Niles gives him a thumbs up. As they ad-lib good-night, Frasier exits.

Daphne   He just snapped like a twig, didn't he?

As Martin and Niles nod agreement, we:

FADE OUT.

END OF ACT ONE

ACT TWO

SCENE E

FADE IN:

INT. CAFÉ NERVOSA — DAY — DAY 4

Roz is putting on her coat. Frasier sits at a table.

Roz   Oh, one last thing. The station wants your okay on this new bumper sticker idea.

Roz takes out a bumper sticker — I ♥ Frasier Crane.

Frasier   "I ♥ Frasier Crane." That's fresh. May I assume that Bell-Bottom Larry is still heading up the promotions department?

He hands it back to Roz.

Frasier   See if he can come up with something that isn't quite so dated.

Roz   Speaking of things that aren't dated...

Frasier   Roz, trust me, I do not need a date. Go.

Roz   I just thought you might be interested in meeting my friend, Tawny. She's cute, she's got a nice personality, and she rolls over like an interest-bearing bond.

Frasier   Out.

Roz crosses to the bathroom as Frasier's cell phone rings. SFX: Cell phone rings. Frasier answers it.

Frasier   Hello... Kelly, I didn't know you were back in town... Well, yes, that would be great. I can't wait... I'll meet you there in, oh, say, half an hour... Me too. 'Bye.

Frasier hangs up, smiling happily. Martin, Niles and Daphne enter. They join Frasier.

Niles   Frasier, I'm glad we caught you. We're off to the Buster Keaton Retrospective. Care to join us?

Frasier   Normally I'd jump at the chance, but I'm dashing to Campagne for a late lunch with Kelly.

Niles   Oh, your supermodel.

Martin   You didn't mention that when you left the house.

Frasier   Oh, she just called. *(He starts dialing)* She flew back a day early from a modeling assignment in Hawaii. *(Into phone)* Bernard? Dr. Crane. I'll need my usual table. In about twenty minutes. Oh, and chill your finest bottle of Pouilly Fuisse. *(He hangs up)* Modeling those swimsuits, she works up quite a thirst.

Frasier exits.

Daphne   Poor old sod.

Niles   Doesn't he realize how outlandish it all sounds?

Martin   Yeah, even a fake supermodel would've dumped him by now.

Daphne   It just seems so unlike him to invent something like this.

Niles   Well, it's not without precedent. When he was seven, he forged letters from Leonard Bernstein, then told everyone they were pen pals.

Martin   Oh, yeah.

Niles   He'd come bounding up the stairs, "Got another one from Lenny." We knew they were fake when Mr. Bernstein wrote that his Broadway debut was "Candide," when everyone knows it was "On The Town."

Martin   The messy kid lettering was also a clue.

Niles   When we finally confronted him, he was actually relieved that once and for all he could give up the charade. I think the time has come to confront him again.

Martin   Well, I guess. What will we even say to him?

Niles   We'll tell him that we know what's going on and that he doesn't have to pretend anymore. It's perfectly okay if you don't have a woman in your life.

Roz re-enters from the bathroom, un-noticed. She hears the following:

Martin   Sure, you don't have to be dating all the time.

Niles   You don't have to be dating at all.

Martin	It doesn't matter if you never have a date the rest of your life.
Roz	What is that? The Crane family creed?

Roz exits, and we:

CUT TO:

SCENE H

INT. CAFÉ CAMPAGNE — AFTERNOON — DAY 4

Frasier sits alone at a table set for two. He waits, trying not to look conspicuous. Kelly enters. Frasier stands to greet her. They kiss.

Kelly	Frasier, hello.
Frasier	Kelly, you look fabulous. I hope you don't mind, but I took the liberty of ordering us a small appetizer.
Kelly	Oh, I feel just terrible. I can't stay. I just had a call from my research lab, there's been an emergency.
Frasier	My God. Is everything all right?
Kelly	Our incubator broke, and my iguana eggs need to be moved to another lab right away. I hope you understand.
Frasier	I'm disappointed, of course, but we'll do it again.

Kelly kisses Frasier as a waiter arrives.

Kelly	I'll call you as soon as I'm done at the lab.
Frasier	My fingers are crossed. Let's hope your eggs are still fertile.

Kelly exits. The waiter removes the second place setting.

Waiter	My wife had trouble conceiving too. (Whispers) It turned out to be me.
Frasier	Well, mystery solved. Off you go.

The waiter exits. Frasier sits alone. Niles, Daphne and Martin enter, unseen by Frasier.

Niles	Oh, that is so sad.
Daphne	I can't even look at him. I'll wait in the car.

Daphne exits.

Martin	Maybe we should just leave him alone.
Niles	No, he needs help.

They cross to Frasier's table.

Niles   *(cheery)* Hello, Frasier.

Frasier   Dad? Niles? Is something the matter?

Martin   Nah, we were in the neighborhood and thought maybe you'd changed your mind about the movies.

Frasier   You're being awfully persistent, but I may just take you up on it. My date canceled at the last minute.

Niles   Oh, Frasier, whatever it is that makes you feel the need to perpetuate this fantasy woman, you don't have to on our account.

Frasier   Fantasy?

Martin   We're your family. We don't care if you haven't been with anyone in a while.

Frasier   My God, you actually think I've invented this relationship.

Martin   Look, it's no crime to go down to Acapulco and come back empty-handed.

Frasier   I didn't come back empty-handed. I came back with two huge handfuls. Kelly was just here. She was simply called away on an emergency.

Niles   That would be a modeling emergency?

Frasier   No, no, she only models in order to pay for her real interest: zoology. You see, she raises iguanas… *(sinking)* and the incubator broke… and the eggs were in danger— *(bails)* Oh, the details are unimportant. The point is, I am having a relationship with this woman.

            Long pause.

Martin   We all love you. Niles, me, Daphne.

Niles   *(gently)* Leonard Bernstein.

Frasier   I knew some day you'd throw that back in my face!

            Frasier stands, throws a wad of money onto the table and storms out. And we:

            CUT TO:

SCENE J

INT. FRASIER'S HALLWAY/LIVING ROOM — NIGHT — NIGHT 4

Frasier steps off the elevator carrying a bag of groceries. Kelly is standing outside his door.

Frasier	Kelly.
Kelly	Oh, hi. I was just leaving you a note. I'm really sorry about lunch.
Frasier	Not to worry. Do you have time to come in?
Kelly	Sure. The good news is, I was able to move all my eggs over to another lab.
Frasier	I hope you didn't put them all in one basket.
Kelly	Why does everyone think that's funny?

They enter the apartment.

RESET TO:

INT. FRASIER'S LIVING ROOM — CONTINUOUS — NIGHT 4

During the following, Frasier crosses to the bar and pours two glasses of wine.

Kelly	What a beautiful apartment.
Frasier	Thank you. Can I interest you in a glass of Beaujolais Nouveau?
Kelly	I'd love some. I actually have something to toast. My doctorate advisor asked me to join his team of researchers going to the Galapagos Islands.
Frasier	That does call for a toast.
Kelly	I'm replacing someone, so it's all very last minute. We leave in the morning and we'll be there for six months inseminating indigenous iguanas. I called my friends, they don't believe it.
Frasier	Nor will mine.
Kelly	I feel terrible leaving town so early in our relationship, but it's an opportunity of a lifetime.
Frasier	Of course. You can't pass up something like this. Besides, I'll be here when you return, and we'll always have one incredible night to look back on fondly.
Kelly	Really? I think we'll have *two* incredible nights.
Frasier	Not to be a stickler, darling, but it was only the one night: Saturday. Remember, Sunday you had to rush off to— *(getting it)* Oh right, right.

As Frasier and Kelly head toward the bedroom, we:

CUT TO:

SCENE K

INT. FRASIER'S BEDROOM — NIGHT — NIGHT 4

Clothes strewn recklessly. The moonlight streams through the curtains on Frasier and Kelly in bed. Frasier stirs, then gazes at fabulous Kelly asleep on his arm beside him. His eyes drift across the room, then settle on his camera resting on the night table. He gets an idea — he'll take a picture or two of them in bed as proof. No, too distasteful. He shakes it off. But he can't resist. Careful not to jostle Kelly, he reaches for the camera with his free hand. He's got it. He quietly opens the flash, then holds the camera as far away as possible, while nuzzling up to Kelly. He smiles, then takes a picture. Nothing happens. He tries again. Still nothing. He brings the camera close to his face to check the problem. It goes off… flash! Right in his eyes. Kelly wakes up.

Kelly   What was that?

Frasier   Nothing.

Kelly   Oh, I must have drifted off there.

Just then, the camera's automatic rewind starts loudly whirring. Frasier shoves the camera under his pillow.

Kelly   What's that noise?

Frasier   I don't hear anything.

Kelly   It sounds like a camera… Under your pillow.

Frasier   No, no, can't be.

Kelly lifts his pillow, revealing the camera.

Kelly   You took a picture of me while I was alseep?

Frasier   Absolutely not.

Kelly   Then what's this?

Frasier   Oh that's … your going away present. Bon voyage.

Kelly   I don't believe this. Are you out of your mind? You're disgusting. Just get out of here. I need to get dressed.

Frasier   You know, you'd think as a professional model, you'd be a little more relaxed about having someone take your—

Kelly   Get out!

Frasier, still holding the camera, grabs his bathrobe and exits.

CUT TO:

SCENE L

INT. FRASIER'S LIVING ROOM — MOMENTS LATER — NIGHT 4

> *Frasier waits for Kelly. She enters, fully dressed and storms across the room.*

Frasier   We have got to talk about this. I won't see you again for six months.

Kelly   You won't see me again for a lot longer than that.

> *Kelly exits, as does Frasier.*
>
> *RESET TO:*

INT. HALLWAY — CONTINUOUS

> *Kelly pushes the button for the elevator.*

Kelly   What, it wasn't enough to just tell people you bagged a model, you had to take a picture? What were you planning to do with it? Sell it to the tabloids? Pass it around the office? Show it to all your friends?

Frasier   No, no, just my immediate family.

Kelly   Forget this, I'm taking the stairs.

> *Kelly heads off down the hall.*

Frasier   Kelly... Kelly...

> *We hear a door slam. The elevator doors open revealing Niles, Daphne and Martin. They're concerned to see Frasier wandering the hallway in just his bathrobe. They treat him gingerly.*

Frasier   Well, you missed her again. She just took off down the stairs. You can go see for yourselves.

Martin   That's okay, Frasier, we believe you. Let's just get your robe cinched up and get you back inside.

> *They escort Frasier in.*
>
> *RESET TO:*

INT. FRASIER'S LIVING ROOM — CONTINUOUS

> *Frasier races over to the wine glasses. Daphne, Martin and Niles follow inside.*

Frasier   I know you're all just patronizing me. But look... *two* wine glasses.

Daphne   Oh yes, one for you, one for her. That proves it all right.

Frasier   Oh, stop it! I am not crazy!

Frasier, now thoroughly frustrated, throws a tantrum on the couch.

Frasier   I am dating a supermodel zoologist whom I stole away from a football player and she is off to the Galapagos Islands to artificially inseminate iguanas. Is that so hard to believe?

The door flies open. Kelly re-enters, extremely pissed off.

Frasier   *(instantly charming)* Kelly.

During the following, Kelly crosses to the camera, rips out the film and exposes it to the light.

Kelly   Oh look, a crowd. Where were you all hiding, under the bed? The more I think about this, the more it makes me sick to think I spent even one night with you, let alone two. You know, I've looked under a lot of rocks in my time, but I've never seen anything slither out that's as slimy and repulsive as you.

Kelly exits, slamming the door for emphasis. Stunned silence.

Frasier   Well, what do you think of me now?

Vindicated, Frasier throws his head back, and marches into his bedroom.

FADE OUT.

END OF ACT TWO

MERRY CHRISTMAS, MRS. MOSKOWITZ

Written by
Jay Kogen

Created and Developed by
David Angell, Peter Casey, David Lee

Directed by
Kelsey Grammer

ACT ONE

SCENE A

> *FADE IN*

INT. DEPT. STORE — DAY — TWO WEEKS BEFORE CHRISTMAS — DAY 1

> *Frasier and Roz stroll through the Christmas section of an upscale department store browsing through Christmas ornaments.*

Roz   I thought your dad was in charge of Christmas decorations.

Frasier Not this year — we're doing it my way. That's why I'm ordering a tasteful tree here. They'll even deliver it on Christmas Eve fully decorated.

Roz   Gee, that'll be fun for Freddie. While they're there, maybe they can open his gifts for him, too, and spare him all that annoying joy.

Frasier For your information, Freddie is not coming this year. He's spending this vacation on an archaeological tour with Lilith.

Roz   He's spending Christmas with dried-up old bones?

Frasier Yes, I just told you. She's taking him on an archaeological tour. *(Checking watch)* Dear God, look how late it's gotten.

Roz   Don't blame me. You're the one who spent twenty minutes looking for that candle-holder thing.

Frasier It's called a menorah. Hanukkah starts this week and I want to send one to Freddie.

Roz   Oh, that's right. I completely forgot Frederick is half-Jewish.

Frasier Between the Crane boy genes and Lilith's contribution, I don't think the NFL is holding its breath.

> *They walk in to the women's clothing section where a few other women shoppers mill about, including an attractive, elegant, middle-aged woman, Jean.*

Roz   Oh, I need to run over to notions and grab a gift for Calvin the security guard.

Frasier What are you getting him?

Roz   If I knew I wouldn't be going to notions.

> *Roz scoots off. Frasier watches to make sure she's gone, then quickly signals a salesman, Sal.*

Frasier Excuse me. I want to buy a gift for that woman I was just with. I was thinking about that yellow sweater there.

Frasier points to a sweater.

Sal	Excellent choice.
Frasier	I'm just not sure about the size. Why don't you bring me a medium? And please hurry before she comes back.
Sal	Of course.

Sal turns away. Roz comes back, unseen by Frasier.

Roz	It's a madhouse in there.
Frasier	Roz!
Roz	People pushing and shoving for nose-hair clippers. Is there a nasal hair epidemic I don't know about?

Sal turns back with the sweater. Frasier ushers Roz away from the counter

Sal	Here we are.
Roz	Is that man talking to you?
Sal	Here's your sweater.
Roz	Frasier, he's looking right at you.

Jean steps between Frasier and Sal.

Jean	No no, that's for me.
Frasier	You see, it's for her.

Frasier and Jean exchange a look, Frasier silently thanking her.

Jean	It's for my niece. I'm just worried about the size. *(To Roz)* You know, she's about your height. Do you mind my asking, would this fit you?
Roz	*(holds it up)* It's a little big for me.
Jean	I'm also a little concerned about the color. What do you think — and be honest.
Roz	Well, personally, yellow washes me out. I like the blue.
Jean	I agree. Thank you so much. *(To Sal)* I'll take a smaller size in the blue.
Sal	Coming right up.

Sal goes to get the blue sweater.

Frasier	You know, Roz, it looks like notions has thinned out.
Roz	Ooh, good. So you think Calvin will like the nose-hair clippers?
Frasier	Well, we can be pretty sure he doesn't own a pair.

Roz nods and exits.

Frasier   *(to Jean)* Thanks for bailing me out there.

Jean   My pleasure. *(Offering hand)* Jean.

Frasier   Frasier.

Jean   Not Frasier Crane — from the radio show? I listen to you whenever I come to Seattle to visit my daughter, Faye.

Frasier   That's very kind.

Jean   You should really know your wife's sizes.

Frasier   Oh, she's not my wife.

Jean   I'm sorry. I didn't mean to pry.

Frasier   Think nothing of it.

Jean   *(quickly)* Girlfriend?

Frasier   Just a friend. *(Off Jean's inquisitive look)* I'm unattached.

Jean   You know, could I ask you about a personal matter?

Frasier   After you rode to my rescue just now, what can I say but "I'm listening."

Jean   It's about my daughter, Faye. She's very attractive and bright, but just can't seem to meet the right man.

Frasier   Well, it's hard to advise you without knowing a little more about her.

Jean   Perfect. So you'll meet for coffee, say about three o'clock? There's a café just around the corner.

Frasier   Oh, so this isn't a professional rendezvous, but more of a fix-up.

Jean   Is that so terrible?

Frasier   Well...

Jean   Oh, I'm sorry. I overstepped. Why would you have coffee with my daughter just because I helped you?

Frasier   Look, I didn't mean to seem unfriendly. Of course I'll have coffee with your daughter.

Jean   Are you sure? I wasn't being too pushy?

Frasier   Of course not.

Jean   Wonderful. Then come with me to the men's department. We've got to do something about that tie.

As Jean starts pulling Frasier out by the arm, we:

FADE OUT.

SCENE B

> *FADE IN:*

INT. CAFÉ NERVOSA — LATER THAT AFTERNOON — DAY 1

> *Frasier and Niles sit at a table.*

Frasier   So once this woman gets here, give me five minutes and then call my cell phone. If I'm miserable, I'll say it's an emergency and excuse myself.

Niles   Ah, yes. The ever-valuable escape call.

Frasier   You've done them.

Niles   No, but I've seen it done.

> *Niles crosses to the bar. Frasier looks around the café. A beautiful woman walks over to Frasier. It's Faye.*

Faye   Excuse me, are you Frasier?

Frasier   Yes, hello. You must be Faye. How did you know it was me?

Faye   You had that horror-stricken look of someone who's met my mother.

Frasier   *(indicating table)* Shall we?

Faye   That's sweet of you, but you don't have to go through with this. I really just came to apologize for my pushy mother.

Frasier   Not at all. Please sit down.

Faye   Are you sure? I'm a total stranger.

Frasier   On the contrary. I spent twenty minutes with your mother in the tie department. You graduated from Vassar, in high school you ran on the track team, and until you were seven you had an imaginary friend called Puffis.

> *Angle on: Niles' table as Daphne enters.*

Daphne   Oh, Dr. Crane — are you here with your brother?

Niles   No, actually he's on a blind date.

> *Daphne moves to get a better look at Frasier and Faye. As she watches them Niles takes the opportunity to stare at Daphne. Daphne's following description of Frasier matches Niles as well.*

Daphne   Oh he is, isn't he? Look at him. I think he really fancies her. It's always so obvious when a man likes a woman. You can tell just by his awkward body language. His arms are open but he's nervous as a hen. *(At Frasier)* Oh, for God's sake, stop fidgeting!

> *Niles stops fidgeting.*

Angle on: Frasier and Faye's table. They sit drinking coffee and getting along fine.

Frasier   So, your mother tells me you're a lawyer.

Faye   That's so typical. I was a lawyer. I quit a year ago. Now I'm a pastry chef.

Frasier   Oh?

Faye   Yes, I work at a little French restaurant in town. Maybe you've heard of it? Le Cigare Volant?

Frasier   Oh my God, it's one of my favorites. I ate there last Friday.

Faye   I worked last Friday. What did you have?

Frasier   The Grand Marnier Soufflé.

Faye   I made that!

Frasier   Well, it was poetry on a plate.

Faye   Thank you. You didn't happen to find my earring in it, did you? *(Off his look)* Kidding.

Frasier   You know, suddenly I'm glad your mother is as pushy as she is. Funny though, you're nothing like her.

Faye   That's the nicest thing anyone's ever said to me.

Angle on: Daphne and Niles at their table.

Daphne   Dr. Crane, can I ask a favor? What are you doing for the next ten nights? Because—

Niles   Yes. Excuse me, finish the question.

Daphne   My neighborhood theater group is putting on a holiday revue — in fact, we're performing in the common room of Dr. Crane's building — but we're still looking for a musical director. I would never ask you, but they put me in charge of the whole thing.

Niles   Count me in. Is the show more religious in tone or secular?

Daphne   Well, we couldn't quite agree so we ended up with a mixed bag. We open with the "No room at the inn" scene, then it's a rousing version of "Let It Snow," a brief medley from "Jesus Christ Superstar," and then the first act ends with Santa's elves and the three wise men all linking arms and singing "Frosty the Snowman."

Niles   Well, it looks like we'll have ourselves a muddled little Christmas. *(Speed-dialing cell phone)* Excuse me, I have a quick call to make.

Angle on: Frasier's table.

Frasier ...and then I moved to Seattle and—

SFX: His cell phone rings.

Frasier Excuse me. *(Answering)* Hello? Yes, those papers. I'll just have to sign them later. I'm going to be here for a while. *(Hangs up)* Office work.

Faye That was an escape call, wasn't it?

Frasier No. What are you talking about?

Faye Oh, come on. It's a blind date. You wanted a way to back out.

Frasier You're sharp aren't you? How in the world did you know that?

SFX: Her cell phone rings. Embarrassed, she takes it out.

Faye I'll tell you after I take this call.

As she answers her phone, we:

FADE OUT.

SCENE C

FADE IN:

INT. FRASIER'S LIVING ROOM — LATE AFTERNOON — CHRISTMAS EVE — DAY 2

Frasier is on the phone. Niles positions a tasteful wreath over the fireplace.

Frasier *(into phone)* No, that would be lovely. I'm looking forward to it. *(Hangs up)* Isn't that nice? Faye's dropping by.

Niles You've been seeing a lot of her lately, haven't you?

Frasier Yes.

Niles I thought she was off to Florida with her mother.

Frasier She is. They're popping up on the way to the airport. I guess someone wants to rack up some more frequent Frasier miles.

Niles You don't ever actually say those things to the woman, do you?

Daphne enters with an armload of costumes.

Daphne Oh Dr. Crane, good, you're here.

Niles The show does begin in half an hour.

Daphne Could you give me a hand? I still have to sew the chains to Jacob Marley's tux for the dance number.

Niles	Be happy to.
	Daphne exits to her room.
Frasier	I didn't know they were doing a scene from *A Christmas Carol*.
Niles	They're not. They worked him into the Nativity scene.
	Niles follows after Daphne. After a beat Martin enters from his room with his Rudolph decoration.
Martin	Hey, Fras. Where's a good spot for Rudolph this year?
Frasier	Dad, we had an agreement about the decorations.
Martin	I know, but what's Christmas without Rudolph?
Frasier	Oh, for God's sake. He's not even one of the original reindeer.
Martin	Do any of the others have a song?
Frasier	I'm not having this discussion again.
	SFX: The doorbell rings. Martin crosses off to his room.
Martin	Okay, fine. I wouldn't want to ruin your designer Christmas.
	Martin exits. Frasier opens the door and Faye enters. They hug hello.
Frasier	Where's Jean?
Faye	Talking to your doorman.
Frasier	Does she know him?
Faye	She does now. She's trying to fix him up with my cousin Janet. I couldn't bear to watch. *(Then, spotting the wreath)* Oh my gosh.
Frasier	What?
Faye	You have a wreath.
Frasier	Yes. I tied the bows on it myself.
Faye	This is kind of an awkward question, but are you… ?
Frasier	Just because a man enjoys decorating and has an eye for color doesn't mean—
Faye	No, Frasier. Are you Jewish?
Frasier	No. Why do you ask?
Faye	That day we met, my mother said she saw you shopping for a menorah.
Frasier	Yes, for my son. My ex-wife is Jewish.
Faye	Oh, God.
Frasier	Is there a problem?

Faye	For me, no. But my mother is another story. And here I was wondering what she and I would talk about on the seven-hour flight to Miami.
Frasier	Look, if this is going to be an issue, I can take this down.
Faye	No. I've got to stop being a child about these things. If she's upset, she's upset.
Frasier	How many stop-overs do you have?
Faye	Two.
Frasier	I'll take it down.
Faye	Thank you.
	Frasier grabs the wreath and hides it in the hallway. There's a knock at the open door.
Faye	I really appreciate this.
Frasier	Don't even worry about it.
Faye	I can't believe I'm actually asking you to pretend to be Jewish on Christmas Eve.
Frasier	It's nothing. The subject probably won't even come up.
	Jean enters.
Jean	Hello, Frasier.
Frasier	Hello, Jean.
Jean	What a beautiful apartment you have.
	Unseen by Jean, Eddie enters dressed as Santa and jumps up onto the back of the couch.
Frasier	*(to Eddie)* Get out! *(To Jean)* — of that coat already. Who wants a little nosh?
	Eddie runs off. As Frasier helps Jean with her coat, we:
	FADE OUT.

END OF ACT ONE

ACT TWO
SCENE D

> *Title card: "Gefilte Fish Out of Water."*

> *FADE IN:*

INT. FRASIER'S LIVING ROOM — LATER — DAY 2

> *Frasier places some refreshments on the coffee table. Faye and Jean are seated on the couch.*

Jean   So, Frasier, you grew up in Seattle?

Frasier   As a matter of fact, I did.

Jean   Such a pretty city. So, I guess you were bar mitzvahed here?

Frasier   Yes, of course. What a proud day that was. Reading from the Torah, before the rabbi, the cantor, the mohel…

Jean   The mohel?

Faye   *(helpfully)* The one who did your circumcision?

Frasier   Yes, well, I just wanted to show him there were no hard feelings.

> *Niles enters from Daphne's room.*

Niles   Hello, you must be Faye.

Jean   And I'm her mother, Jean Moskowitz.

Niles   I'm Frasier's brother, Niles.

Frasier   Niles, can I see you in the kitchen?

Niles   Sure. *(Re: missing wreath)* What happened to the—

Frasier   —Moskowitz family that lived next door? They moved. No relation. So, can I get anybody a drink?

Faye   Nothing for us, we're leaving soon.

Jean   I'll have a glass of wine.

Frasier   Very well.

> *Frasier and Niles enter the kitchen and pour the wine.*

Niles   What is going on?

Frasier   Faye's mother thinks we're Jewish. Just play along.

Niles   What?

Frasier   I'll explain later. It's for Faye and possibly for the future of me and Faye. They'll only be here a few minutes.

Niles   Well, all right.

Frasier	Do you think you can pull it off?
	Niles opens the oven and sniffs.
Niles	Without a doubt. Ooh, ham.
Frasier	Niles. Act more Jewish! *(Then)* Now, as soon as you can we've got to let Dad know.
Niles	You mean Papa?
Frasier	Stop it.
Niles	Frasier, is this for Jean? What if she's expecting Jewish wine?
Frasier	Oh, right. I don't happen to have a bottle of that on hand.
Niles	Well, that's easy enough. It's like regular wine, plus a little of this.
	Niles pours sugar into Jean's glass.
Niles	There. Try that.
	Frasier takes a sip and grimaces.
Frasier	That's dreadful.
Niles	Perfect.
	Niles and Frasier go back into the living room. Frasier distributes the drinks.
Frasier	There we are.
Jean	Thank you. Who's got a nice toast? Niles?
Niles	All right. *(Raising glass)* L'chaim. A blessing on your head. Mazel Tov. Next year in Jerusalem.
Frasier	*(sotto)* Take it down a notch, Tevye.
	They all sip.
Martin	*(o.s.)* Hey, Frasier, seeing as it's the night before—
	Martin comes out from the hallway. Frasier, Niles and Faye freeze with fear.
Frasier	*(panicked)* Dad—
Martin	Oh great. Would it be a crime if someone told me we had guests here? I'm Marty Crane, Frasier's dad *(pointedly, to Frasier)* but you wouldn't know it sometimes with the way I get treated like a second-class citizen around here. But as long as Frasier's happy, why should my feelings matter?
	Martin exits to the kitchen as the rest wait on Jean's reaction.
Jean	And you think Jewish mothers are difficult.
	They breathe a sigh of relief.

Frasier	Niles, maybe you could help Dad in the kitchen.
Niles	Well, all right, but he's just going to kvetch at me, and frankly, I don't need the tsouris.
	Niles exits to the kitchen.
Faye	You know, Mom — we should really be going.
Jean	Always in a rush, just like a lawyer.
Faye	One more time, Mom, I'm a pastry chef.
Jean	*(to Frasier)* Law Review at Stanford and now she's making cupcakes.

RESET TO:

INT. KITCHEN — CONTINUOUS

Niles explains things to Martin.

Martin	But I don't know how to be Jewish.
Niles	Just answer questions with a question.
Martin	Like what?
Niles	What, I have to explain everything?
Martin	Can't you give me an example?
Niles	What, I should give you an example?
Martin	Are you going to help me or not?
Niles	You're saying I'm not being helpful?
Martin	Oh, forget it.
	Niles and Martin exit into the living room, where Jean holds the phone to her ear.
Jean	*(into phone)* Yes, I can hold. *(To Martin)* So, Marty, both your sons are doctors… Aren't you a lucky man?
Martin	Oh, yeah, I'm very proud… aren't I?
	Daphne enters, carrying costumes in garment bags.
Daphne	Well, I just got the phone call every producer dreads.
Niles	What is it?
Daphne	Someone's dropping out of the show. *(Getting an idea)* Actually, do you think you could take over one of the roles?
Niles	I don't know why not, I know all the songs.
Daphne	Wonderful.

Niles	*(to Faye and Jean)* Nice meeting you both.
Faye	Do you mind holding the elevator for us? We're on our way out too.
Jean	I'm still on hold.
Faye	You go ahead, we'll be down in a minute.
Niles	*(to Daphne)* So, who dropped out?
Daphne	Mr. Blanchard.
Niles	I was afraid of that.
	Daphne and Niles exit.
Jean	*(on phone)* Yes, I'm still here. …I see. Well, thank you. *(Hangs up)* It's a good thing I called. The plane's been delayed an hour so I guess we can relax a little.
Frasier	Oh. How lucky.
Jean	*(to Frasier)* So, something smells good. What have you got in the oven?
	On Frasier's reaction, we:
	TIME DISSOLVE TO:

INT. KITCHEN — TWENTY MINUTES LATER

Faye	I can't believe how well you're doing.
Frasier	Thank you, but we're beginning to push our luck. It's Christmas Eve and we're Christians. Any minute, something is going to tip her off.
	They cross into the living room.
Frasier	I don't know what's with this brisket. It just won't cook through.
Jean	Let me take a look.
Faye	No, Mom. It's really time we hit the road.
Jean	All right, all right. *(To the Cranes)* She's such a nudge.
Frasier	Well, I'd love you to stay but I'd feel terrible if you got stuck in traffic and missed your flight.
	Frasier opens the front door to see the fully-decorated Christmas tree being brought off the elevator by Dell, a delivery man. Frasier closes the door.
Frasier	On the other hand, you can't leave without a tour of the apartment.

Faye	What?
Frasier	I insist. Let's start in the bedroom.
	There is a knock on the door.
Frasier	Dad, could you see who that is, and ask them to come back another time.
Martin	Whatever you want. As usual.
	Frasier leads Faye and Jean off to the bedroom. Martin opens the door to see Dell bearing the monochrome tree.
Dell	Hello, Sir. Merry—
Martin	Shhh. Look, you got to bring that thing back in about an hour.
Dell	No way. It's Christmas Eve and I've got a full truck downstairs. So, where do you want it?
Martin	Aw geez, I don't know.
Dell	You know, a lot of people put them in their living rooms.
Martin	Look, just put it in the bathroom.
Dell	The bathroom?
Martin	Hey, this is America and we can worship any way we choose.
Dell	I don't know if it's gonna fit—
Martin	Shhh! Be quiet.
	Martin helps Dell shove the tree into the bathroom and closes the door. There's a beat, then the front door opens and Niles enters dressed as Jesus. He immediately begins searching for something he left behind. In the midst of this he takes out his handkerchief and sneezes. He exits into the kitchen just as Martin opens the bathroom door and looks around to see if the coast is clear. Then he and Dell exit from the bathroom.
Martin	All right, let's go. Quick.
Dell	Okay, you have a M—
	Martin closes the door on Dell as Frasier comes back out with Jean and Faye. They pause on the landing.
Jean	That's a beautiful bedroom, Frasier.
Frasier	Thank you.
Jean	I noticed you were sorta quiet, Faye — almost as though you'd been in there before…
Faye	Oh yeah, I have, Ma, but I was drunk and it was dark — I don't remember so much.

Jean   You see how she talks to her mother?

Niles, dressed as Jesus, appears in the kitchen doorway. Frasier and Martin spot him.

Martin/Frasier Jesus!

Niles, startled to see Faye and Jean still there, ducks back into the kitchen.

Frasier   I just realized you almost finished the tour without seeing the beautiful balcony. Dad, would you do the honors, while I check on the brisket?

Martin   All right. *(Leading them out)* Here's the balcony. That's the view.

Frasier runs into the kitchen.

Frasier   What the hell is going on? Why are you dressed this way?

Niles   The man who was supposed to do the number from "Jesus Christ Superstar" can't go on because he slipped in the shower. A man who walks on water but—

Frasier   Yes, it's loaded with irony. But why are you here?

Niles   I got within ten feet of the hay for that manger scene when my allergies kicked in. I'm pretty sure I left my nasal spray here somewhere.

Frasier   I'm sorry, but just get the hell out.

Niles   I don't think that kind of language is appropriate.

Frasier crosses back up to the balcony.

Frasier   Can you believe it? Still pink in the middle. By the time my brisket is ready, my kugel will be as dry as the Sinai.

Frasier rejoins them on the balcony. Niles pokes his head out of the kitchen and, making sure not to be seen, crosses through the living room, still looking for his nasal spray.

Frasier sees him cross through the living room and, he assumes, out the door.

Niles gets to the front door and decides to take a peek in the powder room. He turns into the bathroom. A beat later, Niles starts out with his nasal spray. Hearing everyone, he realizes he's never going to make it to the front door and pulls the bathroom door shut.

Jean   I'm sorry, it's too cold out there.

Martin   *(cold)* Really? I thought it was refreshing.

Faye   Mom, we've really gotta run. We're cutting it close.

Jean   *(to Frasier)* Well, this was a real pleasure. I can't wait to see you again. Faye, I'll just ring for the elevator.

Jean reaches for the bathroom door. She pulls it open such that Frasier, Faye and Martin can see Niles and the Christmas tree inside, but Jean doesn't.

Faye   Mom! That's the powder room.

Jean   Oh, you're right, what am I doing? *(Indicating it)* That's the front door.

Jean closes the door, leaving her hand on the knob. Frasier and Faye breathe a sigh of relief. Suddenly she opens the door...

Jean   Though I should freshen up before I go.

Jean goes into the powder room, closing the door behind her. There's a beat as Frasier and Faye look at each other in horror. Then the powder room door opens and a startled Jean exits, followed a beat later by Niles.

Jean   I take it you're reformed Jews. *(Then)* What is going on?

Frasier Jean, I'm so sorry about all this.

Faye   Don't apologize, it's my fault.

Niles   I'll let you all sort this out. I really have to go.

Jean   I understand. This is your busy time.

Niles exits.

Faye   Ma — Frasier's not Jewish. I told them to pretend so you wouldn't freak out.

Jean   What? You think I care? You can date anyone you want.

Faye   Since when?

Jean   I just can't believe you'd embarrass me this way.

Faye   You embarrass me on an hourly basis.

Jean   I embarrass you? *(To Frasier and Martin)* Are you hearing this?

Frasier Why don't we give you some privacy?

Martin   Right.

Jean   No one leaves. *(To Faye)* See? You've made them uncomfortable in their own home. You could have trusted me to understand. All I want is for you to be happy.

Faye   Yes, as long as I'm happy in the life you pick out for me.

Jean   Excuse me for being a terrible mother. All I do is care.

Faye	Oh, here it comes, the guilt. Just because I don't want you controlling my whole life.
Jean	So what do you wanna do? Cut me out of it? You hate me?
Faye	Sometimes I do hate you.
	Faye, hearing that out loud, starts to cry.
Jean	Oh my God. That I should have to hear those words.
	Jean starts to cry.
Faye	Ma, I'm sorry. I shouldn't have said that.
Jean	Why not? It's the truth. I am too involved. It's because you're all I have.
Faye	But I can't keep living my life for you!
Frasier	Maybe we should—
	Frasier and Martin start to get up.
Jean	Sit, we're nearly done. *(To Faye)* I have been smothering you. Maybe it's time I learned to let you go.
Faye	I don't want to be let go. I want you in my life, just not controlling it. I do love you, Mom.
Jean	Oh baby, I love you too.
	Jean and Faye hug.
Faye	Well, we should go.
Jean	Right. *(To the Cranes)* Thank you for a lovely visit. You have a beautiful family. Enjoy your holiday.
	Jean exits.
Faye	I'm so sorry about all of this.
Frasier	Forget it. Call me when you get back.
	Frasier kisses Faye and she exits. Frasier and Martin are stunned.
Martin	Boy, that was something.
Frasier	It certainly was. Well, I suppose we should get that tree out of the bathroom.
	Frasier and Martin struggle to take the tree out of the bathroom.
Martin	One minute they're talking about one little problem, suddenly it blows up into their whole lives, then it gets really emotional and messy, then they're hugging and it's all over.
Frasier	Well, I suppose it's a fairly healthy way to deal with those things.
Martin	Right. It's not good keeping things bottled up.

Frasier	Exactly.
Martin	You're better off just laying it on the line.
Frasier	Is there something you'd like to say?
Martin	Uh… Nah. I'm going to get a beer.
	Martin starts for the kitchen.
Frasier	Dad, do you want to have a talk like they just did?
	Martin turns around.
Martin	Uh… not unless you want to have one.
Frasier	I always enjoy talking. It's my livelihood, it's my pleasure, it's my passion.
Martin	I don't want to talk if you're going to talk like that.
Frasier	All right, let's just talk.
Martin	Fine. *(Beat)* I don't remember how they started.
Frasier	Clearly something's on your mind. Just say it.
Martin	You want to know what's on my mind?
Frasier	Yes.
Martin	You really want to know what's on my mind?
Frasier	Yes, Dad.
Martin	I want my Rudolph out for Christmas.
Frasier	That's it?
Martin	Yeah.
Frasier	All right, then put it up. Boy, to think there's been all this angst over such a silly thing.
Martin	I don't think it's silly. It's important to me, isn't that enough?
Frasier	Now, Dad—
Martin	It's pretty darned insulting the way you take a shot at anything I like.
Frasier	You're a fine one to talk. You ridicule my wine club, my clothes, the way I decorate—
Martin	At least you get to decorate. There isn't a single thing here that's mine. Except my chair, and you've gone after that from the start 'cause it doesn't go with all your frou-frou knickknacks.
Frasier	You see there? What you just said? More criticism. It's constant. Do you know how that makes me feel?

Martin	Do you know how it makes me feel to live like a guest in my own home?
Frasier	I've tried to make you feel welcome here, but nothing I ever do is good enough.
Martin	You've got a funny way of trying. Christmas is the one time of year I get to have things my way around here, the way they used to be when you lived in my house. And now I don't even get that. You'd think as a psychiatrist you'd know that was important to me.
Frasier	So now I'm not even a good psychiatrist. I'm just a big, fat let-down, aren't I?
Martin	And all I am to you is a burden. I hate living here.
Frasier	I hate you living here.
	They both start to cry.
Frasier	Oh, God.
Martin	Ah, geez.
Frasier	I feel terrible.
Martin	So do I. But how do we get out of this? They were hugging by now.
Frasier	We never should've tried this. We're not Jewish.
Martin	Maybe Mrs. Shapiro next door can talk us through it.
Frasier	I'm sorry I ever suggested we do this.
Martin	Yeah, it's not in our bones. I shouldn't have said what I said.
Frasier	No, I should've been more sensitive. I'm a psychiatrist.
Martin	And a damned good one. You make me very proud.
Frasier	Really? Dad, I'm sorry, I didn't mean what I said. I love having you here.
Martin	I love being here. I always have.
Frasier	Honestly?
Martin	No, but it might get us to the hug.
Frasier	I'll take it.
	They hug.
Martin	Is it over?
Frasier	Yes, I think it is. You know what? *(Starts to exit to Martin's room)* Why don't we put up the old decorations?

> *Frasier exits.*

Martin (*calling*) Frasier, you don't have to do that. Do it the way you want it.

Frasier (*o.s.*) No, Dad. This is the way I want it.

> *Frasier returns with a box of Christmas items. He pulls a santa out and turns it on. It glows and moves and says "Merry Christmas" in an annoying way. Frasier and Martin look on it warmly as it repeats "Merry Christmas" for a while.*

Martin All right. Nothing that talks this year.

Frasier You're a mensch.

> *Martin flips it off and Frasier and Martin start happily putting up the goofy decorations, as we:*

> FADE OUT.

END OF ACT TWO

DINNER PARTY

Written by
Jeffrey Richman

Created and Developed by
David Angell, Peter Casey, David Lee

Directed by
David Lee

ACT ONE
SCENE A

> *FADE IN:*

INT. FRASIER'S LIVING ROOM — EVENING — NIGHT 1

> *Niles sits on the couch, leafing through a magazine. Frasier is pouring sherry.*

Frasier You know what, Niles? I think I'm going to have a dinner party.

Niles Oh? What's the occasion?

Frasier I got the idea last night after we bumped into Hollis and Walter Ashby at the symphony. I've always wanted to get to know them better but I never manage to find the time.

Niles I feel the same way. They're such a charming couple. Bright, amusing… This dinner party sounds delightful. I almost wish I were hosting it myself.

Frasier Well, you know I suppose we could host it together.

Niles Really?

Frasier Yes, it'll be twice the work and half the fun.

Niles Don't you mean twice the fun and half the work?

Frasier That's what I said.

Niles No, you said twice the work and half the fun.

Frasier Well, if I did I didn't mean it. Let's pick a date.

Niles If you don't want me to co-host, just say so.

Frasier For God's sake, it was a slip of the tongue. Honestly, Niles, you bruise more easily than a champagne grape.

> *SFX: The doorbell rings.*

Frasier As a matter of fact, we should get some of those. They'll be perfect on the cheese platter.

> *Frasier opens the door. It's Roz, in an evening gown. She is carrying a dress in a dry cleaning bag.*

Frasier Roz… what brings you — and your dry cleaning here?

Roz It's Daphne's. We're going out tonight and I had it cleaned for her. She bought it last week and stopped by my place to model it. Then she picked up little Alice and started playing bouncy-bouncy with her.

Frasier And…?

Roz	I forgot to tell her Alice doesn't like playing bouncy-bouncy. Especially after a big lunch. A really big lunch. Strained spinach, strained carrots, strained beets—
Frasier	Keep going and you can add strained friendship.
	Daphne enters in her robe.
Daphne	Hi, Roz. Don't you look gorgeous.
Roz	Thanks. I feel a little guilty, though — I had to dip into my savings to buy this. But hell, if it snags Alice a daddy, *he* can pay for her education.
Niles	Is there any mystery why little Alice has trouble keeping food down?
Daphne	I better get changed. We've got to leave in twenty minutes.
Niles	Where are you going?
Daphne	A friend of mine works for the British Consulate. They're having a big reception tonight and she got us invitations.
Roz	*(as they cross off)* I'm so excited. Who knows? Maybe I'll meet some English lord who'll make me a Lady.
	They exit to Daphne's room.
Niles	At this point, I think it would take the actual Lord to make her a Lady.
Frasier	Where were we? Oh yes, picking a date for the party. You have your book?
	Niles pulls a small date book out of his coat pocket. Frasier gets an identical one from the desk. They start leafing through them.
Frasier	Let's see… not the first—
Niles	Wine club. Or the second—
Frasier	Library fund-raiser. The third no—
Niles	Fourth, fifth, sixth…?
Frasier	*(leafing)* No, no, no, no, no…
	Frasier looks at Niles. Niles quickly starts turning pages like Frasier.
Niles	No, no, no, no, no… what about the eleventh?
Frasier	Concert tickets.
Niles	Really? I don't have that marked.
Frasier	I'm planning on asking a date.

Niles	Oh. That's nice. *(Writing in book)* The eleventh — expect desperate last minute call from F. *(Turning pages)* Anything the next week?
Frasier	No, I'm going to Boston to see Freddie. Oh wait — I've got the nineteenth.
Niles	I've got the nineteenth.
Frasier	The nineteenth it is.
	Martin enters.
Martin	Hey, boys. Well, you look happy.
Frasier	With good reason. After an unusually protracted game of dueling datebooks Niles and I have set upon a mutually acceptable date for an intimate soiree.
Martin	What?
Frasier	We're having a dinner party.
Martin	Sounds fun. Any night but the nineteenth.
Frasier	What's wrong with the nineteenth?
Martin	I'm having my poker game that night. *(Off their looks)* Don't even ask.
Niles	It's the only date Frasier and I both have free for weeks. Can't you reschedule?
Martin	We never reschedule. We made a pact. It's always the third Saturday of the month. Once Jimmy even postponed his daughter's wedding, and if you ever saw Jimmy's daughter, you'd know how risky it was to give the groom any more time to think.
Frasier	Well, can't someone else host it?
Martin	No. We made a pact.
Niles	Another pact? What is this, a night of poker or the Conference at Yalta?
Frasier	Dad, we wouldn't ask if there were any other date that worked.
Martin	Why do I have to change my plans because you want to give one of your intimate soirees?
Niles	I knew he knew what that meant.
Martin	Don't you always tell me this is my house too?
Frasier	Yes. I do. I'm sorry.
Martin	That's better.
Frasier	No, I'm sorry I told you this is your house, too. *(Then)* Dad,

	please. Won't you just make a few calls and see if it's possible to change the date?
Martin	Oh, all right. I'll try. But I'm not promising anything. Those guys lead pretty busy lives and it's not always easy to get in touch with them.
	Martin exits.
Niles	Yes, let's just hope that dog track has a P.A. system.
Frasier	All right, let's get back to the party. Any thoughts on a caterer?
Niles	Well, Cornell Evans is pricey but he is the best. So innovative.
Frasier	Yes, he's the originator of the culinary pun. I was there the night he served a capon with an actual cape on. Let's book him.
	Frasier flips through his address book, looking for the number as Roz and Daphne enter. Daphne is wearing her evening dress.
Frasier	Look, Niles, our two Cinderellas.
Daphne	Yes, we're off to the ball to meet our princes.
	Daphne and Roz cross to the door.
Niles	Daphne, wait. There's something on the back of your dress.
	Niles brushes something off the back of Daphne's dress.
Frasier	You mean other than your hand?
Daphne	*(looking around)* Oh my God, it's a stain. It looks like bleach or something. The dry cleaner must have done it.
Roz	Don't worry. It's hardly noticeable.
Daphne	Dr. Crane noticed it.
Roz	That's only because he's always staring at your—
Niles	Roz! Just because you took that gown to an inferior—
Daphne	Well, I can't go now.
Roz	Why not?
Daphne	This is the only formal dress I've got.
Roz	Wait — the rest of my dry cleaning's down in the car. I bet I have something you can wear. I'll be right back.
	Roz exits. Daphne crosses toward her room.
Daphne	My only good dress. I'm so mad I could just rip it off and crawl into bed.
	She exits. Niles starts to follow.
Niles	You may need a hand with those buttonhooks.

Frasier grabs him by the coat.

Frasier   Niles.

Niles   I'm just trying to be helpful.

Frasier   *(back to address book)* Here it is — Cornell Evans.

He picks up the phone. A beat, then:

Frasier   *(into phone)* Oh, I beg your pardon. *(Hangs up)* Dad's on the phone with one of his poker buddies. At least I assume it's one of them. All I really heard was sort of a choked sob and the words, "Why, Marty, why?"

He takes out his cell phone and dials.

Frasier   *(into phone)* May I speak to Cornell, please? Yes, I'll hold.

FADE OUT.

SCENE B

INT. FRASIER'S LIVING ROOM — EXACTLY THE TIME IT TAKES TO DO A COMMERCIAL LATER — NIGHT 1

Frasier is still on the phone. Niles is nearby.

Frasier   This is ridiculous. How long is he going to keep me on hold?

Roz enters with an armload of dry cleaning.

Niles   Goodness, Roz, you had all those clothes cleaned?

Roz   Yeah. I'm dating the dry cleaner and he promised me a big discount. *(Looks at bill attached to clothes)* Hey, he only took half off. Fine, the next time I see him, I'll do the same.

She exits to Daphne's room.

Frasier   *(into phone)* Hello, Cornell? Frasier Crane… I'm hoping you're free to do a small dinner party on the nineteenth… oh, no… I see… ah, well… you too. Bye. *(Hangs up)* Wouldn't you know, the only date he's free all month is the eleventh. Damn those concert tickets.

Niles   By the way, what time does that concert start?

Frasier   Eight o'clock. Why?

Niles   *(writing in book)* No reason. Oh, you know who might be available? Tyler Wilkins.

Frasier   Doesn't he work with Cornell?

During the following, Niles looks up a number and dials.

Niles	Not anymore. They were catering a seafood banquet when Cornell flew into a rage because Tyler had ordered Mahi Mahi instead of Ahi. Tyler, of course, blamed it on Cornell's stutter and they haven't spoken since. *(Into phone)* Tyler? Niles Crane. Are you free the nineteenth? Excellent… dinner for ten… I'll call later to discuss the menu… Bye. *(Hangs up)*
Frasier	Wonderful. Okay, it's *(writing)* you, me, and the Ashbys. That leaves six chairs to fill.
Niles	Well, we have to have Joan and Ted Berkin. That's a no-brainer.
Frasier	Technically, that's two no-brainers. Forget the Berkins. Who else?
Niles	Wait a minute. You can't just steamroll over me.
Frasier	It's my party too. Don't I get a say who comes?
Niles	I have as much say as you and I want the Berkins.
Frasier	Well, I don't.
Niles	Of all the arbitrary—
Frasier	All right, all right.

During the following, Frasier crosses to a bowl of nuts on the table and plucks out six walnuts.

Frasier	We'll each have the right to blackball three guests. That way we both get an equal voice.
Niles	Fair enough.
Frasier	*(handing over walnuts)* Three for you and three for me. And to get the ball rolling — bye bye Berkins.

Frasier places one of his walnuts in the middle of the table.

Niles	Very well. How about Jon and Carol Petersen? Everyone loves them.
Frasier	Not everyone. Bllllaaaackball!

Frasier puts down another nut.

Niles	But why?
Frasier	Uh uh uh — we do not question the blackball. We just bow to its will.
Niles	All right. Nina and Arch Duncan.
Frasier	The Drunken Duncans? Have you lost your mind? They're gushy, boorish, and they can't even stand up after five o'clock. Why on earth would you — wait a minute. You loathe the Duncans. You just want me to waste a blackball.

Niles	That's insane. I adore the Duncans.
Frasier	Really. Well, perhaps I've misjudged them. The Duncans it is. *(Writing)* Nina and Arch Dunc—
Niles	Oh, stop it, they're hideous. Blackball.

Niles puts down one of his walnuts.

Niles	What about the Wolperts?
Frasier	Oh, I like the Wolperts. *(Writes)*
Niles	Finally. The Gordons?
Frasier	I love the Gordons. *(Writes)* Now we're moving.
Niles	How about the Millers.
Frasier	Blackball. She's a twit. The McGuires?
Niles	Blackball. He's a dolt. The Cromwells?
Frasier	Black—
Niles	*(buzzer sound)* Sorry. I'm afraid you don't have the balls for that. *(Writing)* The Cromwells. There. The guest list is complete.
Frasier	Well, I suppose we should start calling everyone. *(Opens book)* Beginning with our guests of honor: the Ashbys. *(Picks up phone)* Oh, pardon me, Dad. Yes, Duke, hello… Well, I understand you're upset with me… That hardly gives you the right to be vulgar.

Frasier hangs up, takes out his cell phone and begins dialing.

Niles	That Duke has quite a mouth on him, doesn't he?
Frasier	It was Dad. *(Into phone)* Hello, Hollis? Frasier Crane… fine, thanks… oh, he's fine too, he's sitting right here… actually, we're calling to invite you to a dinner party on the nineteenth… oh, you're kidding. *(To Niles)* They're leaving for Africa on the nineteenth. *(Into phone)* What a shame, we were sort of building the evening around you… oh really… *(To Niles)* The only night they have open is the eleventh.

Niles looks in his book.

Niles	That's no good, we have the concert.
Frasier	I didn't ask you to that.
Niles	Yet.
Frasier	*(into phone)* Actually, the eleventh will be fine… Oh? *(To Niles)* Now they have a conflict. *(Into phone)* … is that all? No problem. …yes, in fact they were our next call. Of course — we adore the

Duncans. See you then. *(Hangs up)*

Niles Not the Drunken Duncans? How could you?

Frasier I had no choice. They have plans with the Ashbys on the eleventh so now we have to invite them too.

Niles Then I want my blackball back.

Frasier Sorry, the blackball once dropped can never be—

Niles Oh shut up.

Frasier Anyway, the Ashbys are worth it. And, there's another plus: if we're moving the party to the eleventh, Cornell can cater.

Niles Right. Quick, you call Cornell while I call Tyler and cancel him.

They quickly look up numbers and dial their cell phones.

Niles It's a shame the party is going to conflict with that concert.

Frasier Will you stop that? At the very least, I could have taken Roz.

During the following, Frasier and Niles move around the room as they talk.

Niles *(into phone)* Tyler? Niles Crane again. Listen, we won't be needing you on the nineteenth after all.

Frasier *(into phone)* Hello, Cornell, please.

Niles *(into phone)* No, of course we're not using someone else. Cornell? Where would you get such an idea?

Frasier *(into phone)* Cornell? Frasier Crane. Good news. We're changing the date of our party…

Niles *(into phone)* We're cancelling the entire party… really, Tyler, it's nothing to get upset about…

Niles trips over the ottoman and bumps into Frasier. They both drop their identical cell phones, which now lie near each other on the floor.

Niles Oh, for God's sake. *(Re: phones)* Which is which?

Frasier picks up a phone, sniffs it and then covers the mouthpiece.

Frasier *(sotto)* This one's mine. I smell my cologne.

Niles takes the other phone. They both continue their conversations.

Niles Forgive me, I dropped the phone.

Frasier Sorry, Cornell. Anyway, the party's now on the eleventh so we can use you after all…

> *They both gasp — actually gasp — in horror, then immediately switch phones.*

Niles   *(weakly)* Tyler? *(Quickly pulling phone away from ear)*

Frasier   Cornell? We want you for the eleventh… what?

Niles   *(into phone)* I'm very sorry you feel that way…

Frasier   *(into phone)* You've already booked it? In five minutes?

> *Beat. Beat.*

Niles/Frasier   *(together)* I guess there's nothing more to say. Goodbye. *(They hang up)*

Niles   Thanks to your keen sense of smell it appears we've lost both caterers.

Frasier   It's not my fault. You obviously switched to my cologne without telling me.

Niles   Excuse me, my Notification of Intention to Change Fragrance letter must have gotten lost in the mail.

Frasier   Now what'll we do.

Niles   I suppose we could use Kitty Price.

Frasier   Kitty Price? Is she still in business?

Niles   Yes, they dropped the charges.

Frasier   Really. Well, at least we know she's available. All right, I better call the Duncans. *(Looks up number and dials)* Maybe I can catch them before Happy Hour. *(Into phone)* Hello, Nina? *(Sotto, to Niles)* Too late. *(Into phone)* Frasier Crane… Listen, Niles and I are having the Ashbys and a few others to dinner on the eleventh and we'd like to invite you and Arch… Nina, don't cry… yes, I've always loved you too… what's that? *(For Niles' benefit)* Joaquim is coming in from Argentina that weekend and you'd like to bring him along?

Niles   Joaquim? Joaquim Juarez, the conductor of the Buenos Aires Philharmonic?

Frasier   *(sotto: excited)* Of course, they were just down there, they must have met him. *(Into phone)* Absolutely, we'd love to have Joaquim… We'll see you on the eleventh… the eleventh… take two swizzle sticks and stand them up side by side… that's right, eleven… write it down, love. You know how you forget things. Okay, bye bye.

> *He hangs up and goes into a happy little flamenco.*

Frasier   We've got Joaquim!

	Niles joins him.
Niles	The maestro is coming! The maestro is coming!
Frasier	Don't cry for me Arch and Nina... So, let's see here... *(Writing)* The Duncans and Joaquim are in, which means the Cromwells and... your call, Niles.
Niles	*(re: list)* The Gordons.
Frasier	The Gordons are out. Now we're one short — we need a single woman.
Niles	That's easy. Call that babe you were going to take to the concert.
Frasier	Will you just think?
	A beat of silence. Roz enters, crosses to kitchen.
Niles	Roz! Good timing.
Roz	What's up?
Niles	We're having a dinner party and we need an interesting single woman. Do you know any? We're desperate.
Roz	Excuse me?
Frasier	*(covering)* Well, naturally we thought of you first but this isn't really your kind of crowd.
Roz	What, sophisticated? Cultured? Genteel?
Frasier	Now, Roz...
Roz	Now, Roz, my ass. I'm just as refined as you are. Shut up, Niles. Not that I'm surprised I never make your snooty A-list. The only time you invite me to anything is at the last minute when you can't get a date.
	She exits back to Daphne's room.
Niles	God knows that's enough to keep her calendar filled.
Frasier	Shut up, Niles. Roz, please...
	He starts after her, but stops when Martin enters carrying a pad and pencil.
Martin	Well, don't ask me how, but I got them to change the game. Mel was the big question mark — he had to reschedule his polyp surgery, but the doctor says he's got a two week window before it gets dicey so he's got some play.
Frasier	Oh, I'm sorry I put you to all that trouble. You can have your game on the nineteenth after all. We changed the party to the eleventh.

Martin	That's when I changed the game to!
Niles	So just change it back.
Martin	I can't. *(Re: pad)* Duke gave away his hockey tickets, Arnie switched his kids' visitation night — they'll kill me if I try to change it again.
Frasier	Dad, please, we have some very important people coming.
Martin	My friends are important too. And we don't just go around breaking pacts.
Frasier	I'll cover your losses for a month.
Martin	I'll see what I can do.
	He exits.
Frasier	All right, we still need to call the Wolperts. Why don't you do that while I go talk to Roz.
	He exits to Daphne's room.
	RESET TO:

INT. DAPHNE'S ROOM — CONTINUOUS

Daphne is in her robe, unhappily surveying the clothes strewn all over the bed. Roz stands nearby.

Roz	Come on, we've got to go. Just pick something.
Daphne	Pick what? This one doesn't fit, this one isn't dressy enough, and this one *(holds up very tarty dress)* is hardly appropriate for a posh reception.
	SFX: A knock at the door.
Frasier	*(o.c.)* Everyone decent?
	He enters.
Roz	What are you talking about? I won a SeaBee in that — it's my lucky dress.
Daphne	Oh, yes. I'm sure you got very lucky in that one.
Frasier	Excuse me — Roz, I just came in to apologize.
Roz	*(cold)* Whatever.
Daphne	What happened?
Roz	He told me I wasn't classy enough to come to his fancy dinner party.
Frasier	I didn't mean—

Daphne   Oh, get in line. I've lived here six years and the only time I'm asked to that table is when I'm holding a freaking serving spoon.

Frasier   It's just a silly dinner party. Why is everyone getting so upset?

Daphne   Oh, let's just go. *(Re: dress)* I guess this color might look nice on me after all.

She picks up the tarty dress as Niles enters.

Niles   I left a message for the Wolperts. How's it going in here?

Roz   Fine. Now could you guys please leave so Daphne can change?

Frasier starts to exit.

Niles   *(re: dress)* Oh, Daphne, not that one.

Roz   She's going to accessorize it.

Niles   With what — a lamppost and a public defender?

Frasier   Niles!

Daphne   That's it. *(Throws dress back on bed)* I'm not going.

Roz   What?

Niles   You know, an evening at home isn't such a bad idea. We could light a fire, make popcorn…

Frasier pulls Niles out of the room and closes the door.

RESET TO:

INT. FRASIER'S LIVING ROOM — CONTINUOUS

Frasier and Niles enter just as the answering machine beeps.

Frasier   Was that the answering machine?

Niles   I bet it was the Wolperts. She always screens.

Frasier crosses to the machine, presses button.

Allison Wolpert   *(v.o.)* Hi, it's Allison Wolpert and yes, count us in for the eleventh. Looking forward to it. Bye.

Sound of phone hanging up.

Frasier   Oh, good. I haven't seen them in awhile.

Harry Wolpert   *(v.o.)* Who was that?

Allison Wolpert   *(v.o.)* We just got invited to a dinner party at Dr. Crane's.

Harry Wolpert   *(v.o.)* Which Dr. Crane?

Allison Wolpert   *(v.o.)* Does it matter? You get the one, you get that other one too. Personally, I think it's a little—

Harry Wolpert *(v.o.)* Is that thing off the hook?

Allison Wolpert *(v.o.)* What? Oh my God…

>Sound of the receiver being frantically hung up. As Frasier and Niles stare at the machine, we:

>FADE OUT.

END OF ACT ONE

ACT TWO

SCENE C

INT. FRASIER'S LIVING ROOM — EXACTLY THE TIME IT TAKES TO DO A COMMERCIAL LATER — NIGHT 1

>Frasier and Niles are just as we left them.

Niles How long are we going to stand here staring at this machine?

Frasier Until it takes back what it said.

Niles What do you think she could have meant by that?

Frasier Obviously, she thinks we're always together, that we're some sort of… couple.

Niles That's ridiculous. We spend lots of time apart. Besides, she should talk. What about her and Harry? They go everywhere together.

Frasier They're married, Niles.

Niles So? I was married and I certainly didn't spend all my time with Maris.

Frasier That's because you were with me.

Niles Well, I don't see what's so odd about two people who enjoy each other's company spending time together.

Frasier She didn't say it was odd… did she?

Niles   I thought she did.

>Frasier presses the button and fast forwards to:

Allison *(v.o.)* Does it matter? You get the one, you get that other one, too. Personally, I think it's a little—

Harry *(v.o.)* Is that thing off the hook?

>Niles pushes the button, stops the machine.

Niles You're right, she didn't say odd. We're getting upset over nothing.

Frasier	Nothing? Is there a good end to that sentence? "Personally I think it's a little" what — rare? Charming? Warm outside? Face it, she was heading for odd. And what's worse, she has a point.
Niles	What are you talking about?
Frasier	Well, ever since your divorce, you've become much more socially attached to me. That's probably why she said what she said.
Niles	What?
Frasier	"You get Frasier, you get that Niles, too."
Niles	She didn't say that. She said, "You get the one, you get that other one, too." What makes you think you're the one and I'm that other one?
Frasier	I'm the "one" giving the party. That makes you "that other one."
Niles	Well, I'm the "one" who invited her. That makes you "that other one."
Frasier	Oh, come on, Niles—
Niles	No, you come on—
	They launch into an overlap: "I tell you, I'm the one," "Yes, the one with oversized ego," "How can you be so deluded?" etc. Finally:
Niles	This is absurd. Why don't we just call Allison and ask her what she thinks is so strange about us? We could both get on an extension.
Frasier	Better yet, why don't we both get on a bicycle built for two so we can ride over and ask her in person what's so strange about us?
Niles	Oh, all right. No sense driving ourselves crazy over some silly off-handed comment. Let's just forget about it. We have a party to plan. Where were we?
Frasier	Well, we have the Ashbys, the Duncans, the Wolperts and Joaquim, thank God. We just need a dinner companion for him and we're all set.
	SFX: The phone rings.
	Frasier answers it.
Frasier	*(into phone)* Hello?… Yes, Nina… *(Mimes a drunk)* What is it, dear? No, actually, you called me… oh, yes, we'll be happy to accommodate him. *(To Niles)* Joaquim can only eat certain foods.
Niles	How exotic.
Frasier	*(into phone; writing)* Rice. Beans. Jerked beef… Any special

reason?… Oh, I see… Interesting… Okay… bye.

He hangs up.

Niles Rice and beans? Why is Joaquim on such a strict diet?

Frasier Because the Joaquim they're bringing to dinner is their foster child from a tiny village on the Pampas who speaks no English and gets nauseated if he eats American food.

Niles So he's not the conductor of the Buenos Aires Philharmonic?

Frasier Oh, you are *so* "that other one." Now where the hell are we going to find somebody to baby-sit a nine-year-old?

Roz comes out of Daphne's room.

Roz *(shouting)* Quit your blubbering and pick something, dammit!

She crosses to get her purse on the couch.

Frasier Oh, Roz?

Roz Now what?

Frasier I just wanted to say you were right. You'd be a welcome addition to any party.

Roz Frasier, you don't have to do this.

Frasier No, no, we'd really like you to come to our dinner.

Roz You mean it?

Frasier Yes. In fact, we're having someone who might make a very charming dinner companion for you.

Roz He's not some stuffy old coot, is he?

Niles Oh, no. Young, young, young.

Frasier He's from an old family in South America, but he's quite in touch with the common people. I think you'll find him fascinating.

Roz Okay. Thanks. And don't worry. I've dated some very classy guys. If I can cut it with them, I can cut it with this one.

She exits back to Daphne's.

Niles She may have to cut it *for* this one.

Frasier All right, we have our ten for dinner. It's not my wish list, but at least we've got the Ashbys.

Niles That's really all that matters. Who cares what Allison Wolpert thinks about us? It's just one opinion, right?

Frasier Right.

They sit a beat in silence, then Martin enters.

Frasier   Dad… do you think Niles and I are… odd?

Martin   No, you're not odd. There's nothing wrong with you. You're just special. Your mom told me that when you were kids and I still believe it.

Martin exits into the kitchen then returns with a beer.

Frasier   Do you think we spend too much time together?

Martin   What kinds of questions are these? You're close, lots of brothers are close. Nothing odd about that.

Frasier   You're right. George and Ira Gershwin were close and they didn't turn out too badly.

Niles   Or the Marx Brothers…

Frasier   Or the Wright Brothers…

Martin   'Course then there were the Collier brothers.

Niles   Who were the Collier brothers?

Martin   Oh, they were real close, lived together their whole lives. They built a maze in their apartment out of newspapers that only they could get through. Then the whole thing collapsed on one of them and the other one just sat there with the dead body till the neighbors started complaining about the smell. (*He takes a swig of beer, stares at Frasier and Niles a beat; then*) But there's absolutely nothing wrong with you two. You're just… special.

He exits.

Frasier   You know, maybe it wouldn't be the worst idea if we went our own ways a bit more.

Niles   Yes, perhaps we have become a tad dependent on one another.

Frasier   This could be the warning we need. Today we're planning a dinner party, tomorrow we're wearing matching pajamas and washing each other's hair.

Niles   Oh come on, I hardly think it's as dire as all that.

Frasier   People are starting to talk about us. Right now we may be holding the line at "colorful." If we're not vigilant, we could slip down to "eccentric." From there it's a swift lunge to "creepy" and then the short, final drop to children ringing our doorbell and running away.

Niles   Dear God, how did this happen?

Frasier   It didn't just happen. We let it happen. And if we don't want to end up crushed to death under back issues of the "Seattle Post," we'd better do something about it.

A beat of silence as they both think about what this means. Finally:

Niles   So.

Frasier So.

SFX: The phone rings. Frasier answers it.

Frasier *(into phone)* Hello?… Yes… Oh, no. …well, I'm sorry you won't be able to make it… of course we understand… another time… goodbye. *(Hangs up)*

Niles   *(hopefully)* The Duncans? The Wolperts? Joaquim?

Frasier The Ashbys.

Niles   Nooooo.

Frasier Family emergency. They're leaving tomorrow. *(Hands Niles pen)* Here, you do it. I haven't got the strength.

Niles crosses out the Ashby's name on the guest list as Daphne enters, in the dress Roz was wearing.

Frasier Daphne — isn't that Roz's dress?

Daphne   Yes, it was really the only thing that looked good on me. *(Calling)* Come on, Roz, we don't want to be late.

Roz enters in the tarty dress Daphne wouldn't wear.

Daphne   Doesn't she look beautiful?

Roz   Oh, shove it, Daphne. I know you think I look like a hooker.

Daphne   No, I said it made me look like a hooker. On you it looks… well, it works. Shall we?

Roz   Bye, Frasier. Niles, I guess I'll see you on the eleventh.

Daphne   What's the eleventh?

Roz   Oh, I didn't tell you? They invited me to their dinner party. Shall we?

She exits.

Daphne   I don't believe it. You asked her and not me? How could you be so—

Frasier Oh, ssh. We only invited her because there's a nine-year-old child coming and we need someone to mind him. Satisfied?

Daphne   I will be in a minute. Oh, Roz…

She exits.

Frasier All right, where are we?

Niles   *(re: list)* Here, have a look.

Frasier   Perfect. We have a third rate caterer with a record, two lushes, a couple who think we're nutcases, an Argentine wild child and Roz. Dinner is served.

Niles   I still have one blackball left.

Frasier   At this point, I don't think one is going to make much difference.

Niles   It will to me. I'm using it on myself.

Frasier   You can't self-blackball. The only way you're getting out of this party is over my dead body. *(Then)* Dear God, we are the Collier brothers.

Niles   Frasier, why are we delaying the inevitable? Let's just cancel the whole thing.

Frasier   All I wanted to do was give a civilized dinner party and look what happened: You and I are questioning our whole relationship, Daphne and Roz are at each other's throats, Dad is breaking pacts all over the place…

Niles   Of course, canceling a party after twenty minutes. They'll probably think it's strange.

Frasier   They already think we're strange. You know something? Who cares what they think. So we spend a lot of time together, so what? I enjoy it. And I'll be damned if I'm going to let someone tell me there's something wrong with that.

Niles   I feel the same way.

Frasier   Thank you. Well, shall we start making our calls?

Martin enters.

Martin   Thanks a lot, you two. Nobody could agree on a date so they called off the whole game. They'll "let me know" when the next one is. I hope you enjoy your dinner party.

He exits.

Niles   When do we tell him?

Frasier   Never. We'll send him packing early that night and fill the sink with crème brulee ramikins.

Niles   Done.

Frasier   You know, those calls can wait until tomorrow. I'm famished. How about Le Cigare Volant — my treat.

Niles   You're on.

They get their coats.

Niles   *(joking)* Unless you're afraid it's too "odd" to go to dinner together.

They laugh.

Frasier   I don't think we have anything to worry about. If our relationship ever became truly odd, we're certainly intelligent enough to recognize the signs.

The doorbell rings. Frasier opens the door — there's no one there. Just the faint sound of children giggling. Frasier and Niles look at one another a beat.

Frasier   Maybe I'll pass on dinner.

Niles   Yes, I think I'll call it a night, too.

Niles walks out, then:

Niles   See you tomorrow?

Frasier   We'll talk in the morning.

Niles exits. And we:

FADE OUT.

END OF ACT TWO

DR. NORA

Written by
Joe Keenan

Created and Developed by
David Angell, Peter Casey, David Lee

Directed by
Katy Garretson

ACT ONE

SCENE A

> *FADE IN:*

INT. CAFÉ NERVOSA — DAY — DAY 1

> *Frasier waves goodbye to a rumpled professorial type as Niles crosses over with his coffee.*

Frasier	Bye-bye.
Niles	Frasier, was that the author, Dr. Gordon Edelstein? I wasn't aware you knew him.
Frasier	We just met. The station's hiring a second call-in psychiatrist for a week-long trial. They've asked me to choose among the finalists.
Niles	He'd be wonderful. I just read his book on victims of obsessive compulsive disorder. *(Meticulously wiping his chair)* Poor tic-ridden devils.
Frasier	Niles, before you get out your utensil chamois, I should warn you I've got another interview coming. Though, I must say, it's going to be hard to top Dr. Edelstein.
Niles	You're certainly taking this all very well.
Frasier	What do you mean?
Niles	Well, many in your position might feel threatened at the thought of, well… another cat sharing the litterbox.
Frasier	Your flattering analogy aside, I view it as a tribute. Obviously, the station's so pleased with my show they want more of the same. And they could hardly ask me to talk for an extra three hours. Can you imagine how exhausting that would be?
Niles	Yes, and for you as well. Anyway, moving on to me — what's the verdict?
Frasier	The verdict?
Niles	On my new look. And, by the way, you deserve some of the credit.
Frasier	*(at a loss)* Really.
Niles	You keep telling me I should accept Daphne's relationship with Donny and find a paramour of my own. Well, the hunt is on. I thought I'd bolster my self-confidence by adopting this raffish new look.
Frasier	*(at sea)* Well… it suits you. It's dashing, yet understated, and… Oh, I give up, what are we talking about?

Niles	My moustache. I'll grant you, it's at an early stage.
Frasier	What stage? Research and development? I can't even see i...
Niles	It must be covered in cappuccino foam. *(Wipes his lip)* Now wh... do you think?
Frasier	I think next time you should order your cappuccino with a dash of Rogaine.
Dr. Nora	Dr. Crane.

Dr. Nora Fairchild has entered. She's an attractive woman dressed in a crisp yet sexy business suit.

Dr. Nora	Dr. Nora Fairchild.
Frasier	Oh, welcome.
Dr. Nora	I can't tell you what a privilege this is. I listened to your show today and… I was amazed. I'm sorry if that sounds too fawning.
Frasier	No. Fawning is fine. Fawning is fun.
Dr. Nora	Am I interrupting another interview?
Frasier	Oh, no, this is my brother, Niles. And he was just going.
Dr. Nora	I should have known you were brothers — the same superb fashion sense, the same refined yet masculine good looks. *(To Niles)* You must be so proud of your kid brother, the radio star.
Niles	Oh, yes. *(Rising)* Congratulations. I hope you'll be happy at KACL.
Dr. Nora	That's a little premature, isn't it?
Niles	Let's just say I know my little brother.

As Niles exits, we:

FADE OUT.

SCENE B

Title card: "The Tricks of the Trade."

FADE IN:

INT. RADIO STUDIO — DAY — DAY 2

Frasier's on the air. Roz is in her booth.

Frasier	Well, that's all for today. Coming up next is a new member of our KACL team, Dr. Nora Fairchild. I had a long chat with her yesterday and I'm confident that she'll bring to Seattle the same

insight and compassion she brought to her award-winning stints on "Wake Up, Wichita" and "Up and At 'Em Albuquerque."

Kenny ushers Dr. Nora into the booth. With her is George, her call screener, a tall nice-looking man in his twenties.

Kenny   Here's where it all happens.

Frasier   Dr. Nora, come in. I see you've met our crack station manager.

Dr. Nora   Yes, and I just want to thank you both for making me and my producer feel so welcome. Is everyone around here as friendly as you two?

Roz enters from her booth, seeing Nora and George.

Roz   *(to George)* Well, hi there.

Frasier   Some are even friendlier. My producer, Roz Doyle.

Dr. Nora   *(shaking Roz's hand)* Dr. Nora. And this is my producer George.

Roz   Nice to meet you. *(To George)* Follow me and I'll give you the lay of the land.

Roz steers George into her booth.

Frasier   Let's hope that was a figure of speech and not a sales pitch.

Frasier guides Nora into her chair and shows her the console.

Frasier   At any rate, here's your headset, phone lines, cough button. And remember, it's normal to be nervous. Even my own first show was a tad bumpy.

Kenny   *(laughs)* Bumpy? It was a train wreck! Medic! We got incoming!

Frasier   As I recall, you weren't even working here then.

Kenny   I got a tape of it from my secret Santa. Break a leg, Dr. Nora.

Kenny exits the booth.

Dr. Nora   *(taking Frasier's hand)* All my life I've wanted to help people and now, thanks to you, I can do that on a scale I never could before. I am so lucky I met you.

Frasier   I'd say the lucky ones are the people of Seattle. Godspeed, Dr. Nora.

Frasier withdraws and stands watching Dr. Nora benevolently though the glass. Roz comes around the corner from her booth.

Roz   What are you smirking about?

Frasier   It's just nice having a protégée.

Frasier gives Dr. Nora a thumbs-up. She smiles back.

Frasier	You see the way she acts toward me? Like a shy Japanese novice bowing before her Frasier sensei.
Roz	I feel a bow coming on myself. Can you hand me that bucket?
Frasier	Shh, she's starting. I just want to hear the beginning, make sure she's got those first-show jitters under control.
	Dr. Nora's show has begun.
Dr. Nora	Well, let's get right to our first caller. Whom do we have?
George	We have Jenny from Tacoma on line one.
Dr. Nora	Hello, Jenny. I'm Dr. Nora and I'm here to help.
Jenny	*(v.o.)* Hi, Dr. Nora. My boyfriend and I have been living together about two years and we're really happy.
Dr. Nora	Are you having sex?
Jenny	*(v.o.)* Oh, our sex life's not the problem. It's great. But whenever I mention marriage he changes the subject. Do you think he's afraid of commitment?
Dr. Nora	No, that's not it.
Frasier	*(to Roz)* She'll be fine.
	Satisfied that Dr. Nora is off and running, Frasier heads down the hallway and offscreen.
Dr. Nora	Let me help you see this from a different perspective… You're a whore, Jenny.
Jenny	*(v.o.)* Huh?
	A wide-eyed Frasier reappears at the window and listens incredulously.
Dr. Nora	You're sleeping with a man you're not married to. In my book, that's a whore.
Jenny	*(v.o.) (starting to cry)* I'm not a whore. I'm a stewardess.
Dr. Nora	You think there's no overlap?
	Dr. Nora laughs at her own joke.
Roz	Well, she's got those jitters under control.
Dr. Nora	Why are you crying, Jenny? A minute ago you were a happy whore. Now you're a sad whore. Maybe it's because you're learning that men marry wives, not prostitutes.
Jenny	*(v.o.) (crying)* But, you don't understand. I love him and he loves me too and—
	SFX: Dr. Nora cuts Jenny's lament off with a sound effect cart; a

cranky baby crying.

Dr. Nora No crybabies! Wake up, Jenny. You've blown it. Dump this creep, find a new guy, and until you're Mrs. New Guy you keep those knees together, okay? Staple 'em! I don't care if you have to hop to the altar! *(She laughs)* God bless, honey. *(Hangs up)* Who's next?

George We have Amber on line two.

Dr. Nora Hey, Amber. I'm Dr. Nora and I'm here to help.

And as Frasier and Roz look on in appalled amazement we:

FADE OUT.

SCENE C

FADE IN:

INT. FRASIER'S LIVING ROOM — DAY — DAY 2

Daphne is tidying the kitchen. Niles enters.

Daphne Dr. Crane, I didn't hear you come in.

He strikes a casual yet debonair pose.

Niles Hello, Daphne. Notice anything?

Daphne Oh, yes. Don't you look dashing? *(Off his tie)* Blue really is your color. Hold still, though, there's something on your lip.

She takes a cloth and tries to wipe off Niles' moustache.

Daphne Eating tapioca, were we?... No, wait, it's some sort of hair.

Niles Actually, it's a moustache.

Daphne Oh, so it is. Still a bit on the wispy side. Puts me in my mind of my Grammy Moon... or rather it will once it's grown in a bit.

She exits into the living room where Martin sits in his chair as Frasier enters from outside. He is in high dudgeon.

Frasier Turn on the radio.

Martin Is something the matter?

Frasier Just turn the radio on to KACL.

Daphne turns on the radio. We hear Dr. Nora.

Dr. Nora *(v.o.)* Listen to me! You have a child! You think you have the right to get divorced just because you're tired of your husband?

Jill *(v.o.)* But he's gay!

Dr. Nora *(v.o.)* You picked him. You made a baby with him. Maybe you got him drunk, maybe you dressed up as Antonio Banderas. I don't care. Just make it work!

Frasier turns off the radio.

Niles   My God, that's a bit harsh.

Frasier   If you think that's bad, you should hear her on premarital sex. This afternoon she told a teenage girl from Bainbridge her parents should have had her spayed.

Martin   We had her on earlier when I was doing my exercises, and I don't think she's so bad.

Frasier   Excuse me?

Martin   It's nice to hear someone stick up for old-fashioned values. I mean like sex. I'm not a prude or anything, but in my day, sex was still something sacred, mysterious. Nowadays, you can't turn on the television without seeing all that "ooh-ooh, ahh-ahh" stuff.

Frasier   I think that explains our ninety dollar cable bill last month.

Daphne   I liked her too. I know she's a bit of a terror. She'll call a girl a tramp, tell her she'll never amount to anything, then laugh in her face when she cries. But if you listen to her very carefully you can hear all the love underneath… she's like my mother that way. I think I'll go give mum a call.

Daphne exits to her room. Niles addresses Frasier.

Niles   Well, I'm with you. She's a monster. It makes you wonder what sort of person would hire her.

Frasier   You can hardly blame me for that. I interviewed her at length and she said all the right things.

Martin   Buttered you up like a pancake, didn't she?

Niles   I'll say — she complimented his clothes, his looks. She even pretended to think I was the older brother. Of course the moustache could have clouded her judgment on that one.

Martin   She has a moustache?

Frasier   No, Dad, Niles' moustache.

Martin   Niles doesn't have a moustache.

Frasier   Shh. He doesn't know yet. *(Then)* Well, like it or not, I am responsible for her being here. I'll just have to sit her down and tell her that when it comes to sex advice people want Dr. Ruth, not Dr. Ruthless. It's for her own good. At the rate she's going, she'll be out of callers by Wednesday. How many people will phone some harridan just to be abused?

Daphne enters from the hall conversing on a portable phone.

Daphne No, mum, my boyfriend hasn't dumped me for someone prettier. He loves me… Oh come on, that can't be the only reason he's staying with me. He loves me, just like you do… Oh, stop it, you old tease. If you keep saying those things I'll start to think you mean them.

Daphne wanders into the kitchen.

Frasier Well, maybe by Thursday.

And we:

FADE OUT.

SCENE D

Title card: "Dr. Virago."

FADE IN:

INT. RADIO STUDIO — DAY — DAY 3

Frasier is on the air.

Frasier Until tomorrow this is Dr. Frasier Crane wishing you good mental health.

Dr. Nora enters the booth.

Fraser *(coldly)* Ah, Dr. Nora.

Dr. Nora Such a frosty tone — is something the matter?

Frasier I have just one question for you—

Roz enters from her booth.

Roz *(to Dr. Nora)* What kind of vicious, name-calling, judgmental, machete-mouthed bitch are you?

Frasier I was going for the less feisty version—

Roz I heard what you said to that single mother yesterday. Well, for your information, I'm a single mom too!

Dr. Nora I'm not surprised after watching you pounce on poor George like a Kodiak bear on a salmon.

Roz *(advancing on her)* That does it—

Frasier Roz! I need to talk to Dr. Nora before her show, so just pencil in the hair-pulling for later.

Roz	This isn't over between us. If you want to I'll take it out in the street.
Dr. Nora	That would hardly be fair. You'd have the home field advantage.
	Frasier pushes a struggling Roz out of the booth and closes the door.
Frasier	I hardly know where to begin.
Dr. Nora	Save it. Whatever it is, I've heard it. "Dr. Nora is mean." "Dr. Nora hurts people's feelings." Well, too bad. I'm not here to coddle people, I'm here to help them.
Frasier	"Help?" Just how are you helping a confused bisexual woman by calling her an "equal opportunity slut?"
Dr. Nora	I don't mince words.
Frasier	No, just people. Doesn't it bother you that you misrepresented yourself to get this job? You clearly implied your show would be similar to mine.
Dr. Nora	When did I do that?
Frasier	You said you admired my show.
Dr. Nora	I didn't say I admired it. I said it amazed me — which it does. You're a fine one to question my ethics. We both know you only hired me because you hoped I might sleep with you.
Frasier	That thought never crossed my mind.
Dr. Nora	Now who's lying? You won't admit that, like most men, you leave all major decisions to your penis. Fortunately for Seattle, your penis chose right. It just didn't know why.
Frasier	Well, you forget one thing, Dr. Nora. You're here on my recommendation. You may consider it withdrawn.
	Kenny enters.
Kenny	Hey, Dr. Crane.
Frasier	Kenny! Just the man I want to see.
Kenny	Dr. Nora — *(comically cowering)* Don't hit me!
Frasier	I wanted to share my thoughts on Dr. Nora's show.
Kenny	Get in line. The switchboard's been goin' nuts.
Frasier	I don't doubt it.
Kenny	*(to Dr. Nora)* They love you.
Frasier	Excuse me?
Kenny	Except for the ones that hate you — either way, they're listening.

So consider that option picked up.

George   Ten seconds.

Dr. Nora   Thank you, Kenny. Now get out of my booth.

Kenny   *(cringing)* Yes, ma'am.

He exits. Frasier follows.

Frasier   You can't seriously intend to hire her full-time?

Kenny   Sorry, Doc. Ratings are ratings.

Frasier   We're talking about a woman who thinks the Spanish Inquisition was tough love for heretics.

Kenny goes. Frasier peers furiously into Dr. Nora's booth.

Tom   *(v.o.)* Hello, Dr. Nora. My name is Tom and I have this co-worker who's really driving me up the wall. What can I do about it?

Dr. Nora smiles at Frasier.

Dr. Nora   Not a thing, Tom. Not one damn thing.

As Frasier glowers through the glass, we:

FADE OUT.

END OF ACT ONE

ACT TWO

SCENE E

FADE IN:

INT. RADIO STUDIO — DAY — DAY 4

Frasier is on the air listening to a caller, Denise. Dr. Nora lurks in the hall waiting for her show.

Denise   *(v.o.)* ...Nothing I ever do is good enough for her. I baked a cake for her birthday and she said it tasted like sawdust. I know she's my mother but sometimes I just want to shut her out of my life.

Frasier   Now Denise, burning bridges solves nothing. What you need is a good family counselor who can help you and your mother get to the root of these issues — provided your mother is willing. Will you stay on the line so Roz can give you some names?

Denise   *(v.o.)* Okay. Thank you, Dr. Crane.

Frasier   I'd love to take more of your calls but the sight of Dr. Nora outside daintily donning her brass knuckles tells me our time is up. Till tomorrow, this is Dr. Frasier Crane. Now let's go to

Chopper Dave for a traffic report.

Angle on: Roz's booth.

Frasier enters Roz's booth as George also enters from the hall. Roz is still on the phone with Denise. She looks through her address book.

Roz (on phone) Okay, Denise, I've got some names for you. Have you got a pencil?

Frasier Let's hurry it up, Roz. I'd like to be gone before her trainer brings in the bucket of live mice for her pre-show feeding.

Dr. Nora is now on the air.

Dr. Nora Sorry to cut you off, Chopper Dave, but I've got a therapy emergency here. (Hits button) Denise, are you still there?

Denise (tentatively) Yes.

Frasier What is she doing? That's my caller.

Dr. Nora Denise, I want you to ignore everything Dr. Crane told you. I know a lot more about mothers than he does and here's fact number one — *they don't change.* Cut this woman out of your life.

Frasier Give me that phone.

Frasier presses a button and starts dialing.

Roz What are you doing?

Frasier (dialing) I'm calling in.

Denise (v.o.) You don't think that with counseling—?

Dr. Nora Denise, when you have a tumor what do you do? Do you sit down and say, "Hey, tumor, let's get along, okay?" No. You take a knife and you *cut it out.* Well, Denise, your mother is a tumor — (getting maudlin) My heart bleeds for you, Denise, because I have been there and I know how hard it is to look in your mother's face and say, "Bye-bye, you toxic harpy. You're not hurting me again." But that is what you have to do.

Denise (v.o.) (teary) I think maybe you're right.

Dr. Nora I'm always right. And you know what else. I bet your cake was yummy. God bless, honey. Who's next?

George We have Frasier from here.

Frasier How dare you ambush Denise that way? She called for my advice, not yours!

Dr. Nora Well, what a surprise. I dare to give one of Frasier's callers a second opinion and what does Frasier say—?

SFX: She hits a button and we hear the crying baby.

Frasier   Ah, sound effects — the therapist's best friend. You'll want to get a nice kerplop sound on there in case a jumper should call in.

Dr. Nora   You know, Dr. Crane, all your gassing on reminds me we cut off Chopper Dave. Let's get back to the traffic report.

Dr. Nora hits a button and goes off the air.

Frasier   I don't believe it — she cut me off!

Frasier barges into her booth.

Frasier   All right, let's just settle this. We don't like each other, but we do have to coexist here, so why don't we agree that I won't criticize you and you won't criticize me. Do we have a deal?

Dr. Nora   No.

Frasier   No?

Dr. Nora   No. I will undermine you every chance I get. Because you, Dr. Crane, are a dangerous man.

Frasier   *I'm* dangerous?!

Dr. Nora   Yes. Seattle's great Enabler. You tell tramps and fornicators their problem is low self-esteem. They *should* have low self-esteem — they're going to Hell! A positive self-image won't help them there!

Frasier   I take it back. You're not unprofessional — you're a freaking loon.

George   Five seconds.

Frasier returns to Roz's booth and crosses to the door.

Frasier   I've had it. *(To George)* If it's war you two want, it's war you'll get. Right, Roz?

Frasier charges out.

Roz   *(to George)* You don't actually buy all that no sex stuff of hers, do you?

George   Of course I do.

Roz   Well, it's war!

She exits after Frasier. And we:

FADE OUT.

SCENE H

> *FADE IN:*

INT. FRASIER'S LIVING ROOM — EVENING — DAY 4

> *SFX: The doorbell rings.*
>
> *Martin opens the door to Niles.*

Martin   Hey, Niles.

Niles   Hello, Dad.

> *Niles enters.*

Niles   As you've probably noticed, I shaved my moustache. I decided a better way to change my look is to pump some iron.

Martin   So what, you joined a gym?

Niles   Indeed I have. The minute my weight belt is back from the monogrammers I begin.

> *Frasier enters.*

Niles   Frasier, are you free for dinner?

Frasier   Yes, I suppose so.

> *Daphne and Roz enter through the front door. Daphne has a basket of dark laundry. During the following, she folds them at the table.*

Daphne   Look who I ran into on the elevator.

Roz   I've been on the phone all day looking for dirt on Dr. Nora. You won't believe what I found.

Frasier   Sorry, Niles, dinner may have to wait.

Roz   I called the station where she used to work. They couldn't wait to dish her. *(Sits and opens a file)* For starters, she has no medical degree. Her doctorate's in Physical Education.

Frasier   She's a gym teacher?

Niles   You didn't want to be the chubby kid in that gym class.

Martin   Or the boy in the monogrammed weight belt.

Frasier   Well done, Roz.

Roz   That's not the half of it. Her name isn't Fairchild. She was born Mulhern. And Miss Family Values has two divorces behind her and an affair with a married man.

Niles   *(folding Daphne's underwear)* How does a person live with herself hiding all those secrets?

Frasier   Well, I think I'll use this little bombshell to open my show tomorrow. Better yet, I'll use it to end my show… and hers. *(He laughs villainously)* If only I had your moustache, Niles, I'd be twirling it right now.

Martin   If you use this stuff you're just gonna make things worse. I know 'cause when I was on the force I had a feud just like this with Charlie Drucker. I started it by making a joke about his chest.

Daphne   His chest?

Martin   He was a heavyset guy and he had those, you know, man bosoms. He heard what I said, so he wrote something about me on the men's room wall. I should've called it even right there, but his name being Drucker just brought out the poet in me. It just got worse from there and we both wound up looking like idiots.

Frasier   I don't intend to get into a feud with her. I just want to get her off the air.

Niles   But if you attack her like this aren't you just descending to her level?

Roz   Yeah, that's what makes it fun.

Frasier   You know, they do have a point, Roz. Look what she's already reduced me to: trading barbs, yelling on the air. Now I'm spreading gossip about her. Is that any way for a psychiatrist to deal with conflict?

Roz   Yes!

Frasier   I disagree. There's a better way. Dr. Nora is clearly a very damaged, angry person. If I could figure out what's at the root of that anger I could simultaneously tame the beast and prove that my whole school of therapy is the more valid one.

Roz   I don't believe this. I didn't even tell you about the year she lived in Vegas.

Niles   You know, if you want to analyze her, I'd start with her whole mother thing. I heard her show yesterday and it certainly seemed like a hot button issue.

Frasier   It did, didn't it? They've been estranged for years. Perhaps I could find the woman, see how the rift started.

Niles   Maybe even effect a reconciliation—

Roz   You're killing me!

Frasier   Of course, it won't be easy. We don't even know if her mother's still alive.

Daphne   Yes. All sorts of things could happen to a woman her age. Her mother could have a heart attack or a stroke…

Frasier   Exactly.

Daphne   She could be hit by a bus as she's coming out of a pub… or fall asleep smoking a cigarette and burn to a crisp right there in her smelly bed. She could fall off a ferry and be pulled down under the briny, the roar of the waves drowning out her cries for help, until no one could hear that shrill voice, not ever again. *(Then)* Well, I'm all done with my darks.

Daphne exits cheerfully with her laundry basket.

Frasier   Let's hope so.

And we:

FADE OUT.

SCENE J

FADE IN:

INT. RADIO STUDIO — DAY — DAY 5

Dr. Nora is on the air.

Dr. Nora   No, listen to me. You should be *shunning* this woman, not rewarding her with gifts! *(Hangs up)* A baby shower for an unwed mother. Now I've heard it all. Who's next?

RESET TO:

INT. HALLWAY OUTSIDE FRASIER'S BOOTH — CONTINUOUS

Frasier appears in the hallway and joins Roz at the vending machine.

Frasier   Did her mother get here all right?

Roz   I'm begging you. Let's not do this. We could blow her out of the water.

Frasier   Trust me. My way is better.

They exit through the double doors into—

RESET TO:

INT. HALLWAY — CONTINUOUS

Dr. Nora's mother, Mrs. Mulhern, waits patiently on a bench.

Frasier   Mrs. Mulhern? I'm Frasier Crane. So nice to meet you in person.

Mrs. Mulhern   Dr. Crane, I can't thank you enough for finding me and bringing me here.

Frasier   Your story so moved me on the phone. It's a joy for me to do this.

Mrs. Mulhern   *(to Roz)* For twenty years I've wondered where my little girl was and if I'd ever see her again.

Roz   Why did you two fight to begin with?

Mrs. Mulhern   I thought the man she wanted to marry wasn't good enough for her. So she eloped. I've been so afraid the emphysema would finish me before I could ask her forgiveness and tell her I love her.

Frasier   Well, tell her you shall. Follow us.

Frasier leads Mrs. Mulhern back to the…

RESET TO:

INT. HALLWAY OUTSIDE FRASIER'S BOOTH — CONTINUOUS

Frasier makes a call using the phone in the hall. In the booth, Nora is on the air.

Dr. Nora   Forget couples therapy, Allison. He's a loser. If you don't drop him right now then you deserve every bit of misery that you get. God bless, honey. *(Hangs up)* Who's next?

George   We have Frasier Crane on line one.

Dr. Nora   He's turning into quite a fan. *(Pushes a button)* Frasier. You want to yell at me for that last call?

Frasier   No. Though I do believe a gifted therapist can help two people put aside anger and heal the wounds that divide them.

Dr. Nora puts in a cart.

SFX: snoring.

Frasier   Very amusing. But I think I may be able to sway you over to my side. I have someone with me you haven't seen for quite a while.

Unseen by Frasier, Nora's mother advances to the booth.

Frasier   She has something to say to you, something she's wanted to say to you for a long, long time. Go ahead.

Mrs. Mulhern   *(barging into the booth)* You little WHORE!

Dr. Nora   *(horror-stricken)* Mother!

Frasier sees that Mrs. Mulhern is in the booth. She tears into her daughter, unleashing two decades' worth of pent-up rage and hostility. Dr. Nora cowers like the scared little girl she once was.

Mrs. Mulhern   So, you thought you could get away from me, did you?! Thought you could leave me to rot in that dump with barely enough cash for a bottle of Matteus! You'll pay for that, Missy.

Roz   I was wrong — your way is better.

Frasier   Mrs. Mulhern!

Frasier starts into the booth. Mrs. Mulhern slams the door and locks it. Frasier runs around to the hallway entrance.

Mrs. Mulhern   *(to Frasier)* Keep out of this, you gullible wimp!

Dr. Nora   Mother, please! I'm doing my show!

Mrs. Mulhern   Oh, yes, you're Miss Perfect now, ain'tcha? Tellin' everyone else how wicked they are. They should hear about your past!

Frasier starts in from the hall.

Frasier   Mrs. Mulhern, if you'd just let me help you with these issues.

Mrs. Mulhern slams the door.

Mrs. Mulhern   The shame you brought on *me*, alley-cattin' around.

Dr. Nora   *(near tears)* Mother, please! I'm a good girl now!

Mrs. Mulhern   How you were paid, *paid* to leave town by that nice boy's family!

Frasier   For God's sake, Nora, go to commercial!

Dr. Nora   *(into mike)* There, Seattle. Now you know what I mean when I say there are people you just *don't need in your life*!

Mrs. Mulhern   You want me to leave you can pay me! Same as they paid you!

Dr. Nora   *(bravely composed)* Now for this word from our sponsor.

Mrs. Mulhern   What do they pay you here? I want my cut!

Dr. Nora flees the booth, closing the door behind her. Mrs. Mulhern tries to get out but Frasier holds the door shut.

Dr. Nora   *(to Frasier)* I knew you hated me but I never dreamed you could be so cruel.

Frasier   I was trying to help! She was delightful on the phone.

Mrs. Mulhern   *(banging on the door)* I want fifty dollars right now!

Dr. Nora   How many times will I have to move before I'm finally free of her!

Dr. Nora flees down the hall.

Roz   Frasier, we've got dead air.

Frasier opens the door, letting Mrs. Mulhern out. She chases after Dr. Nora. Frasier calls down the hall.

Frasier   Sorry! *(Then)* Mrs. Mulhern, how could you?

Mrs. Mulhern   You owe me, Missy! I gave you life!

Frasier takes his seat and puts on his headphones.

Frasier   This is Dr. Frasier Crane. I'm sure Dr. Nora's listeners join me in hoping that she and her mother resolve their issues very soon. They're off to a bumpy start, but at least the lines of communication are open. Even the longest emotional journey begins with a single step…

Roz   *(looking out booth window)* Oh my God, the old lady's got her foot on her neck.

Frasier   …And apparently, they've taken it.

And we:

FADE OUT.

END OF ACT TWO

OUT WITH DAD

Written by
Joe Keenan

Created and Developed by
David Angell, Peter Casey, David Lee

Directed by
David Lee

ACT ONE

SCENE A

> *FADE IN:*

INT. FRASIER'S LIVING ROOM — NIGHT — NIGHT 1

> *Daphne is on the couch inspecting video boxes. Martin enters with Eddie on a leash as Roz exits the kitchen carrying a bowl of popcorn.*

Roz   Hey, Martin. Happy Valentine's Day.

Martin   Thanks Roz. So, you're with us tonight? It's not like you not to have a date on Valentine's Day.

Roz   You're telling me. Most years I try for a second seating. *(Then)* I had one but he got the flu.

Daphne   And you'd think that, being engaged, I'd have a guaranteed date, but, no — Donny had to go to Florida for his grandmother. She'll do anything to come between us.

Martin   What'd she do this time?

Daphne   She died.

Roz   So we're going to sit here all night and watch sad chick movies. Can you imagine a more pathetic way to spend Valentine's Day?

> *Frasier enters from the hall.*

Frasier Where's Niles? We'll be late for the opera.

Roz   You're going out with Niles on Valentine's Day?

Frasier It's a subscription series. We got these tickets months ago. We didn't realize what day this one fell on.

Daphne   So Dr. Crane's not spending tonight with Mel?

Frasier No, she had to leave town. Some conference on safer surgical techniques.

> *SFX: The doorbell rings.*
> *Frasier crosses to answer it.*

Frasier I'm sorry for Niles, but it'll be nice for us to have an old-fashioned boys' night out.

> *He opens the door to Niles who's on his cell phone.*

Niles   *(on phone)* I can't wait, either. See you in twenty minutes, darling.

> *He makes a loud kiss and hangs up.*

Frasier That better be the seat duster in our opera box.

Niles	No, it was Mel. Is it any wonder I'm mad for that impetuous little minx? She was halfway to the airport when she said "Surgical safety be damned — I want my huggle bunny."
Frasier	I take it you won't be joining me at the opera?
Niles	Sorry to leave you by your lonesome, but it is Valentine's Day. Wait — here's a thought: if you give Mel your ticket, you don't have to be alone. You can stay here and watch fun movies with Roz and Daphne. *(Reading a video box)* Ooh, "Dying Young" — a classic.
Roz	That is so unfair, Niles.
Frasier	Thank you, Roz.
Roz	I meant to us.
Frasier	I'm sorry, Niles. And frankly I'm surprised at your gall. We made these plans months ago. And now at the last minute, you not only bail on me, you expect me to give up my ticket.
Niles	Please Frasier, put yourself in my shoes. I have to do something for Mel. Every restaurant in town's been booked for weeks. I ran into Archie Wilfong today. He told me he had to settle for two at the counter at The Salad Experience. What do you suggest I do?
Frasier	Bring your own wine and order the spicy caesar.
	Niles storms to the door.
Niles	May your opera box be filled with cellophane crinklers and the stage swarming with standbys.
Frasier	Get out!
	Niles exits.
Frasier	He goes too far.
Roz	Yeah, ditching you to spend Valentine's Day with a girl. That's just weird.
Martin	Look, Fras, I don't blame you for being a little jealous that he's got someone and you don't, but—
Frasier	I am not jealous — just appalled at his rudeness. I was looking forward to tonight. I thought we'd have a nice drink, enjoy the opera. Then a late supper, a nice wine, perhaps a dessert soufflé and — oh God, I need a woman.
Martin	And you'll find one. You just gotta start looking a little harder.
Daphne	Remember my friend Rowena? She's much prettier since her surgery. You look at her now and you can't even tell where the extra one was.

Frasier	Thank you, Daphne, but I had someone else in mind. There's this stunning woman who's always at the opera when we are. She has a box across the way from ours. We've flirted a bit from a distance.
Martin	Have you spoken to her?
Frasier	Not yet, but I feel like I know her. I've laughed with her during "Figaro", cried with her during "Tosca". I even had a dream about her during "Einstein on the Beach".
Roz	Well, don't just stare at her. Make a move.
Frasier	I will, Roz. Tonight's the night. By the finale, I'll make my overture. I've been timid long enough.
Martin	That's the spirit.
Frasier	Will you come with me, Dad?
Martin	To the opera? What do you need me for?
Frasier	I can hardly make my move after she's seen me sitting alone all night, an empty chair next to me.
Roz	He would look pretty pathetic.
Martin	Aw, geez.
Daphne	Or you can stay home with us and watch sad movies.
Frasier	*(reading another video box)* "Sophie's Choice".
Martin	I'll say it is.
Frasier	Please. You would really be helping me out.
Martin	Oh, okay, I'll go. But I'm not getting all dressed up.
	Martin rises and exits to his room. As he goes:
Frasier	Wear anything you like. Opera needn't be stuffy. I trust your taste. *(Then aside to Daphne)* That plaid sports jacket went to Goodwill, right?
Daphne	Yesterday morning.
Frasier	*(calling after him)* Anything you like, Dad!
	And we:
	FADE OUT.

SCENE B

FADE IN:

INT. OPERA BOX — LATER THAT NIGHT — NIGHT 1

Martin and Frasier sit in the box. Both have opera glasses. Frasier peers anxiously across at his intended's opera box. He checks his watch.

Martin You see her, yet?

Frasier That's her box over there, the empty one.

Martin Well, I'm not sitting through a whole opera for some woman who's not even here.

Frasier Give it a chance, Dad. You might learn to enjoy opera if you'd actually listen to one.

Martin Hey, your mom dragged me to plenty when we were dating and they were all stupid. The stories make no sense whatsoever.

Frasier That's not true.

Martin Okay, what's this one about?

Frasier It's about Rigoletto, a hunchbacked jester in the court of the Duke. He has a daughter, Gilda, secretly living with him, though everyone at court thinks she's his mistress. In this first scene, Rigoletto mocks the Duke's enemy, who places a curse on him.

Martin A cursed hunchback who's dating his daughter. Nothing screwy so far.

Frasier He's not dating her. Gilda's being courted by the Duke, but he's disguised himself as a humble student.

Martin See, that's what I'm talking about. It's so unrealistic. Everyone's in love and pretending to be someone they're not. And they're all swooning and gasping—

Frasier gasps.

Martin Exactly. Who acts that way?

Frasier She's here. And not with a date. That must be her mother she's with.

Martin *(peers over)* You weren't kidding. She's a looker all right.

Frasier Don't gawk. She'll notice.

Martin I thought that was the point. You have to get her attention.

Martin waves to the other box.

Frasier Stop that. Just keep your eyes on the stage.

The lights dim.

Martin *(complying)* Okay, but I'll bet you that gets results.

Frasier *(peeks over)* Yes, Dad, it did.

SFX: Applause.

Frasier nudges Martin, who sneaks a peek.

Martin   I was waving to the daughter, not her.

Frasier   *(through a frozen smile)* Well, that's not what she seems to think. Wave back to her.

Martin   *(frozen smile)* I don't want to.

Frasier   You started it. Wave back.

Martin glances shyly at the other box and gives a little wave back. Frasier smiles over too.

Martin   *("smiling" back)* Aw, geez.

SFX: The orchestra plays the prelude.

And as Martin smiles and squirms, we:

FADE OUT.

SCENE C

FADE IN:

INT. OPERA HOUSE — UPSTAIRS LOBBY — LATER — NIGHT 1

It's intermission. Frasier scans the crowd for his dream woman while Martin reads his program.

Martin   The hunchback's got a nice voice, but the daughter's kinda screechy.

Frasier   She's no Renata Tebaldi. Damn, where are they?

Martin   Betcha the mother's in the ladies room, puttin' on more war paint.

Frasier   Oh, calm down. You might like her.

Martin   That's what you said about the opera. I can tell by looking at her she's one of those high-maintenance society types.

Frasier   *(sees them)* They're coming. *(Sotto to Martin)* Just be nice to her, all right? If you're rude to her you'll ruin my chances with the daughter.

They are joined by the very beautiful Emily and her mother, Helen. Both women are elegantly dressed.

Frasier   Well, hello. We meet at last.

Emily   I feel like we're practically old friends.

Frasier   Yes, do forgive us for all that distracting waving. It's just that—

Martin	He was so relieved you showed up.

Frasier shoots Martin a look and begins to jabber nervously.

Frasier	I was afraid you may have been ill. I mean, you're usually so punctual. Except for "Carmen" when you were three minutes late. Not that I've been watching you. Not that you're not… watchable.

Frasier, embarrassed, falls silent.

Helen	You're much calmer on the radio. *(Then)* I'm Helen Browning. And this is my daughter, Emily.

They all shake hands. Helen's eyes linger on Martin, making him nervous.

Frasier	Frasier Crane. And my father, Martin. So you know my show?
Emily	Yes, we both listen. In fact, I own an art gallery and right in front there's a bus shelter with a poster of you.
Frasier	*(modestly)* With a graffiti moustache, no doubt, and my front teeth blacked out.
Emily	Oh, you've seen it?
Frasier	May we offer you ladies a glass of champagne.
Helen	We'd love one, thank you.
Martin	Here, let me give you a hand.
Frasier	We can manage, Dad. You two just stay here and have a nice chat.

Frasier takes Emily's arm and escorts her to the bar.

Helen	Lovely production, isn't it? I adore Verdi.
Martin	He's my favorite.
Helen	Though the woman singing Gilda's a bit off.
Martin	She's no Renata Tebaldi.
Helen	You know, if you like Verdi so much, I have a spare ticket for "Aida" next week.
Martin	Gee, I'd love that, but if it's a week from tonight I'm kinda busy.
Helen	Actually, it's next Thursday.
Martin	Thursday, gosh, there's this thing at my… wine club—
Helen	It's all right, Martin. We just met. I shouldn't have asked.
Martin	No, it has nothing to do with you. It's me. I think I've given you the wrong impression about myself. The truth is, I'm—

Helen	Gay.
	A moment.
Martin	Right. Gay.
Helen	I thought you might be. How many straight men remember Renata Tebaldi?
Martin	Not many.
Helen	Well, I think it's lovely that you're so close to your son. I know a lot of men in your shoes who aren't as lucky. Men who married back in the fifties, started families then woke up one day and said—
Martin	Whoops, I'm playing for the wrong team here.
Helen	I'm sorry if I seemed forward. It's just so hard sometimes to meet nice men.
Martin	Tell me.
	Frasier and Emily rejoin them with the champagne.
Frasier	Here we are. Good news, Dad. Emily's agreed to come for a night cap after the opera and cast her expert eye over my African art collection.
	SFX: Chimes announcing the end of intermission.
Emily	*(re: champagne)* I guess we'll have to smuggle these back to our seats.
Helen	So nice meeting you both.
	The ladies withdraw.
Frasier	How'd it go with Helen? You didn't offend her, did you?
Martin	Not a bit. Turns out I'm not her type.
	Angle on: Helen and Emily. They walk toward the entrance to the boxes.
Emily	*(re: Martin)* Well…?
Helen	Opera queen.
Emily	Sorry.
Helen	Though, you know who he'd be perfect for?
Emily	*(excited)* Yes! You know, he's here tonight. I'll bring him along.
	Angle on: Frasier and Martin.
	SFX: The chimes ring again.
Frasier	Hurry up, Dad. We don't want to miss Act Two.

Martin	Who cares? It's just going to be more goofy stuff that never happens in real life.

FADE OUT.

END OF ACT ONE

ACT TWO

SCENE D

    FADE IN:

INT. FRASIER'S LIVING ROOM — LATER THAT NIGHT — NIGHT 1

Roz and Daphne are on the third hankie of a four hankie film when Frasier enters with Martin. Eddie is there.

Daphne	I low was the opera?
Frasier	Lovely. Get out.

Frasier picks up the remote and turns off the TV. Martin crosses into the kitchen.

Roz	Hey, the movie's not over.
Frasier	Too bad. There's a stunning woman on the way over and I won't have her thinking I'm running some maudlin sorority house.
Roz	You actually spoke to her? You didn't wimp out?
Frasier	You've never seen me so suave.
Roz	Some Valentine's Day. First my date bails and now I owe Daphne fifty bucks.

Roz and Daphne exit. Martin enters with a can of beer and addresses it affectionately.

Martin	(to the beer) Well, hello there. Will you be my Ballantine?
Frasier	Use a glass.
Martin	Oh, all right.

SFX: The doorbell rings.

Frasier crosses to the door, calling back to Martin.

Frasier	And drink fast. The last thing I need tonight is a third wheel cramping my style.

Frasier opens the door to Emily and her dapper Uncle Edward.

Edward	Hello.
Frasier	(baffled) Hello.

Emily	I hope you don't mind. Edward here was at the opera, too. And as he's sort of my partner—
Frasier	Your partner?
Edward	At the gallery. I'm also her uncle.
Frasier	Oh, I see. When you said partner, at first I thought you meant romantic partner.
Edward	Hardly.
Frasier	I'm Frasier.
Edward	Pleasure. What a marvelous view you have. May I?
Frasier	Please.
	Edward crosses upstage to check out the balcony. Emily pulls Frasier aside.
Emily	Your father, is he dating anyone at the moment?
Frasier	No…. though if you're thinking of your mother, I don't think they're quite right for each other.
Emily	*(laughs)* Yes, I know. I meant Edward.
Frasier	Your uncle?
Emily	Yes.
Frasier	And my father?
Emily	They're both single, they love opera, and they were both married with kids when they came out of the closet. Your dad told my mother all about it.
Frasier	Oh, did he?
Emily	Well, she asked him to be honest.
	Martin enters with his beer.
Martin	Hey there.
Frasier	Nothing like a little honesty to head off an awkward situation.
Martin	*(re: Edward)* So, who's this?
Frasier	Dad, I'd like you to meet Emily's uncle. They're partners in her gallery. Edward, this is my father, Martin.
Edward	*(shaking his hand)* A pleasure to meet you, Martin.
Martin	Same here. And my friends call me Marty.
Edward	Then Marty it is. I love what you've done with this place. It's the perfect blend of sleek elegance — *(re: Martin's chair)* — and audacious whimsy.

Martin	*(re: chair; proudly)* You like it, huh? *(Gives Frasier a "so there" look; back to Edward)* You know, Edward's my favorite name.
Edward	Really?
Martin	It's what I named my dog. Here he is.
	Eddie trots in.
Emily	A Jack Russell. *(Re: Edward)* He loves Jack Russells.
Edward	I have three. All girls.
Martin	We should get 'em together some time. Who knows, maybe a little romance will bloom.
	Emily smiles at Frasier as if to say "It's really going well, isn't it?".
Frasier	Dad, why don't we go fetch our new friends some drinks.
Emily	I'd love some white wine.
Martin	How about you, Ed?
Edward	*(noting Martin's mug)* Why not a beer?
Martin	A man after my own heart.
	Martin and Frasier exit to the kitchen.
	RESET TO:

INT. KITCHEN — CONTINUOUS

	They fetch drinks. Frasier whispers to Martin.
Frasier	I don't believe you.
Martin	What?
Frasier	You actually told Emily's mother you were gay?
Martin	Well, you said not to offend her. If you ask me it was a pretty good way to cool her jets without hurting her feelings.
Frasier	Dad, there's something you don't understand. She told Emily.
Martin	Oh, I get it… You're worried Emily will see I'm straight and she'll know I lied to her mother.
Frasier	Dad—
Martin	Damn this beer, I shoulda had a sherry.
Frasier	Dad—
Martin	I get it already. Don't worry, I'll gay it up a little.
	Martin exits the kitchen.
	RESET TO:

INT. LIVING ROOM — CONTINUOUS

> *Martin enters. He brings Edward his beer and sits next to him on the couch. Frasier enters with white wine for himself and Emily, who's inspecting Frasier's art work.*

Martin   Here's your beer, Ed. Emily, have I told you how much I love your hair?

Emily   Thank you, Martin.

Martin   It's divine.

Emily   Frasier, these pieces are wonderful. You have exquisite taste.

Martin   He gets that from me. It was worth all the hours I spent dragging him around to museums and antique shops, teaching him about art and, you know, upholstery.

Edward   Were you in the arts?

Martin   Well, since you ask, Ed—

Frasier   Dad was a cop.

Edward   *(intrigued)* Really?… The, uh, uniform and everything?

Martin   Yup. That's what happened to my hip. I took a bullet breaking up a robbery. I called for back-up but it never showed.

Emily   *(moved)* Because you were gay?

Martin   Don't think I didn't wonder. That was the day I came out. Lying there, bleeding in that alley, a bullet in my hip, I said to myself, "That's it, I'm gay, I like myself and I'm not living a lie any more."

> *Edward, moved, places a hand on Martin's knee.*

Edward   I had exactly the same experience when I came out.

Martin   *(very aware of the hand)* Oh?

Edward   Well, not exactly perhaps. Different things inspired us. For you it was a bullet in your hip, for me it was a Lufthansa steward named Gunter, but believe me, they struck with the same impact.

Emily   *(an arm around Frasier)* What did I tell you? I knew they'd hit it off.

Frasier   I had a feeling myself.

Martin   And you never said a thing about it, you scamp. Fras, why don't we get some snacks for everybody.

> *Frasier and Martin exit to the kitchen.*
>
> RESET TO:

INT. KITCHEN — CONTINUOUS

> *Frasier and Martin again whisper furiously as they prepare some nuts or cheese to put out.*

Martin You didn't tell me this was a set-up!

Frasier Well how blind can you be? You didn't think he seemed gay?

Martin He's English. They all seem gay. Look, let's just tell 'em the truth.

Frasier What? That you found her mother so unappealing you pretended to be gay? Emily is the most fabulous woman I've met in ages and if you screw this up for me I will never forgive you. Now just be nice.

Martin What if he asks me for a date?

Frasier I have news for you — you're on a date.

> *CUT TO:*

SCENE E

INT. FRASIER'S LIVING ROOM — CONTINUOUS — NIGHT 1

> *Martin and Frasier re-enter to discover that Daphne has joined the party.*

Frasier Daphne!

Edward We've just been chatting with your delightful physical therapist.

Daphne *(re: Edward)* Oh, he's a charmer, this one. *(To Martin)* Now aren't you glad you went to the opera? *(To Edward)* I keep telling him he should get out more, meet people. Most nights he just sits here watching tely with his dog in his lap.

Emily *(re: Edward)* He's the exact same way. He'll watch anything.

Daphne *(re: Martin)* With him it's mostly sports. Just give him a bunch of sweaty men chasing each other around a field and—

Frasier *(to Daphne)* Daphne, could you show me where we're keeping the Camembert these days?

Daphne The same place we always do.

> *Frasier violently jerks his head indicating "Get in the kitchen." They exit to the kitchen.*

Emily *(to Martin, confidentially)* You were smart to hire a woman for physical therapy. Much safer than a man. Edward sprained his leg last year—

Edward	All right, Emily.
Emily	I never trusted that man.
Edward	All right, Emily.
Emily	And why you loaned him your boat—
Edward	All right, Emily.

We hear Daphne laughing loudly in the kitchen. All heads turn that way. Frasier enters with an hors d'oeuvres tray.

Frasier	Here we are.
Emily	Thank you, Frasier. I'd love to see the rest of the apartment. If it's no trouble.
Frasier	No. No trouble at all. *(To Edward)* If you'll excuse us a moment.
Edward	Take your time.
Martin	Uh, Frasier.
Frasier	Right, Dad. I'll close the door to your room. *(To Emily as they go)* The mess he makes dressing for the opera. Clothes everywhere!

Frasier and Emily exit to the hall. Daphne enters from the kitchen still stifling giggles.

Daphne	Well, I'm off to bed.
Martin	No, join us.
Daphne	No, no, I've had a long day. Besides, three's a crowd.

Daphne exits, leaving them alone.

Edward	So…
Martin	So…
Edward	Our loved ones seem determined to thrust us together.
Martin	Well, don't let 'em pressure you.
Edward	Congratulations on having raised such a splendid son. I envy you your bond.
Martin	You have kids?
Edward	Just one. George. He's thirty-five and he has consecrated his life to bowling. Never tires of it. I join him when I can, but…
Martin	You're not wild about it.
Edward	No. I mean… the shoes. Strange, isn't it, the things we'll do to be close to our children?
Martin	I hear you.

MERRY CHRISTMAS, MRS. MOSKOWITZ
Niles The man who was supposed to do the number from "Jesus Christ Superstar" can't go on because he slipped in the shower.

MERRY CHRISTMAS, MRS. MOSKOWITZ
Resplendent in his santa outfit, Eddie nearly gives the game away.

DINNER PARTY
Niles Daphne, wait. There's something on the back of your dress.
Frasier You mean other than your hand?

DINNER PARTY
Frasier Dad... do you think Niles and I are... odd?

DR. NORA

Dr. Nora I'm not here to coddle people, I'm here to help them.

Frasier "Help?" Just how are you helping a confused bisexual woman by calling her an "equal opportunity slut?"

OUT WITH DAD

Frasier I was afraid you may have been ill. I mean, you're usually so punctual. Except for "Carmen" when you were three minutes late. Not that I've been watching you. Not that you're not… watchable.

OUT WITH DAD

Martin That was the day I came out. Lying there, bleeding in that alley, a bullet in my hip, I said to myself, "That's it, I'm gay, I like myself and I'm not living a lie any more."

SOMETHING BORROWED, SOMEONE BLUE

Mrs. Moon We were starting to think our Daphne would never find herself a young man. *(Taking Donny in)* And I see she hasn't.

SOMETHING BORROWED, SOMEONE BLUE

Daphne I love this song.
Niles Where are my manners? Would you like to dance?

SOMETHING BORROWED, SOMEONE BLUE

Daphne How come you never said anything before?

Niles Don't you think I wanted to? The timing just never seemed right.

Daphne And the timing's right, now? I'm twelve hours from the altar and you're on your honeymoon.

SLIDING FRASIERS

Frasier There are twelve men and twelve women in a room. You talk to one person for eight minutes, and when the bell rings, you move along and talk to the next one. Essentially it's all the stress and humiliation of a blind date, times twelve.

AND THE DISH RAN AWAY WITH THE SPOON

Niles Mel, I never meant to—

Mel What? Hurt me? If that was the case, you never would have run off with your little maid-whore leaving me holding the brochures to our honeymoon.

AND THE DISH RAN AWAY WITH THE SPOON

Niles I... I...

Mel I love you too.

AND THE DISH RAN AWAY WITH THE SPOON

Daphne It looks like we're having that first date after all.

**AND THE DISH RAN
AWAY WITH THE SPOON**

Daphne I'm sorry. I guess
I'm just not used to kissing
my boss's brother in the
kitchen. Not that I'm used to
kissing him any other place. I
mean any other room.

Edward	Would you happen to be free this weekend?
Martin	This weekend? Well, uh, actually…
Edward	Never mind. Forget I asked.
Martin	No, I'd love to, really. It's just that…
Edward	It's all right. Nothing ventured, nothing gained.
Martin	No, it's not you. I'm just… dating someone. Because if I weren't—
Edward	Marty, you don't have to spare my feelings—
Martin	No, it's the truth.

Niles lets himself in. He carries a bottle of champagne.

Niles	Hello.
Martin	Darling!

Niles regards Martin quizzically, then sees Edward.

Niles	Sorry, I'm not interrupting anything, am I?
Martin	No, not a thing, dear. Take your coat off, stay a while.
Niles	*(baffled)* Okay.

Niles crosses upstage to hang up his coat.

Niles	*(re: champagne)* I felt bad about that squabble earlier so I thought I'd drop off this peace offering.
Martin	As if I could stay mad at you. Edward, this is Niles, my boyfriend. Niles, this is Edward. We met tonight at the opera.
Edward	Charmed… and you needn't look so startled. I assure you, there's nothing funny going on.
Niles	Oh, good.
Martin	Excuse us while we put this on ice.

Martin hustles the thoroughly bewildered Niles off to the kitchen. Frasier and Emily enter from the hall.

Frasier	Of course, the most moving Gilda ever sung was by the great Mathilde DeCagny. I have the recording.
Emily	I'd love to hear it.
Frasier	*(to Edward)* By the way, where is Dad?
Edward	He's in the kitchen with his boyfriend. He just arrived.
Frasier	What?

Niles and Martin exit the kitchen, Martin's arm around Niles' shoulder. *Niles is still reeling from the role playing, but doing his best to act the boy toy.*

Frasier Niles! What are you doing here?

Martin It's my place too. I can have company. Emily, this is Niles.

Emily *(coldly)* Hello. *(Then, quietly, to Frasier)* You said your father was single.

Frasier I thought he was. *(To Martin)* Since when are you two an item?

Martin A few weeks. We didn't want to say anything yet, because, well…

Niles So many reasons.

Edward You know, it's getting late, Emily—

Emily Yes. We should be going.

Frasier No! Please stay just five more minutes. I have this marvelous old port you really must taste.

He crosses to the kitchen jerking his head toward Niles to indicate that he should follow.

RESET TO:

INT. KITCHEN — CONTINUOUS

Frasier and Niles enter. Frasier fetches an old bottle of port and hastily pours a few glasses.

Frasier How could you do this to me?

Niles You think this was my idea?

Frasier Emily just kissed me in the bedroom and now she's leaving. I've never been so embarrassed.

Niles You're embarrassed? They think the best I can do is an old man with a cane.

Frasier You've got to fix this.

Niles How am I supposed to do that?

Frasier Isn't it obvious? You have to dump Dad.

RESET TO:

INT. LIVING ROOM — CONTINUOUS

Frasier enters and gives the port to Edward and Emily.

Frasier Here you are. You must try this.

They each take an obligatory sip.

Edward   Very nice.

Emily   Yes, lovely.

Frasier   So Niles, you missed quite an opera tonight.

Niles   Perhaps I'll catch it this weekend with Mel.

Martin   *("jealous")* Hey, who's Mel?

Niles   *(explodes)* Damn you and your jealous questions. You don't own me!

Martin   *(thrown)* I was just asking.

Niles   You're always asking! Badgering, spying on me. Well, I won't be suffocated any more. I'm tired of being your trophy boy. It's over, you hear me? Over!

He crosses to the door.

Niles   And I'm keeping the jewelry.

Niles storms out slamming the door. After a shocked, embarrassed silence:

Frasier   I'm so sorry, Dad.

Emily   We all are.

Edward   An appalling exhibition. Familiar, but appalling.

Emily   Can we get you anything?

Martin   No, I'll be fine. I guess I always knew it wouldn't last.

Edward   The young ones never stay.

Emily   I know what will cheer you up. A nice spot of "Rigoletto". Frasier, play that recording.

Frasier   Yes, why not?

Edward   You know, Emily, I'd really love to hear it, but that shipment's coming in bright and early.

Emily   Oh, damn. *(To Frasier)* I wish I could stay, Frasier, but I'm Edward's ride.

Frasier   Ah, what a shame. Well, then, I guess this is good night.

Martin   You know what, Emily? You stay here with Frasier. Enjoy the music. I'll drive Edward home.

Frasier   You would do that, Dad?

Martin   Happy Valentine's Day, son.

Frasier   Thank you, Dad.

Martin and Edward head for the door.

Edward And don't give Niles another thought. He wasn't your first love and he won't be your last.

Martin I know. I'm just going to need a little time before I'm ready to dive in again. Who am I kidding? A lot of time.

And they exit. Frasier puts on the CD and joins Emily on the couch.

Emily It was so sweet of your father to do that. He really loves you, doesn't he?

Frasier You have no idea.

Emily smiles. Frasier smiles back, clicks the stereo on with his remote. As a romantic aria fills the air we:

FADE OUT.

END OF ACT TWO

SOMETHING BORROWED, SOMEONE BLUE, PARTS I & II

Written by
Christopher Lloyd & Joe Keenan

Created and Developed by
David Angell, Peter Casey, David Lee

Directed by
Pamela Fryman

ACT ONE

SCENE A

    FADE IN:

INT. ELEVATOR — DAY — DAY/1

    Frasier, Daphne, Niles, and Mel are there. They all wear dark mourning clothes. Daphne is very emotional.

Daphne   It'll be so hard to walk through the lobby and not see Morrie there. He always had the same warm smile for everyone.

Mel   He didn't seem very old. Was it sudden?

Niles   Heart attack. Right there at his desk in the lobby.

Frasier   Really makes you see how precious life is when someone goes just like that. From doorman to dormant.

Daphne   It's so sad.

Frasier   From Morrie to memento mori… I really should've given the eulogy.

Niles   Oh yes, what new widow doesn't enjoy a string of morbid puns about her dead husband?

    The doors open. They exit.

    RESET TO:

INT. HALLWAY — CONTINUOUS

    Roz is there. She holds a small box.

Frasier   Roz.

Roz   There you are. I brought this for Daphne. I was just about to leave it with your doorman.

    Daphne whimpers. Frasier opens the door.

    RESET TO:

INT. LIVING ROOM — CONTINUOUS

    They enter. Daphne exits to the powder room.

Roz   What's wrong with her?

Frasier   Morrie passed away this week. We're just coming back from his funeral.

Roz   My gosh, I'm sorry.

Frasier	It's not your fault, Roz. She's been very emotional all week, even before Morrie died.
	Daphne re-enters.
Daphne	So you brought something, Roz?
Roz	Yeah, I figured you can't get married without wearing something borrowed.
	Roz hands the box to Daphne, who opens it.
Daphne	What a beautiful garter. Look at all the lovely detail.
Niles	I especially like the little odometer.
Daphne	Thank you so much, Roz.
Mel	Does anyone besides me feel like coffee?
Frasier	I'll brew a pot.
Mel	Don't be silly. I've been here enough times to know how to get coffee made. Daphne, make us some coffee. *(Then)* Kidding!
	Mel exits to the kitchen. Roz picks up a brochure from the coffee table.
Roz	The Wayside Inn. Is this where you're having your wedding? It's beautiful.
Daphne	I hope it is. The planning's been a nightmare. *(Indicating chart)* I spent an hour today on the seating chart. Everyone has some demand: "Don't put me near the band!" "Do you mind if I bring a friend?"
Roz	*(looking at chart)* Oh God, you can't seat me next to him!
Daphne	Exactly. Every selfish, whiney little—
Roz	No, you can't seat me next to Tim Walsh. I dated him all last summer then he dumped me.
Daphne	He's going with my bridesmaid Annie. I have to seat the bridesmaids together.
Roz	This always happens to me. Is there no place I can go without running into guys I've dated?
Niles	I was reading about a Trappist Monastery in the Amazon that they somehow built into the treetops.
Roz	Oh, shut up, you big doily. *(Then)* This is going to be awful. There I am at a wedding sitting with some guy who dumped me and his date.
Frasier	Now now, Roz, it's not as if you're showing up alone. You'll be on

the arm of a well-known Seattle boulevardier and radio star.

Roz I can't go with you now. I need a real date.

Frasier Excuse me?

Roz I'm sorry. Taking your boss to a wedding's like going to the prom with your brother.

Frasier Niles and I did not go to our prom together. Our dates were sick and we went stag.

Niles In retrospect, yes, we should have cancelled the horse-drawn carriage, but hindsight's twenty-twenty.

Martin enters carrying a bag.

Martin Hey, Roz.

Roz Hey Martin. Sorry about your friend Morrie.

Martin Yeah, his wife just did the nicest thing. I guess she knew that Eddie and I used to stop and shoot the breeze with him, so she gave me something to remember him by.

Frasier *(reading card)* "For Martin and Eddie." Isn't that nice?

Martin I think it's some kind of wine.

Frasier pulls the bottle from the bag.

Frasier Dear God! It's a 1945 Chateau Petrus!

Martin She said he got it from an uncle of his who was in France after the war.

Frasier This is one of the rarest wines in the world.

Martin Well, if you're nice, maybe Eddie will give you a glass from his half.

Martin exits to the kitchen.

Niles I've never even seen a '45 Petrus.

Roz Poor Morrie. He probably spent his whole life waiting for an occasion special enough to open that bottle.

Frasier Well, perhaps there's a lesson here. Morrie may have moved on to stand guard at the door to heaven, but he's buzzing us right now with one last message: don't put life off. I'm reminded of a parable—

SFX: A knock at the door.

Niles/Roz/Daphne Come in!

Simon enters through the front door with his duffel bag.

Simon   Hello, all.

Daphne   Simon, I thought you were in California.

Simon   Turns out those friends I went to surprise were out of town. So I decided to house-sit for them, which was lovely until they came home last night. I don't know what they were all upset about — I was the one in the tub. *(Re: duffel bag)* Where should I put this?

Frasier   By the door so you don't forget it when you leave.

Simon   I think I know everyone here *(spotting Roz)* or do I? What would your name be, Miss?

Roz   Simon, you low-life idiot, you made a date with me last week and you stood me up.

Simon   Sorry, love, need a bit more to go on.

Roz   Maybe this'll refresh your memory.

           Roz exits, slamming the door in his face.

Simon   Roz! Of course.

           Martin enters.

Martin   Hey, look who's back!

Simon   And who's that, then? I'd say it was Marty Crane but he's too young and trim.

Martin   Oh, go on. Can I get you a beer?

Simon   I do hate to drink alone. How about a sandwich with that?

           Martin and Simon exit into the kitchen. During the following, Mel exits the kitchen.

Frasier   If that beer-swilling boomerang thinks he's staying here again, he can think again.

           SFX: The phone rings.

           Daphne crosses to answer it.

Niles   *(looking at Simon's duffel)* Better move fast. He already has your address on his duffel bag.

Daphne   *(into phone)* Hello? Mummy! No, it's never a bad time.

           Daphne slumps dejectedly and exits to her room.

Mel   We should be off if we're going to reach the cabin by dark.

Frasier   Cabin?

Niles   Yes, Mel and I are celebrating our six month anniversary with a little getaway to her friend's country place.

Mel   No phones, no stress, just two days of rest and relaxation. I do have to pick up a little anniversary gift. Give me nine minutes, then meet me on the northwest corner of Pike and Elm at *(checks watch)* four forty-two. Coming up on four forty-three…

Niles   *(checks watch)* Synchronizing…

Mel   Now! Good. I'm relaxing already.

Mel kisses Niles, ad libs goodbye to Frasier, and exits. Martin and Simon enter from the kitchen.

Simon   Thank you, Marty. That's downright hospitable of you.

Martin   Well, you need a place to stay—

Frasier   Stop right there. I'm sorry, Dad, but the man snores like a locomotive, has the table manners of a Visigoth, and last time he killed a ficus on the downstairs neighbor's balcony by means that are best left to the imagination.

Martin   Frasier, I just invited Simon to stay in my Winnebago. *(To Simon)* Come on, I'll show you your new digs.

Frasier   Simon, what I was saying before—

Simon   Forget it. It's no worse than what I was just saying about you in the kitchen.

Frasier   *(laughs)* Very good, Simon.

Simon   *(sotto, to Martin)* He thinks I'm joking.

Simon and Martin exit.

Niles   Join me in a sherry, Frasier?

Frasier   I think I will.

Niles   I have to admit I am just a bit nervous about this trip. Given that it's our six month anniversary, I have a feeling Mel may make another push for us living together.

Frasier   Oh my.

Niles   She's been bringing it up quite a bit lately. She says it's a good way to test our relationship.

Frasier   And you're worried you'll discover things about each other you may not like?

Niles   No, we're past that stage. She knows my likes and dislikes. And I've become attuned to her various quirks, allergies, eccentricities, bugaboos, foibles, bête noires, night terrors… That's the fun of being in love. I'm not sure what's bothering me.

Frasier   I wonder if your foot dragging has anything to do with some lingering feelings for Daphne?

Niles   Oh, Frasier. Surely, you must realize I put that behind me months ago.

Frasier   Just asking.

Niles   I'm very happy with Mel.

Frasier   Then what's your problem?

Niles   Well, it could be any number of things. I just got through a rough divorce, I do have a tendency toward being overly cautious.

Frasier   This might be your chance to change that.

Niles   Then you're in favor of it?

Frasier   Well, I've never been the president of the Mel fan club but she does make you happy. And, as we were reminded this morning, life is not to be taken in baby steps. Ask not for whom the doorman buzzes, he buzzes for thee.

Niles   Thank you, Frasier. That was well-needed therapy.

Frasier   The best part is, you're my brother. You get the family discount.

Niles   *(checks watch)* Well, I should be off.

Niles opens the door to see Martin step off the elevator and enter.

Martin   Got down to the Winnebago and realized I had the wrong keys.

Niles   Bye, Dad. See you in a few days.

Niles exits as Daphne enters still on the phone.

Daphne   *(into phone)* You don't say? Your phlebitis again?

Daphne waves frantically at Frasier to save her.

Frasier   Daphne!

Daphne   *(into phone)* Got to go, Mum. Dr. Crane's on the warpath again. Bye. *(Hangs up)*

Martin   Daph, I'm glad you're here. I was thinking about that wine of Morrie's and how it really is meant for a special occasion. I thought you should have it for your wedding. Enjoy it on your honeymoon.

Daphne   Oh, Mr. Crane!

Daphne bursts into tears and hugs Martin.

Martin   *(uncomfortable)* Come on, Daph. It's just a bottle of wine. I don't even know anything about it. Help me out here, Fras.

Frasier	Well, Dad, Chateau Petrus is a premier cru Bordeaux—
Martin	I mean with her.
Frasier	Oh.
	Martin moves the still sobbing Daphne onto Frasier and exits.
Frasier	It's all right, Daphne.
Daphne	I'm sorry about this.
Frasier	The funeral this morning certainly has affected you.
Daphne	It's not about that.
Frasier	Daphne?
Daphne	Dr. Crane, I've wanted to talk about this with you all week, but I haven't known what to say. Can you promise me you'll keep this just between us?
Frasier	Of course.
Daphne	It's about your brother. You see, I know.
Frasier	Know what?
Daphne	I know about his feelings for me.
Frasier	My God. How did you find out?
Daphne	It's not important.
Frasier	Someone babbled, didn't they? I knew it. Why can't people mind their own business? Who was the nattering gossip? Roz? Dad?
Daphne	You.
Frasier	What?
Daphne	When you were taking those pills for your back. You blurted it out while I was giving you a massage.
Frasier	Oh. Well they were very strong pills.
Daphne	Needless to say, it completely took my breath away. I didn't know what to make of it. I tried to forget about it, you know, pretend it didn't happen—
Frasier	The bottle said to take one, but I'm a big man—
Daphne	Will you shut up about the pills?
Frasier	Sorry.
Daphne	Anyway, after a while, I couldn't put it out of my mind anymore. I find myself thinking about him all the time.
Frasier	So you have feelings for Niles.

Daphne   I think I do. I don't know. Even if I did, he may not feel that way about me anymore… unless you know better? Oh, listen to me, I sound like a bloody teenager.

Frasier   Daphne, I can't speak for Niles. The best thing may just be for you to talk this over with him.

Daphne   That's not an easy conversation to have.

Frasier   Easier now than after you're married.

Daphne   You're right. I have to talk to him. And soon. I'm already climbing the walls over this. If I wait any longer I'll be a complete basket case. Did he mention where he was going just now?

Frasier   Uh, actually…

    RESET TO:

INT. HALLWAY — CONTINUOUS

    Martin and Simon step off the elevator.

Martin   I'll get you some towels and you'll be all set down there.

    RESET TO:

INT. LIVING ROOM — CONTINUOUS

    Martin and Simon enter. Daphne is sobbing on Frasier's shoulder.

Martin   Geez, Daph, it's just a bottle of wine.

    FADE OUT.

END OF ACT ONE

ACT TWO

SCENE B

    FADE IN:

INT. FRASIER'S LIVING ROOM — DAY — DAY 2

    SFX: The doorbell rings.

Daphne   *(o.s.)* I'll get it.

    A nervous-looking Daphne enters from the kitchen holding a bag of cookies from which she's eating and crosses through the empty living room. She sets the cookies down on the table, takes a moment to compose herself, and opens the door. It's Frasier with an armload of packages.

Daphne   Oh. I didn't even know you'd gone out. I thought you might be your brother.

Frasier   I went down for the mail and these wedding presents were there for you. But don't worry. Niles called and he's coming by this afternoon.

Daphne picks up the bag of cookies and starts eating again.

Daphne   I'm not even sure how I'm going to have this conversation.

Frasier   Those chocolate chip blackened teeth will make for a nice ice breaker.

Daphne   When I get nervous, I tend to nibble a bit. For the past two days I haven't been able to stop eating junk food.

Frasier   That would account for the tamale husk I sat on this morning in my silk robe.

SFX: The doorbell rings.

Daphne   It's him!

Frasier   You'll be fine. Just speak from the heart.

Daphne once again goes through the process of composing herself and opens the door. It's Donny.

Daphne   Donny.

Donny   Hey, honey, Fras. It turns out my tux won't be ready for an hour, so I thought I'd take my sweetie to lunch.

Daphne   Oh, Donny, that's lovely, but I have no appetite whatsoever.

Daphne sees Donny noticing the cookies.

Daphne   I'm afraid I've been snacking a bit today.

Donny   Ah, look how nervous she is about getting married. You're so sweet. *(He kisses her)* And also kind of Cool-Ranch flavored.

Donny plants himself on the couch and takes his shoes off.

Donny   I've been running around all day, it feels good to sit down.

Daphne   You know, Donny, we never did get the disposable cameras for the rehearsal dinner tomorrow. Could you run out?

Donny   Now?

Daphne   Well, it doesn't have to be this second—

SFX: The doorbell rings.

Daphne   —but why put it off?

Donny   Oh, all right.

> *As Donny puts his shoes back on, Daphne, after an abbreviated self-composing, opens the door. It's Martin.*

Daphne   Mr. Crane.

Martin   Thanks — Eddie starting doing his "I don't know how much longer I can hold this" dance and I ran out without my keys. You ever see him do that dance?

Frasier   Just that droll impression of it you do at parties.

Donny   See ya, honey.

> *Donny exits.*

Daphne   You know, Mr. Crane, Eddie seems awfully fidgety. I'm not sure he got enough exercise on that walk.

Martin   If anyone could use some exercise, it's you. When they put "Party Size" on the cookie bag, they don't mean party of one.

> *SFX: The doorbell rings.*

> *Daphne, composing herself once again, opens the door. It's Simon.*

Daphne   Simon. What do you want?

Simon   Easy now. I've just come to borrow a pen so I can fill out this job application.

Frasier   You're applying for work? Well done! We'll miss having you around here, but onward and upward. *(Hands him a pen)* So, what's the job?

Simon   Doorman.

Frasier   Oh, dear God.

Simon   It's ideal for me, really. Nice cozy chair, plenty of time to think the long, long thoughts of youth. Not to mention what the uniform does to the ladies, eh? Memory serves, a certain bellhop back in Manchester found that out with a young lady who will remain nameless.

Daphne   Simon!

> *Daphne starts towards Simon but Frasier stops her.*

Daphne   *(to Frasier)* I'm this close to just popping him one — I did it enough when we were kids to know how good it feels.

Frasier   You're just a little emotional, Daphne.

> *Daphne digs into the cookies as Simon notices.*

Simon   I'll say. And she's got the appetite too. What are you, knocked up or something?

Again, Daphne goes for him, but Frasier pulls her back.

Daphne   No.

Simon   Now, now, you'd hardly be the first in our family to walk down the aisle carrying more than a bouquet.

SFX: The doorbell rings.

Again, Daphne turns to face the door nervously.

Martin   C'mon with me, Simon. We'll grab a couple of beers while you fill that thing out.

They exit to the kitchen. Daphne composes herself once again, and opens the door. It's Roz.

Daphne   Roz.

Roz   Hey, guys. Frasier, I felt kind of bad about the other day — you know, dumping you as my wedding date—

Frasier   You want me back, don't you?

Roz   And I'm sick about it, but I couldn't find anyone.

Frasier   I've already asked someone else. She's driving up Saturday to join me.

Simon enters with a beer.

Roz   Well, get rid of her. I need a date. I'm desperate.

Simon   Well, someone here is singing my favorite song.

Roz   Simon, there's a man who lives in the park across the street from me. He wears a cat suit and meows at people. If he's busy, maybe I'll call you.

Simon   I'll be here. Speaking of that, Daphne, I borrowed your blow-dryer to pretty myself up for my job interview.

Daphne   I spent an hour this morning looking for that. I was losing my mind.

Simon   That does happen to women in your condition.

Daphne   I'm not pregnant!

Simon   Just another scare, then? Like you had back in school with that Pakistani chap?

Daphne   That's it!

She lunges for him but Frasier catches her mid-air and carries her toward the door.

Frasier   Daphne and I are just going to get a little fresh air, maybe retrieve her blow-dryer. If Niles stops by, keep him here, all right? It's very important that I speak to him.

Frasier and Daphne exit.

RESET TO:

INT. HALLWAY — CONTINUOUS

Frasier carries Daphne to the elevator and presses the button.

Daphne   For God's sake, put me down.

The doors open. A middle-aged woman, Mrs. Richman, is there. She holds a laundry basket.

Frasier   Not until you promise not to kill Simon.

RESET TO:

INT. ELEVATOR — CONTINUOUS

They enter. Frasier puts Daphne down.

Daphne   It's not as if he doesn't deserve it — telling everyone I'm carrying Donny's baby. Like I don't have enough to worry about, waiting for Dr. Crane.

Mrs. Richman's interest is piqued, though she attempts to conceal it.

Frasier   You just need to calm down.

Daphne   It's not easy. I don't even know how to begin with him: "Would you like steak or salmon at my wedding, and by the way, I think I might be in love with you?"

Frasier   You'll find the words when the moment comes. *(To Mrs. Richman)* And don't pretend you're not listening, Mrs. Richman. Your laundry isn't that interesting.

RESET TO:

INT. LIVING ROOM — CONTINUOUS

Roz is on the phone.

Roz   *(into phone)* C'mon George, I'm in a bind here. I know it'd only be our second date, but I'd give you an upgrade to third date, if you get my meaning. … No, you can't take a raincheck. What kind of a woman do you think I am? *(Hangs up)*

Simon	Listen to what you're doing, Roz. Not very dignified, is it?
Martin	C'mon, Roz, give Simon a chance.
Roz	So he can stand me up again?
Simon	Miss my own sister's wedding? Never. And if you're worried about my appearance, I happen to know where I can lay my hands on some very nice Armani suits.
Martin	Or you could just grab one out of Frasier's closet.
Roz	What do you think he was talking about? *(Then)* Oh, all right. Just remember, my ex-boyfriend'll be there, so if anyone asks you're an internet millionaire.
Simon	Right. I'll be the perfect, well-bred, upmarket gentleman. Now, I'll see you to the garage.
Roz	You don't have to.
Simon	It's no trouble, I live there.
	They open the door to reveal Niles who stands there beaming.
Niles	*(cheerfully)* Roz, Simon!
Simon	Judging by that smile on your face I'd say someone got himself a bit last night.
Niles	I find that remark rude, boorish and impossible to deny.
Simon	Brilliant!
	Simon laughs heartily. Roz and Simon go. Niles enters.
Martin	Hey, Niles. Have a nice trip?
Niles	Fantastic. Is Frasier here?
Martin	No, he stepped out.
Niles	I was hoping he'd be here. I have some news.
Martin	He'll be back in a bit. What's up?
Niles	*(deep breath)* Well— *(Then)* No, I should wait for Frasier. It was really his idea. Do you mind?
Martin	I can wait.
Niles	Well, I can't!
Martin	What is it?
Niles	I'm married!
Martin	Married?
Niles	Yes! Mel and I eloped yesterday! …Well?

Martin	*(with difficulty)* Congratulations, son. That's great.
	They hug.
Niles	Thanks, Dad.
Martin	So… You're happy, right?
Niles	Happy? I'm delirious.
Martin	You'd have to be, wouldn't ya? So this was Frasier's idea?
Niles	Well, indirectly. Oh, before I forget, it occurs to me we should keep this from Daphne. And Donny. I'd hate for them to think we were stealing their thunder.
	Frasier enters.
Frasier	Niles.
Niles	Frasier. Three guesses what I did yesterday!
Frasier	What?
	Daphne enters with a hair dryer.
Niles	Daphne.
Daphne	Dr. Crane.
Niles	*(sotto to Martin)* Send Daphne away.
Daphne	*(sotto to Frasier)* Get rid of your father.
Martin	Daphne, you mind going to the drugstore for me? We're all out of liniment and my back's kinda stiff.
	Daphne looks to Frasier in alarm.
Frasier	No doubt from sitting in that chair all day. A walk to the pharmacy's just what you need to work the kinks out. *(Hustling him out)* I'll join you.
Martin	Wait. Niles, why don't you come, too?
Niles	Oh good idea. We'll all go.
Frasier	No! Sorry, I have a personal matter to discuss with Dad. I'm sure you understand, Niles. *(Grabbing Martin)*
Martin	Fras—
	Frasier hustles Martin out.
Daphne	Well, Dr. Crane—
	SFX: Niles' cell phone rings.
Niles	Oh, excuse me. *(Answering)* Hello? …Mel, darling. I'm just hangin' out with Daphne.

> RESET TO:

INT HALLWAY — CONTINUOUS

> *Frasier presses the button for the elevator.*

Frasier Honestly, Dad, when will you learn to take a hint?

> *The elevator doors open and they enter.*
> RESET TO:

INT ELEVATOR — CONTINUOUS

> *Mrs. Richman is there.*

Martin I can't take a hint? Couldn't you see Niles wanted to talk to you?

Frasier Well, whatever it was I'm sure it can wait.

Martin Oh, yeah, it's no big deal. He just got married, that's all.

Frasier What?!

Martin He and Mel eloped yesterday.

Mrs. Richman Poor Daphne.

Frasier Would you please keep out of this, Mrs. Richman? *(To Martin)* We have to get back up there.

Martin Well, this thing's going to the basement.

Frasier I can't wait that long.

> *Frasier presses the button for the floor they're closest to.*
> RESET TO:

INT TWELFTH FLOOR HALLWAY — CONTINUOUS

> *Frasier exits the elevator and rounds the corner, heading for the stairs.*
> RESET TO:

INT. LIVING ROOM — CONTINUOUS

> *Niles is on his cell phone. Daphne waits anxiously.*

Niles *(on phone)* See you soon, dear. *(Hangs up)* Sorry about that.

Daphne Oh, it's all right.

Niles So, forty-eight hours 'til the big day. You must be excited.

Daphne	Funny you should bring that up. You see, Dr. Crane…
Niles	Yes, Daphne?

Frasier bursts in the door out of breath.

Frasier	Niles!
Daphne	Dr. Crane! You're back awfully soon.
Niles	You're all out of breath. Is something wrong?
Frasier	No, I just remembered, I need to talk with Niles.
Daphne	What, now? We were just having a chat.
Frasier	Nothing that can't wait, I'm sure.
Niles	Actually, Daphne, I needed to speak to Frasier too. If you don't mind?
Daphne	No, of course not. Why should I mind? It's not like I had anything important to talk about.

Daphne snatches the cookie bag off the table and exits to her room. Martin enters.

Niles	Is Daphne all right?
Frasier	Oh, just wedding stuff. Speaking of which, I hear you have a little news. You're married?
Niles	I guess Dad couldn't contain himself anymore than I could.
Frasier	Niles, I thought you were just moving in together.
Niles	That's what I thought, too, but the strangest thing happened. As we talked about it, we started getting more and more excited about the idea of being together. I remembered your advice to stop taking baby steps through life, and, well, before we knew it, we were asking the waitress for a phone book so we could find a justice of the peace.

SFX: The doorbell rings.

Frasier	What can I say, Niles, but congratulations.

Frasier hugs Niles as Martin opens the door to Mel. She carries a bottle of champagne.

Mel	Martin. Or should I say Dad?
Martin	Yeah, I heard.

Daphne enters.

Niles	Darling, I'm thinking perhaps we should try and keep this quiet from Daphne.

Daphne	Keep what quiet?
Mel	Oh, we can't keep something like this secret. *(To Daphne)* We got married.
Daphne	Did you?
Niles	Yes, while we were out of town. But the last thing we want to do is upstage you and Donny, so we're not even mentioning it outside this room.

Daphne takes them by the hands and gives them friendly squeezes.

Daphne	Well, I'm so happy for you both.
Niles	We're having champagne. Would you like to join us?
Daphne	I'd love to, but I need to get a check down to the caterers. They're closing early today.
Frasier	Why don't I drive you over?
Daphne	No, no, I'll be fine. Congratulations again. Save a glass for me.

Daphne smiles and exits.

RESET TO:

INT. HALLWAY — CONTINUOUS

> *She instantly bursts into tears. The elevator doors open. Mrs. Richman stands there holding a laundry bag. Seeing Daphne, she drops the bag and opens her arms. Daphne looks up, steps into the elevator and into Mrs. Richman's sympathetic hug as we:*

FADE OUT.

END OF ACT TWO

ACT THREE

SCENE C

> *FADE IN:*

INT. BAR/LOUNGE — THE WAYSIDE INN — DAY — DAY 3

> *The lounge of a charming country hotel a few hours outside Seattle. There's a bar, tables and a small dance floor with room for a combo to play. Windows give on to lovely countryside. An archway leads to the hotel's lobby and double doors lead to the hotel's dining room. A bartender is on duty. Frasier is led into the room by the hotel manager, Miss Carney.*

Miss Carney   We've set up the lounge here as a hospitality area for the wedding guests.

Frasier   Lovely. *(Then)* By the way, did you happen to notice if the bride-to-be has arrived yet? I'm quite anxious to speak to her.

Miss Carney   Yes, she and the groom are right in the dining room helping set up for the rehearsal dinner tonight.

Frasier   Thank you.

Frasier starts toward the dining room. She stops him.

Miss Carney   Dr. Crane, I'm sorry for being so giggly when you checked in. See, we don't get many celebrities up here and—

Frasier   Miss Carney, please. I understand.

Miss Carney   Then you know Phil Corbett's staying with us? He's so much handsomer when he's not in front of that weather map.

Miss Carney exits. Daphne and Donny enter from the dining room.

Donny   ...so I thought we'd do the toasts right before dessert.

Frasier   Daphne. Donny.

They ad lib hellos.

Frasier   Daphne, I was wondering where you'd gotten to yesterday.

Daphne   Oh, after the caterer's, I went straight to Donny's so we could leave together bright and early. Lovely up here, isn't it?

Frasier   Yes.

Daphne   Anyway, help yourself to the buffet.

Donny   I think I'm going to help myself to a Scotch on the rocks. *(Signals bartender)*

Daphne   Donny, it's barely noon.

Donny   Isn't that when your mom said she'd be here?

Daphne   *(to bartender)* Make it a double.

The bartender pours a drink.

Frasier   So, um... Daphne—

Roz enters and calls across the room to the bartender.

Roz   I'll have whatever he's having.

Daphne   *(turning away from Frasier)* Roz.

Roz   I don't know why I even came to this wedding. Hi Daphne. *(Then)* I'm all ready to drive up here myself and I think, "Wait. I can't walk into the lobby alone. What if my ex-boyfriend's there?" So I agree to drive up with Simon. What does he pick me up in? Your father's Winnebago.

The bartender sets out her drink.

Roz   Thanks. Don't go anywhere. *(Then)* Next thing I know, we're heading down the highway to the airport. *(The bartender starts to move)* Hey! I wasn't kidding.

The bartender stops dead in his tracks.

Roz   *(to Daphne)* Turns out, he's promised to ferry your entire family up here.

Daphne   All fourteen of them?

Roz   Fifteen. Your aunt Ida got the weekend off at the bakery — judging by the size of her, it'll be the first Saturday they turn a profit.

Frasier   Donny, would you mind taking Roz out for a breath of that rejuvenating country air while I have a word with your fiancée?

Donny   Yeah, all right. Let's go, Roz.

Roz   *(to bartender, re: drink)* You don't mind if I take this with me?

Bartender Well—

Roz   I didn't think so.

Roz and Donny exit.

Frasier   Daphne, I just want you to know I'm devastated about what happened.

Daphne   It's all right, Dr. Crane.

Frasier   When I encouraged you to speak to Niles, I had no idea he'd run off and get married.

Daphne   I know you're concerned for me, but I'm fine with all this. I thought about it all last night and I realized what I was feeling was just wedding jitters. I do love your brother, but I'm in love with Donny.

Frasier   You're not just putting a brave face on this?

Daphne   No. But thank you for worrying about me. You've always been such a wonderful friend to me, Dr. Crane. In fact, I brought this for the honeymoon, but I'd like you to have it.

Daphne pulls the bottle of Chateau Petrus from her bag.

Frasier   Oh, Daphne, I couldn't.

Daphne Donny and I aren't wine drinkers.

Frasier No, Daphne, I simply—

Daphne Turn it down again and I'll keep it.

Frasier I accept. *(Takes bottle)* But I assure you, when I do drink it, I'll think of you.

Daphne Come here.

They hug. Daphne's mother, Mrs. Gertrude Moon, enters.

Mrs. Moon There's my baby.

Daphne Mummy!

Daphne and her mother greet each other.

Daphne Mum, this is—

Mrs. Moon I know who he is, love. *(To Frasier)* I want to thank you, Donny, for rescuing my baby from that horrible Dr. Crane.

Frasier Actually—

Mrs. Moon Every time I call her, I'm not on the phone five minutes before that tyrant's ordering her to hang up. *(To bartender)* Cup of tea, please. I thought my daughter might get me one, but she didn't. *(Re: chair)* Oh, this seat is worse than that Winnebago. Though it's not half as bad as that sardine tin of a room you've arranged for me. *(Re: mug of tea)* Oh, God, I can't even bear the smell of that. Take it away. Reminds me of the salmon they served on the airplane. If it doesn't have me hurling my guts up, it'll be by God's own intervention. *(To Frasier)* Now, give your new mum a kiss, Donny.

Daphne Actually, Mum, this isn't Donny.

Donny enters.

Donny Is that Mom?

Daphne This is Donny.

Mrs. Moon Oh, well, come here. Let's have a look at you. We were starting to think our Daphne would never find herself a young man. *(Taking Donny in)* And I see she hasn't, but beggars can't be choosers. *(Then)* Well, I'll see if your father's stomach is feeling any better. He says it's tension but what he's got to be tense about I'll never know.

Mrs. Moon leaves.

Donny Whew.

Daphne I'm relieved, too. I was worried she'd be in one of her dark moods.

Niles and Mel appear in the doorway talking to Miss Carney.

Donny   Oh, look who's here. The newlyweds.

Daphne   *(calling)* Dr. Crane!

Niles and Mel turn simultaneously.

Mel/Niles   Yes.

Mel   Isn't that funny?

Niles   Yes, I keep forgetting you're Dr. Crane, too.

Mel   Better get used to it.

Donny   *(calling)* Hey, get over here, you two. Congratulations.

Niles and Mel come over. Donny greets Niles with a big hug. Mel holds open her arms to Daphne and they embrace. As Frasier looks on this tableau, we:

DISSOLVE TO:

SCENE D

FADE IN:

INT. BAR/LOUNGE — THE WAYSIDE INN — NIGHT — NIGHT 3

Frasier sits at the bar. A waitress, carrying many drinks on a tray, crosses into the dining area. When she opens the doors, we hear a burst of raucous laughter. After a moment, Donny and Martin enter.

Donny   Those brothers of Daphne's sure know how to let loose.

Martin   I'll say. Help me with the names though — the one who'll eat anything on a bet, that's Nigel, right?

Donny   No, that's Peter. Nigel's the one whose band-aid he ate.

Donny exits to the men's room. Martin crosses to the bar and sits down next to Frasier.

Martin   Hey, Fras. Had enough, huh?

Frasier   I think I hit my limit when I was offering my toast and I looked down to see someone chewing on my boutonniere.

Martin   It has been a hell of a week. I still can't get over Niles and Mel.

Frasier   Didn't see that coming.

Martin   But he says she makes him happy. Nothing you can do about it, right?

Frasier	Well, actually…
Martin	Frasier, don't even think of trying to talk him out of it. He's married. End of story.
Frasier	It's not that simple, Dad. You see… I shouldn't be talking about it.
Martin	Is this about Daphne?
Frasier	Why do you say that?
Martin	I've got eyes. I know something's been going on, the way she's been looking at him lately…
Frasier	She knows, Dad. She found out how Niles has felt about her all these years.
Martin	You're kidding. How'd she find out? Some idiot blab to her?
Frasier	That's not important. The problem is, she came to me saying she thought she might have the same feelings for him.
Martin	Aw, geez.
Frasier	Of course, then Niles showed up married. Now she claims it was nothing but jitters.
Martin	You can't go telling Niles all this. He says he's happy with Mel.
Frasier	Yes, and Daphne says she's happy with Donny, but I'm not sure I believe either one of them.
Martin	All I know is, you've got two marriages on the line here. Before you get involved, you better be damn sure you know what you're doing.
	A long beat as Frasier thinks this over.
Martin	So who blabbed? Roz?
Frasier	Yes, but don't tell her you know.
	Simon enters from the back and joins them at the bar.
Simon	Hello, boys. *(To bartender)* Pack of smokes, please. *(To Frasier and Martin)* Lovely spot, isn't it? Just took a nice little stroll outside around the wishing well.
Bartender	That'll be four dollars.
	Simon pulls two handfuls of wet coins from his pockets and slaps them down on the bar.
Simon	This should cover it.
	Roz enters with Tim Walsh.
Roz	This is so funny, Tim. I had no idea you'd be here. Simon, come here!

Simon	*(sotto, to Martin)* Showtime.
	Simon crosses to Roz and Tim.
Roz	This is my old friend, Tim. We met last year when he put in the new computer system at the station.
Simon	What a coincidence, with me owning my own software company.
Tim	Really? What sort of applications do you focus on?
Simon	Applications?
Roz	Let's not get into all that, you two geeks.
Simon	Voice recognition, data encryption, a little something for NASA — can't discuss that one.
Tim	Wow, that's impressive. And Roz, are you still producing?
Simon	I'll say she is. *(Slaps her ass)*
	Daphne enters from the dining area at the same time Donny re-enters from the lobby. By this time, three or four couples have wandered into the lounge.
Donny	Hi, honey. *(Kisses her)*
	They move to the bar by Martin and Frasier.
Frasier	Things getting a little raucous inside?
Daphne	No more than usual. Aunt Rose dozed off like always from the whiskey. Now the boys have made a slingshot out of Michael's suspenders and they're launching butter curls into her cleavage.
	Daphne sits down next to Martin, Donny next to Frasier.
Martin	*(to bartender)* Give me a beer.
Daphne	*(to Martin)* Sorry we didn't get a toast out of you.
Martin	I was just feeling kind of uncomfortable.
Daphne	Oh, it's all right. Anyway, I should be toasting you. I'm going to miss you, you rotten old bastard.
Bartender	Ballantine okay?
Martin	Yeah, that's my beer. You know, they just decided to stop making this stuff. Boy, that's going to be a sad day, when I get down to my last one. It's funny, you get used to having something in your life, it's a part of your day, you take it for granted. Then, suddenly, it's not there anymore and you realize how much it meant to you.
	Daphne is touched.
	SFX: The band starts playing.

Niles and Mel enter from the dining area, Mel closely inspecting the strap of her dress.

Mel   You don't think it will stain, do you?

Niles   I wouldn't worry. It's just a little butter. *(To Donny)* May we join you?

Frasier   Why don't you take my seat. I may just move to that table by the band.

Martin   I'll join you. Take my beer over, will you? I'm gonna use the rest room.

Martin exits and Frasier crosses to a table by the band.

Donny   Seeing as how this is my last night as a carefree bachelor, I'm going to have some fun. *(To Mel)* Care to dance, Miss?

Mel   I'd love to.

Donny leads Mel to the dance floor, leaving Niles and Daphne alone.

Niles   You certainly picked the perfect spot for your wedding.

Daphne   It is, isn't it? We're doing the ceremony in the garden.

Niles   It should be beautiful.

A beat.

Daphne   I love this song.

Niles   Where are my manners? Would you like to dance?

Daphne   All right. It'll give us a chance to keep an eye on those two.

They share a laugh, then head for the dance floor and begin to dance.

Niles   It's been a long time since we danced together.

Daphne   Yes it has.

Frasier watches with interest.

Niles   Thank you for the dinner tonight. It's been a wonderful evening.

Daphne   Yes, it's one of those times you just don't want to end.

Niles draws her in; they dance in earnest. Frasier watches as Niles and Daphne become more and more lost in their dance. The song ends. Applause, then another song begins.

Donny   Niles, that's a pretty cute date you have. Mind if I cut in?

Niles   Not at all.

They switch partners — Donny now with Daphne, Niles with Mel.

> *After a moment, Frasier notices Niles looking over Mel's shoulder to Daphne, who is turned away. A moment later, Daphne glances over at Niles, who by then has turned away. Martin enters and crosses over to the table.*

Martin   I just ran into a couple of Daphne's brothers in the hallway. Boy, those Brits and their bathroom humor.

Frasier   Uh, Dad…

Martin   I'm no snitch, but let's just say if you're planning on leaving your shoes out to be shined, you may want to think twice. *(Then)* Music's nice.

Frasier   I'm glad you think so, because I need you to dance with Mel.

Martin   What for?

Frasier   I need to talk to Niles.

Martin   Frasier, are you sure about this?

Frasier   I am, Dad.

Martin   All right. But let's not forget, Mel's a fragile woman.

Frasier   I realize this could be devastating to her.

Martin   No, I mean she's fragile for me to be dancing with. If my hip gives out, she's gonna fold like a lawn chair.

> *As Martin crosses onto the dance floor, we:*
> FADE OUT.

END OF ACT THREE

ACT FOUR

SCENE E

> FADE IN:

INT. FRASIER AND MARTIN'S HOTEL ROOM — NIGHT — NIGHT 3

> *Frasier and Niles enter Frasier and Martin's hotel room. There are twin beds and a small seating area. Doors lead to adjoining rooms — Mel and Niles' room is stage right, Daphne and Donny's room stage left. French doors lead out onto a balcony.*

Niles   My gosh — wasn't that Phil Corbett, the weather man, we just passed?

Frasier   I didn't notice.

Niles   He's even better looking in person. You could fit a pimento in that chin dimple.

Frasier   All right, Niles. That's not why we're here. You see, I was watching you just now on the dance floor. The look in your eye was unmistakable.

Niles   Can you blame me? Mel's quite the little dancer, though her vertigo does rule out any serious twirling.

Frasier   I'm talking about Daphne. The way you were looking at her… Well, it breaks my heart.

Niles takes this in.

Niles   Frasier, it was one thing the other day when you were beating this drum, but now, with me here on my honeymoon, you're still insisting I haven't gotten over her?

Frasier   Niles—

Niles   What will it take to convince you?

Frasier   Niles, she knows.

Niles   What?

Frasier   She knows about your feelings for her. She's known for some time.

Niles   How?

Frasier   It's a long story. I think Roz said something. Anyway, she knows.

Niles   Why are you telling me this? I know you think my marriage to Mel was hasty, but to try and poison it this way is just… I'm not going to listen to this.

Niles starts for the door.

Frasier   Niles, Daphne feels the same way about you.

Niles turns back.

Frasier   At least I think she does. She told me as much the other day, but then denied it once you got married. But I saw the way she looked at you downstairs.

Niles   My God…

Frasier   I'm not in the habit of trying to break up people's marriages, and I know this won't win me any ethics awards, but I had to tell you, Niles. You're my brother and you deserve to be happy.

SFX: A knock at the door.

Mel   (o.s.) Niles? Darling?

Niles   Yes, honey.

He opens the door to Mel.

Mel	You left with our only room key.
Niles	Here, I'll let you in this way. So sorry.
Mel	It's all right. I could never be mad at you.
	He closes the door.
Niles	Oh, this is awful. I love Mel. It's just…
Frasier	I understand.
Niles	I have to talk to Daphne. Come with me.
	Niles starts out, opening the door. As he talks Donny and Daphne pass by in the hall.
Niles	Maybe while I speak with her you can occupy *(noticing)* Donny! Daphne.
Donny	Hey Doc. Things were getting a little too wild for us down there.
Niles	Just as well — we all have a big day tomorrow. *(To Daphne)* Oh, about that, may I have a word with you, Daphne?
Daphne	All right.
Donny	I got to get out of these shoes. See you in a few minutes.
	Donny goes.
Frasier	Well, maybe I'll just brave the hordes and head down for a nightcap.
	They ad lib goodnights and Frasier exits…
Frasier	*(o.s.)* Oh, Sir, I wouldn't put your shoes out there.
	…leaving Daphne and Niles alone. They both look a little nervous.
Niles	So, Daphne…
Daphne	Yes?
Niles	May I offer you something to drink?
Daphne	Um… no, thank you.
Niles	All right. *(Then)* Anyway, Daphne—
Daphne	Perhaps an Orangina.
Niles	All right. Maybe I'll join you.
	He gets them from the mini bar.
Daphne	Funny thing about Orangina, I never buy Orangina at home, but whenever I'm in a hotel, and there's a mini bar, it's the first thing I go for. Orangina.

Niles	Anyway, Daphne, I was speaking to Frasier just now and he told me about a conversation you two had.
Daphne	Oh, dear.
Niles	No, don't get upset—
Daphne	I specifically asked him not to say anything. What was he thinking?
Niles	I'm glad he told me.
Daphne	Oh yes, so we can have a big talk. That's what you psychiatrists always do, drag everything out in the open so we can "work through it," no matter how awkward it might be. Well, I just don't see the point in—
Niles	Daphne, I'm glad he told me because I love you.

A moment passes before Martin enters. He's all wet.

Martin	'Scuse me.
Niles	Dad!
Martin	Oh, I'm sorry, I thought you were in here with Frasier. The boys started playing this game they call William Tell with the seltzer hose. And, well... you two go on doing whatever you were doing and I'll be down in the lobby, by the fireplace.

Martin exits.

Daphne	Dr. Crane, you shouldn't say such things.
Niles	But it's the truth. Lord knows I've tried to deny it, tried to pretend I'm over you. But not a day has gone by when I haven't thought of you, your smile, your beautiful eyes, what it would be like to hold your hands and ask you the question I didn't dare ask...

Donny enters, in a bathrobe, from the adjoining room door.

Donny	What's the difference between a blister and a boil?
Daphne	Donny!
Donny	*(re: foot)* I got my shoe off and it was like I was growing another ankle bone. You went to med school, do I lance this thing or what?
Niles	As I recall, the thing for that is to soak it in tepid water for at least half an hour.
Donny	Oh. Okay. Some luck, huh? Can you imagine a worse thing to have happen on the night before my wedding?

Donny exits.

Daphne	I don't understand. How come you never said anything before?
Niles	Don't you think I wanted to? The timing just never seemed right.
Daphne	And the timing's right, now? I'm twelve hours from the altar and you're on your honeymoon.
Niles	I never would have gotten married if I thought there was the slightest chance you shared my feelings. Trust me, Daphne, say the word and I'll leave Mel in a heartbeat.

Mel enters from the door to her room.

Mel	Niles.
Niles	Darling!
Mel	I was just looking over these brochures for our honeymoon. Now, the Danieli has a step-down tub, but the Gritti has the most romantic view of the Grand Canal. What do you think?
Niles	I think any woman with your exquisite taste can handle this decision.
Mel	He says that now, but wait till the honeymoon's over.

She exits back to her room.

Daphne	Don't the doors in this bloody place lock?
Niles	You get that one, I'll get this one.

They split and lock the doors to the adjoining rooms.

Niles	Daphne, it's not too late for us. I meant it when I said I'd leave her.
Daphne	That's crazy.
Niles	It's not crazy if you feel the way I do. But I need you to tell me. And I can accept it if the answer is no. How do you feel about me?

Simon enters from the front door.

Simon	Pardon!
Daphne	Simon!
Niles	How did you get in here?
Simon	Frasier loaned me his key, in a manner of speaking. I just need a few things from the mini bar. Don't want to be caught empty handed when last call comes. *(Then)* You're not having a little last call of your own in here, are you, Stilts?
Daphne	We're just talking.
Simon	Right. He's not the one whose baby you're having, is he?
Niles	Excuse me?

Daphne	I'm not pregnant!
Simon	No need to get touchy. Just hand me that pillow case.
Daphne	No! Get out of here!

During the following, Simon takes a pillow case and starts emptying the mini bar into it. Nigel, another of Daphne's brothers, pushes open the door.

Nigel	Bit of bad news, Simon.
Daphne	Nigel!
Nigel	Oh, hello Stilts. *(To Simon)* Owing to Peter getting sick into the piano, we've been ordered to vacate the bar.
Simon	Bloody hell! Nice hotel you picked, Daphne. *(To Nigel)* Well, I'm sure Daphne wouldn't mind if we helped ourselves to her mini bar as well.
Nigel	*(into corridor)* All right, give us a hand, lads.

Nigel enters, followed by the rest of Daphne's brothers, who fan out in the room toward the adjoining doors.

Daphne	Nigel… Michael, Peter, David, Stephen, Billy! What are you all doing here?

Nigel goes to Niles and Mel's door and unlocks it.

Niles	Wait! That's my room.

But Nigel exits into Niles' room. Mel screams.

Nigel	*(o.s.)* Sorry, love. Nothing I haven't seen before.

Mrs. Moon enters through the front door.

Mrs. Moon	Here you all are. What's the point of bringing the party down to the Winnebago when there's a perfectly nice room right here.
Daphne	You're not moving the party in here.
Mrs. Moon	Now, Daphne, don't get your blood pressure up. You've got your baby to think of.

Daphne moves off in disgust as we:

CUT TO:

SCENE H

EXT. HOTEL TERRACE — MOMENTS LATER — NIGHT 3

Niles stands on the moonlit terrace. Daphne enters from the party and closes the door.

Daphne I'm sorry about all that.

Niles I must be in love. It doesn't even bother me that you come with them. *(Then)* Lovely night, isn't it?

Daphne Mmm.

Niles Stars are out. There's a nice breeze blowing. *(Smells)* Night blooming jasmine. And of course, there's the beautiful girl.

Daphne Dr. Crane, I still haven't answered your question.

Niles I know. That's why I keep talking. In case I don't get the answer I want, I can at least make this moment last a little longer. *(Then)* I'm not sure if it's the jasmine or orange blossom. A lot of times—

Daphne Oh, for God's sake, Dr. Crane.

Daphne grabs Niles and kisses him. They stare at each other.

Niles I think you can call me Niles, now.

He grabs her and kisses her.

Daphne No. I don't think I can. I do love you. But this can't happen.

Niles Why not? I realize it won't be easy, but I'll get a divorce. You can call off the wedding—

Daphne I can't. Donny is a dear, wonderful man and I made a promise to him. And Mel, you made more than a promise to her. We're supposed to forget all that? And for what? We have no idea how we'd be together. For heaven's sake, we've never even been on a date. I'm sorry.

Niles Daphne, please, take it from someone who knows, you don't want to spend half your life thinking about a chance you didn't take.

Daphne I'm sorry. My mind's made up. I think we should say good night now.

Niles Good night, Daphne.

Daphne Good night, Dr. Crane.

She opens the door and exits into the room. Raucous laughter erupts from within. As the door closes, leaving Niles alone in the moonlight, we:

DISSOLVE TO:

SCENE J

Close up on Niles, staring into the middle distance. Widen to reveal:

INT. MARTIN'S WINNEBAGO — THE NEXT MORNING — DAY 4

> *Niles, in a suit, is in the captain's chair behind the wheel of the Winnebago, his feet up on the dash. He shifts his position and finds he has been sitting on a mini bar bottle. The door opens and Frasier and Martin enter.*

Martin Hey, Niles.

Niles Don't tell me the ceremony's over already.

Martin No, it hasn't even started yet.

Frasier We saw you heading over this way and thought you might like a little company.

Niles I just felt like some privacy. This is one wedding I couldn't see myself handling very well.

Martin Lots of people cry at weddings.

Niles But not so many end up wailing and rending their garments. *(Then)* I appreciate your coming over, but I don't want you to miss it on my account.

Frasier Actually, there's been a delay. The justice of the peace began by asking the witnesses to step forward, and three of Daphne's brothers ran off into the woods.

> *SFX: There's a knock on the door. It's a waiter with a bottle of wine, a corkscrew and three glasses.*

Waiter Here's your wine, sir.

Frasier Thank you. *(Tips him)* There you are.

> *The waiter goes.*

Niles What's this?

Frasier Well Niles, I was thinking about how our friend Morrie kept this bottle his whole life waiting for a special occasion. And I thought, what occasion am I keeping it for? And then I thought what a courageous thing you did last night, taking that chance. *(Taking corkscrew)* That's worth a toast.

Niles Frasier, you can't—

Frasier Too late. The foil is pierced.

> *Frasier opens the wine and pours out three glasses.*

Martin I'm sure things between you and Mel look kind of bad right now—

Niles Oh, now why do you say that, Dad? Because I spent the third night of my marriage proposing to another woman?

Martin	I'm just saying marriages survive all kinds of stuff. You still might end up happy. Ten years from now, this could all be ancient history.
Niles	I hope you're right.
	They each take a glass.
Frasier	Here we are. *(Toasting)* To better days.
	They drink. Frasier really savors.
Frasier	Ah, yes…Unmistakably Bordeaux, unmistakably very old, and unmistakably — God-awful.
Niles	I was going to say. Dad, where did Morrie keep this?
Martin	In his wine rack.
Frasier	Which is…?
Martin	In the boiler room.
Frasier	Well, maybe we can save the rest of this treat for later.
Niles	Thanks for the thought, Frasier, but you two should run along. I'll be fine.
Martin	Take care, Niles.
Frasier	I did see a waiter passing champagne just outside. Maybe I'll have him bring you a glass to—
Niles	Get the taste out. Thank you, Frasier.
	Frasier and Martin exit. Niles returns to his reclining position. He assumes a pensive pose, staring out the window. After a beat, there's a knock on the door.
Niles	Come in.
	Daphne enters in her wedding dress.
Daphne	Hello.
Niles	Daphne!
Daphne	I was wondering… if you were free for a date.
Niles	Oh my God! Yes.
	They fall into each others arms.
Daphne	Plenty of time for that, later. Let's get this bloody boat moving.
Niles	You mean now?
Daphne	There's about a hundred people back there I'm not so keen on seeing.
Niles	Well, all right. Let's go then.

They take their seats and Niles starts the engine.

Niles   Fasten your seat belt, Daphne.

Daphne Fasten yours, Niles.

And as they drive off for points unknown, we:

FADE OUT.

END OF ACT FOUR

AND THE DISH RAN AWAY WITH THE SPOON, PARTS I & II

Written by

David Angell & Peter Casey

Created and Developed by

David Angell, Peter Casey, David Lee

Directed by

Pamela Fryman

ACT ONE

SCENE A

> *FADE IN:*

INT. MARTIN'S WINNEBAGO — DAY — DAY 1

> *It's a few moments after the season finale. Niles is driving the Winnebago down the long driveway of the inn escaping the wedding. Daphne is seated next to him in her wedding dress. They're giddy with excitement.*

Niles   I can't believe this.

Daphne   Neither can I.

Niles   What made you change your mind?

Daphne   My little niece, Audrey, the flower girl. She looked up at me and said, "You're the saddest bride I've ever seen." I figured who was I kidding if I couldn't fool a four-year-old with an eyepatch.

Niles   Remind me to give her a car for her preschool graduation.

Daphne   Next thing I knew I was climbing out the window of the loo.

Niles   You mean you didn't tell Donny?

Daphne   I didn't tell anyone! Can't you get this bloody boat going any faster?

Niles   Well, I would but you have to watch out for speed…

> *The whole Winnebago bounces violently.*

Niles   …bumps.

> *It bounces again as the rear tires go over the speed bump.*

Daphne   I've never done anything this crazy. Are you nervous?

Niles   Only that I'm going to wake up.

> *SFX: Niles' cell phone.*

> *Niles take the phone out of his jacket.*

Daphne   Don't answer it! It's probably your brother wondering if you've seen me, or maybe someone saw me climb in here and put two and two together.

Niles   Or maybe it's Mel wondering why it's taken me half an hour to put on insect repellent.

> *They listen to the phone ring once more. Then it stops.*

Niles   Good.

> *He puts it down on the console and slows the Winnebago to a*

stop.

Niles   Well, here we are. The end of the driveway. Which way shall we go?

Daphne   Well, Seattle's to the right and to the left, I guess, is Canada.

Niles   Any thoughts?

Daphne looks to her right.

Daphne   Well, what's left for us in Seattle? Ex-wives, an ex-fiancee, a tangled mess of bitterness and hurt feelings.

Niles   Yes, but an excellent symphony and world class dining.

Daphne looks to her left.

Daphne   And then there's Canada. A fresh start. A chance for adventure.

Niles   Grizzly bears.

SFX: Niles' cell phone.

Daphne   *(Urgently)* Pick one. I don't care. Let's just go.

Niles just sits there as the phone continues ringing.

Daphne   We're not moving.

Niles   I just keep picturing all those people back there… wondering… Maybe we—

Daphne   No! Don't. We can't think about that.

The phone stops ringing.

Daphne   I just ran out on my wedding. I can't go back. I need you to be strong.

Niles   I will. You'll see. For you, I'll have the strength of Hercules.

He moves in for a kiss, but is trapped by his seat belt.

Niles   I love you.

He blows her a kiss.

Daphne   And I love you.

SFX: Phone starts ringing again.

Daphne   They're not going away, are they?

Niles   I don't think so.

Daphne   Why do you have to carry that bloody thing around all the time?

Niles   If you want to keep going, I'll go.

Daphne   No. We better go back and face the music. We should make things right.

Niles takes her hand.

Niles   Okay.

Niles impatiently grabs the phone and answers it.

Niles   (into phone) All right, all right! We're on our way back! … Excuse me?… No, there is no Wendell Fong here.

He hangs up.

Daphne   Oh God, this is going to be friggin' awful.

Niles   Maybe. Maybe not. Sometimes you build these things up in your mind and they turn out not half as bad as you thought.

CUT TO:

SCENE B

CLOSE UP — DAPHNE'S FACE — DAY 1

It's Donny's POV. Daphne speaks directly into the camera.

Daphne   …So that being said, I guess there's no easy way to tell you this. I'm in love with Niles and I can't marry you.

Daphne's face gets blurred and the camera wobbles a bit.

Daphne   (concerned) Donny? Are you all right?

Camera goes to black. We hear a thud.

Daphne   (o.s.) Donny?

CUT TO:

SCENE C

CLOSE UP — NILES' FACE — DAY 1

It's Mel's POV. Niles speaks directly into the camera.

Niles   …Mel? Did you hear what I just said? Say something. Anything.

We hear Mel let out a blood-curdling scream as Niles tries to shush her, looking around hoping they haven't attracted attention.

CUT TO:

SCENE D

INT. FRASIER'S CAR — DAY — DAY 1

A short time later. Frasier is driving. Martin is next to him in the

front seat. Daphne (still wearing her wedding dress) and Niles are
in the back seat. They all look shell-shocked, especially Daphne
and Niles. After a long beat:

Niles   (softly) Wow.

FADE OUT.

END OF TEASER

SCENE E

INT. FRASIER'S CAR — CONTINUOUS — DAY 1

Our merry band as before.

Daphne   (softly) Wow.

Another pregnant pause.

Martin   Did anyone try those little crab cakes? (Off Frasier's look) What?
They were good. (After a beat) I think they had curry in them.

Frasier   All right, Dad! We've just had front-row seats for what is arguably
the most disastrous wedding in history. We can't just ignore it
with a lot of inane chitchat.

Niles   Did you try the mustard dip that went with them?

Frasier   Niles?

Niles   Frankly, I'd prefer a little inane chitchat to talking about what
actually happened back there.

Daphne   Poor Donny. I've never seen him so upset. I just wish I'd broken
the news to him in a carpeted room instead of the rock garden.

Martin   At least the birdbath slowed him down.

Daphne   I just can't help feeling guilty that our happiness has come at the
expense of Mel and Donny.

Niles puts a comforting arm around her.

Martin   Listen, there was no easy way out of this, but you did the right
thing by coming back. I'm proud of you both.

Niles   Thanks, Dad. And thank you, Frasier. As painful as all that was,
we owe you a debt of gratitude. Daphne and I are here right now
because of you.

Frasier   Oh please, Niles. I didn't do much. Just a minor pluck of Cupid's
bow.

Daphne   Nonsense. You set this whole thing in motion.

Frasier   Stop it! I'm blushing! Just seeing you kids together is thanks enough for me. *(Chuckling)* Although I wouldn't turn down a bottle of '82 Latour.

Niles   *(to Daphne)* He's not kidding.

Daphne   I know.

Martin   *(pointing)* Hey, isn't that my Winnebago pulling out from that gas station.

Frasier   I'd say so, judging from that clever bumper sticker. "Watch my rear end, not hers."

Martin laughs.

Martin   It's even funnier when you're behind it.

Frasier   I still can't believe you let Simon drive that thing, Dad.

Martin   Oh, he'll be fine. I gave him a lecture about drinking and driving.

Frasier   He did understand you were discouraging it?

Martin   Of course. *(Thinks a beat)* Uh-oh.

Daphne   I hope he gets my family to the airport on time. I wouldn't want them to miss their plane, if you get my drift.

Martin   Yeah, that's them. There's all your brothers waving from the back.

All wave and ad lib "hi" and "hey guys", etc. Suddenly, their happy expressions turn to disgust, as they attempt to shield their eyes. They ad lib "eeww", "aw geez", etc.

Martin   Tell you one thing, I'm not cleaning that window.

DISSOLVE TO:

SCENE H

FADE IN:

INT. FRASIER'S LIVING ROOM/KITCHEN — MORNING — DAY 2

Daphne and Roz sit on the couch. There are a number of brown cardboard shipping boxes ready for mailing stacked nearby along with a few beautifully wrapped wedding gifts. They are in the process of boxing gifts to be returned. Martin is at the table having breakfast and reading the paper.

Daphne   So, did Simon get you home all right after dropping my family at the airport?

Roz   Oh yeah. He really entertained my neighbours trying to parallel park the Winnebago. The highlight was when he flattened a row of newspaper racks.

Martin	How many did he get? My record's five.
Daphne	And I suppose he followed that up with some sort of clumsy advance.
Roz	Oh, he tried, but I told him to get lost. Then my baby-sitter shot him down, too. As he was leaving I saw Mrs. Henshaw from across the hall coming back from the Senior Center. The last thing I heard was him saying, (*as Simon*) "Third time's the charm."
Daphne	I can't thank you enough for helping me return these wedding gifts. I've been dreading it. It reminds me how many people I've disappointed.
Martin	Hey, Daph, you really outdid yourself with these corn muffins. They're light, moist … corny.
Daphne	Oh, you don't have to keep going on about them, Mr. Crane. (*To Roz*) He's just being sweet to me because of all this.
Martin	No, I mean it. These should be sold in stores. You could make a bundle.
Daphne	Well in that case I'll make you some more tomorrow.
Martin	Aw, darn. Tomorrow's cereal day.
Daphne	Then how about—
Martin	Bagel day.
	Martin surreptitiously feeds Eddie the corn muffin. Simon pushes open the door and enters carrying a load of presents.
Simon	That's the lot of them. The Winnebago is now cleaned out. Look sharp, Daphne.
	He throws a box at her. She misses. We hear breaking glass.
Daphne	Simon, you idiot!
Simon	Don't get your knickers in a twist. I already dropped it in the elevator.
Daphne	I think you've helped enough for one day, Simon.
Simon	Now now, if I didn't help my baby sister in her hour of need, I couldn't look at myself in the mirror… which would make shaving a sight more dangerous!
	He roars at his joke.
Simon	Oh, by the by, Roz, your neighbour Mrs. Henshaw is in remarkable physical condition for a woman her age.
Roz	Oh, God.

Martin   How about some breakfast, Simon?

Simon   Thanks ever so, Marty, but I had a crisp golden waffle and a foamy cappuccino down in your Winnebago.

Martin   The Winnebago? It doesn't have a waffle iron or a cappuccino maker.

Daphne   Wait a minute… this box looks like it's been unwrapped and then wrapped again. Simon…

Simon   It's a bread maker, which we didn't register for. People can be so thoughtless.

SFX: Doorbell.

Daphne crosses to answer the door.

Daphne   That's stealing. Those gifts are going back.

Simon   Never! Returning used merchandise is unethical, and I, for one, refuse to be a party to it.

Daphne opens the door to Niles. He enters and ad-libs greetings to everyone. He awkwardly kisses Daphne, painfully aware that everyone is watching them. He casually puts his arm around her, then takes it back down.

Niles   Ah, returning wedding presents, I take it. That's one thing Mel and I avoided by eloping, no presents to return when… when…

Simon   When you shag someone else's wife?

Daphne   Simon!

Simon   Just trying to help.

Daphne   *(to Niles)* Would you like some coffee?

Niles   Love some. I'll help you.

They cross toward the kitchen. Daphne exits first.

Niles   *(re: muffins)* Those look good, Dad. What are they?

Martin   Doorstops.

Niles   *(sotto)* Thanks for the warning.

He exits to the kitchen.

RESET TO:

INT. KITCHEN — CONTINUOUS

Daphne is tending to the coffee.

Niles   How did you sleep last night?

Daphne   I didn't. How about you?

Niles   Not a wink. (*Beat*) You know, as pleasant as our ride back and forth down the driveway was yesterday, I'm not sure it qualifies as a first date. So I have a surprise for you. I made reservations for tonight at Au Pied du Cochon. Then, afterward, we'll go dancing at the Starlight Room. Are you free?

Daphne   This is awfully short notice. Can I get back to you?

Niles   (*flustered*) Oh. Well… certainly. Whenever you…

She whacks him playfully.

Daphne   Of course I'm free, you silly sausage. It sounds wonderful.

Niles   Listen, Daphne, about um… us. This is all pretty new, and I don't know how you feel, but I think we shouldn't rush into anything, like living together or even physical relations until the situation is resolved with Mel. (*Beat*) Do you have any thoughts on that?

Daphne   Oh, I'm so relieved. I feel exactly the same way. We need to get to know each other in this whole new light first.

Niles   We are totally simpatico.

Daphne turns around to deal with the coffee. Unseen by her, Niles clenches his fists in an exasperated "darn!"

Daphne   Although in some respects we're much further ahead than most couples. I already know how you take your coffee… cream, no sugar.

Niles   (*playfully*) But I do like a little sweet now and then.

They kiss. Frasier enters in his robe.

Frasier   Good morning.

Startled, Niles and Daphne awkwardly break off the kiss.

Niles   (*to Daphne*) No, I don't see anything in your eye.

Frasier   Oh, for God's sake. I hate to break it to you — the cat's out of the bag.

Daphne   I'm sorry. I guess I'm just not used to kissing my boss's brother in the kitchen. Not that I'm used to kissing him any other place. I mean any other room.

Frasier   I know what you mean. So, how are you two doing?

Niles   Well, deliriously happy, of course. But I can't stop thinking about Mel and how she must be feeling today.

SFX: Niles' cell phone rings.

Niles Excuse me.

Niles goes to the corner to answer it.

Daphne Donny must be devastated. I'll never forgive myself for that. Maybe I should go see him.

Frasier Daphne, you're not thinking clearly, so let me do it for you. Donny and Mel have suffered a tremendous blow. What they really need is space, time to lick their wounds. The last thing they want right now is to speak to you… Niles should really be getting some of this.

Niles Frasier, keep it down, it's Mel.

Frasier Ah. *(Then to Daphne)* You'll tell him what I said.

Frasier crosses out.

Roz (o.s) Daphne, Simon's opening your gifts!

Daphne Bloody hell!

Daphne exits.

RESET TO:

INT. LIVING ROOM — CONTINUOUS

Simon is sitting on the couch carefully trying to open a package without ripping it. Daphne quickly crosses and grabs the gift away from Simon.

Daphne Give me that!

Simon Roz, you little snitch! I'm starting to wonder if you really are the future mother of my children.

Roz Somewhere out there, the real future mother of your children just lifted her head from a puddle of drool.

SFX: Doorbell.

Daphne crosses to answer it.

Simon But I bet she's got a ripper body.

Daphne opens the door to a man with a large bouquet of flowers.

Man Daphne Moon?

Daphne Yes?

Man These are for you.

Daphne Oh my goodness.

The man hands her the flowers. Then he hands her an envelope.

Man   And so is this. Consider yourself served.

Daphne   What?!

The man scampers off. Daphne opens the envelope. Niles enters.

Niles   You won't believe this. Mel wants to meet with me tomorrow. (*Noticing flowers*) Who are the flowers from?

Frasier   I can't see the card, but I believe they're from Donny.

Niles   Is he trying to get you back?

Daphne   Oh, he's getting me back, all right. He's suing me.

Martin   Daph, I'm really sorry.

Silence.

Simon   Call me crazy, but you know what I think we could all use right now? A nice pot of fondue. (*Shaking boxes*) I know there's one here somewhere.

Simon continues shaking boxes, and we:

FADE OUT.

END OF ACT ONE

ACT TWO

SCENE J

FADE IN:

INT. DONNY'S OFFICE — LATER THAT DAY — DAY 2

The office is darkened, just slivers of light coming through the blinds on the window. Donny is seated at his desk, but we can't see him because his chair is turned away toward the window. There is a knock on the door and it opens. Frasier sticks his head in.

Frasier   Donny? Are you in here?

Donny   (*softly*) Hi, Fras.

Frasier steps in and closes the door behind him.

Frasier   It's kind of dark in here. What are you doing?

Donny's tone of voice is in the calm, measured tones of the sedated.

Donny   Just sittin' here... thinkin'.

Frasier   Can we maybe... turn on a light?

Donny	Okay.

Frasier turns on a light.

Frasier	There. That's better. Donny, you're going to have to turn around. I can't see you.
Donny	We can't see you either.
Frasier	*(a beat)* We?
Donny	Oh, that's right. You haven't met my friend.

Donny swivels his chair around to face Frasier. He's not very together. He's in his rumpled, dishevelled tuxedo. His tie is undone and his shirt is partially unbuttoned revealing an undershirt. He's unshaven. In his hand he holds the miniature groom from the top of the wedding cake.

Donny	Remember him? From the top of the wedding cake? I call him Mr. Chump. Say hello to Mr. Chump.
Frasier	Oh, well, Donny, I don't—
Donny	*(screams)* I said say hello!

Frasier jumps, startled.

Frasier	Hello, Mr... Chump. Donny, are you all right?
Donny	*(calm again)* Well, I wasn't feeling too well yesterday, but my doctor gave me some pills and now I'm feeling much better. *(Then)* So, what can I do for you?
Frasier	Before I explain why I'm here, you should know that this visit was my idea. Daphne doesn't know about it.

Donny nods.

Frasier	What happened to you yesterday was devastating and, in many ways, unforgivable. Those aren't just hollow words, for I too have been abandoned at the altar. You're feeling hurt, angry, and consider yourself totally alone.
Donny	Aren't you forgetting someone?

Donny holds up Mr. Chump.

Frasier	Just so we're clear, all my remarks refer to human relationships.
Donny	Okeydoke.
Frasier	Now, Daphne realizes you went to great expense for this wedding and she's prepared to repay you over time, but this hundred thousand dollars in punitive damages for emotional distress... that's not you. That's not the Donny Douglas I know.

After a long beat:

Donny   *(coldly)* You don't know me. No one knows me, especially Daphne Moon. Because if she did, she never would have run out on me. She's going to pay, Fras. That's all I have left.

Frasier   Donny, listen, perhaps some of your anger is misdirected. Although not responsible for the choices people made here, I, myself, played a part in these events.

Donny   You?

Frasier   Albeit a small one. Insignificant, really. I scarcely know why I bring it up.

Donny   No, go on. This is interesting.

Frasier   I may have mentioned in passing to Niles and Daphne how they felt about each other, and in so doing, conceivably set this whole thing in motion. Perhaps. So if you want to yell at someone, yell at me. If you want to take a swing at someone, here's my chin. But don't take it out on Daphne.

Donny stands up and looks at Frasier threateningly.

Frasier   Are you going to hit me?

Donny   Yeah. I'm going to hit you with tortious interference with a contract and intentionally negligent infliction of emotional distress. In layman's terms, I'm going to sue your ass off.

Frasier   Me?! I didn't leave you at the altar.

Donny   No you didn't. That was Daphne. I'm suing her for breach of contract.

Frasier   Now Donny, you're reacting emotionally. Give yourself a few days. You'll feel much better.

Donny   Actually, I feel better already. Thanks, Frasier. This lawsuit really was the ticket.

Donny crosses to put his jacket on.

Donny   You know what? I'm starved. I haven't eaten in twenty-four hours. Well, see you in court. Turn the light out when you leave.

Donny starts to exit.

Donny   By the way, Frasier, who's Mr. Chump now?

Donny sticks Mr. Chump into Frasier's pocket and exits, as we:
FADE OUT.

SCENE K

FADE IN:

INT. CAFE NERVOSA — LATER THAT DAY — DAY 2

Niles and Martin are seated at a table having coffee. Niles is tapping his fingers nervously on the table.

Niles   Where is Mel? The woman is punctual to a fault. This is a bad sign.

Martin   *(re: his watch)* She's only five minutes late.

Niles   Five! I thought it was only two! She's doing this intentionally to make me squirm.

Martin   Yeah, but you're showing her. *(Beat)* Would you calm down?

Niles   You're right, Dad. I've always been a bit of an alarmist.

Frasier enters and crosses to them.

Frasier   Sorry I'm late.

Martin   Mel's late, too.

Frasier   Oh dear God! What's bubbling in that woman's cauldron now?

Niles hyperventilates.

Frasier   Steady, Niles.

Frasier takes him by the back of his neck to push his head between his legs. In doing so he bangs his head against the table.

Martin   Aw geez. Nice going. So, how'd it go with Donny?

Frasier   Well, I used all the psychological tricks in my bag to get myself added to the lawsuit.

Niles   *(head still under the table)* That's unforgiveable.

Frasier   Tell me about it.

Niles   No, no. That kiwi tart Dad dropped last Thursday is still down here.

Martin   *(looking out window)* I think I see Mel pulling up.

Niles   You better not let her see you. Thank you both for your moral support.

Frasier   We'll be right up here if you need us.

Martin and Frasier move to a table upstage, sit, and feign reading newspapers to hide themselves. Mel enters and crosses to Niles' table. She's wearing over-sized sunglasses. Niles gets up

	and pulls out a chair for her.
Niles	Hello, Mel.
Mel	(*sitting*) Niles.
	Niles sits.
Mel	Well… here we are. Our four day anniversary.
Niles	You probably hate me.
Mel	No. I wouldn't say that. I definitely hate you.
Niles	Mel, I never meant to—
Mel	What? Hurt me? If that was the case, you never would have run off with your little maid-whore leaving me holding the brochures to our honeymoon.
	A beat.
Niles	Technically, she's a physical therapist. (*Off Mel's look*) You were saying?
Mel	I'll tell you one thing. If you think that I—
	Mel chokes on her words and tries to hold back her tears. Niles take out his handkerchief and offers it to her. She suddenly pulls herself together.
Mel	No!
	She slams her palm on the table, sending crockery and utensils clattering. Startled, Niles sends his handkerchief flying into the air.
Mel	I promised myself I wouldn't cry, damnit!
	As other customers turn to them, Niles scrambles to put the silverware and cups back in their place. He looks to the other tables to assure them everything is fine. Mel takes a cut-out article from the newspaper from her purse and puts it on the table.
Mel	Have you seen this?
Niles	(*reading*) Oh no.
Mel	Yes. News of our marriage has hit the society page.
Niles	What wretched gossip monger leaked this to the press?
Mel	I did. Three days ago. Before you stuck a dagger in my heart and twisted it.
Niles	It's a nice picture of you.
Mel	I want you to listen to me very carefully. Last night as I was lying

in bed awake, I decided I was either going to kill you or kill myself.

Niles   Well here you are, so I guess that leaves…

Mel   Will you shut up and let me finish? I realized that wouldn't solve anything. So, I've decided to make this as painless as possible. You will have your divorce, Niles, and it will be quick and clean.

Niles   That's very generous of you.

Mel   Hold your applause. There are some conditions. As you know, I have a certain standing in my social circle that's important for me to uphold. Having my husband of three days run off with some cockney tart is a humiliation I'd prefer to avoid.

Niles   I understand completely.

Mel   Now, here's how this is going to play out. For the next few weeks, as far as the rest of the world is concerned, we're still happily married.

Niles   Check.

Mel   We'll appear together in public at various social functions.

Niles   Check.

Mel   In private I don't want to lay eyes on you.

Niles   Check, check.

Mel   When a suitable amount of time has passed, *I* will file for divorce.

Niles   Looks like you thought of everything.

Mel hands Niles a box.

Mel   I did. Here's the watch I was going to give you as a wedding present. Wear it when we're together.

Niles takes a watch from the box and tries to read something on the back.

Mel   It said "Forever Yours." I scratched it out with a screwdriver.

Niles looks closer.

Niles   There's something else crudely carved here. (*Getting it*) Ah. Well, at least you were able to use the "F" from "forever."

Angle on: Frasier and Martin.

They're peering around their newspapers.

Martin   Maybe it's not going so badly after all. She just gave him a watch.

Frasier   Well, isn't this all too typical? Niles leaves his wife for another woman and he gets gifts. I try to do the right thing and I get Mr.

	Chump and a lawsuit.
Martin	I know you meant well, but I told you not to go see Donny, didn't I?
Frasier	Yes, you did.
Martin	But you went down there anyway, didn't you?
Frasier	Yes, I did.
Martin	I told you not to screw around with lawyers.
Frasier	All right, Dad!

There's a moment of uncomfortable silence.

Martin	*(to himself)* I told him not to go down there.

Frasier rolls his eyes, then notices Mel getting up.

Frasier	Look. She's leaving.

CUT TO:

Angle on: Niles at table.

Niles is standing at the table watching Mel as she exits. Frasier and Martin move down to him.

Martin	So?
Niles	All things considered, it wasn't so bad. In exchange for a neat and tidy divorce, all I have to do is play the doting husband at some social functions for a few weeks.
Martin	That doesn't sound so bad.
Frasier	*(leery)* What kind of social functions?
Niles	Well, for instance, tonight's our wedding reception.
Frasier	What?!
Niles	Since we eloped, some of Mel's colleagues decided to throw a little last-minute get-together to toast our nuptials.
Martin	Not to be insensitive, but after Donny gets through with Frasier, you won't be the only one getting your nuptials toasted.

On their reactions, We:

FADE OUT.

END OF ACT TWO.

ACT THREE

SCENE L

FADE IN:

INT. FRASIER'S LIVING ROOM — EARLY EVENING — DAY 2

> *Daphne is in her robe with her hair up in curlers in preparation for her evening with Niles. She and Niles are sitting on the sofa. Frasier sits on the arm of Martin's chair.*

Daphne   Explain to me again how you and Mel masquerading as husband and wife is a good thing?

Niles   Well…

Frasier   If I may? It's basically to give Mel some wiggle room so she can emerge from this debacle with her dignity intact.

Daphne   And what about Niles' dignity?

Frasier   Maris got that in the divorce. *(Off Niles' look)* Sorry. Niles, how about some sherry?

Niles   Yes, thank you.

> *Frasier moves toward the sherry.*

Frasier   Daphne?

> *Daphne gets up begrudgingly.*

Daphne   Oh, all right. I'll get your precious wedge of brie and your imported water crackers.

Frasier   No. I meant, would you like some sherry?

Daphne   *(delighted)* Oh. Love some, thanks.

> *Happy, she sits back down. Niles takes Daphne's hand in his.*

Niles   Listen, Daphne, I know this is all very awkward, but if it speeds up the divorce process and avoids the misery I went through with Maris, isn't it worth it?

Daphne   Well…

Niles   Come on, Snookums, we'll get through this together. What do you say?

Daphne   What did you just call me?

Niles   *(hesitant)* Snookums.

Daphne   Snookums?

Niles   Just an attempt at a pet name.

Daphne   If it's all the same to you, can we keep looking?

Niles   Absolutely. There is no rush whatsoever… Truffles. *(Off her look)* The chocolates, not the fungus. *(No response)* It's a work in progress.

Frasier returns with the sherries. He lifts his glass to toast.

Frasier   Here's to better days… for all of us.

Daphne   Why, what happened to you?

Frasier   I tried to get Donny to drop his lawsuit against you. Instead, he's now suing me as well.

Daphne   I'm so sorry, Dr. Crane. This is turning into such a horrible mess. Not that I expected it all to be roses, mind you, but it's gotten so you wonder what God-awful calamity is going to befall us next.

Simon enters the front door.

Simon   Something smells in your elevator. *(Sniffs)* Now it smells in here, too. I'm starting to wonder if this is such a ritzy building after all.

Daphne   Did you get my wedding gifts down to the post?

Simon   As we speak, they are winging their way to their rightful owners.

Daphne   Thank you, Simon.

Simon   And in a completely unrelated matter, I am pleased to announce that the Winnebago is now equipped with a state-of-the-art DVD player complete with surround sound.

Daphne   I don't believe this.

Simon   Tonight's feature is "Braveheart" starring Australia's favorite son, Mr. Mel Gibson. Showtime's at eight sharp. Everyone's invited.

Frasier   Ah, yes. Nothing like a nine inch screen to make you feel part of those epic battle scenes.

Daphne   As tempting as that sounds, I've got a date. Niles is taking me to dinner and dancing. At least this day will end on a high note.

Niles   I guess I can't avoid telling you this any longer.

Martin enters from the hall.

Martin   I just want you to know I'm attending this wedding reception under protest.

Daphne   Wedding reception?

Niles   Thank you, Dad. *(To Daphne)* You know those social obligations I talked about? Well, one of them is tonight.

Daphne   A wedding reception?! For you and Mel?

Niles   It's at the Equestrian Center. Nothing major. Very impromptu. Champagne, cake, we pet the horses, we're out of there by eleven.

Martin   We'd better be! I'm not missing Sports Center for something this stupid.

Daphne   But what about …

Frasier   (*re: his watch*) Oh, dear lord. Niles, do you have any idea what time it is? We have to be across town in an hour. You better go home and get changed.

    He exits. Martin follows Frasier.

Martin   And don't forget to wear that watch she gave you.

    He exits.

Daphne   Watch?

Niles   Thanks again, Dad. (*To Daphne*) I can explain that. And I will… tomorrow night. It's just a twenty-four hour delay. I switched all the reservations… dining, dancing, everything. I'll make it up to you. I promise… Tadpole. (*Another look from Daphne*) Even I hate that one.

    He exits out the front door.

Daphne   (*to herself*) But what about our date…

    She starts crying. Simon comes over and puts his arms around her.

Simon   There, there, Stilts. This sounds like a job for "Braveheart."

    She cries all the louder, as we:

    DISSOLVE TO:

SCENE N

    FADE IN:

INT. LOUNGE AREA — BELLEVUE EQUESTRIAN CLUB — NIGHT — NIGHT 2

    An upscale bar and lounge for the horsey set that looks like Ralph Lauren blew up in it. The wedding reception is in progress. A few dozen well-heeled guests are mingling about with cocktails. Niles and Mel are greeting well-wishers in a receiving line. Frasier and Martin are standing by the bar having a drink.

Martin   Don't look now, but there's a guy over there with a bow tie who's been checking me out for the last twenty minutes.

    Frasier turns to look.

Martin   I said don't look!

Frasier quickly turns back toward Martin.

Martin   Okay, look now.

Frasier   Oh, for Pete's sake. *(Looking)* That's one of Mel's colleagues. I met him earlier.

Martin   Why's he keep starting at me?

Frasier   He's a plastic surgeon. He's probably looking at your eyelids and planning his next trip to Maui.

Martin shudders and pushes his glass toward the bartender.

Martin   Another draft. *(Looking around warily)* I feel like a wounded antelope on the African veldt.

They hear a loud phoney laugh from across the room. They look over and see Niles giddily squeezing Mel and feigning affection for the benefit of those in the receiving line.

Frasier   Oh, God. Look at him ham it up. It's our prep school production of "The Sound of Music" all over again.

Martin   He never forgave me for walking out on that. *(A beat)* I still say he was miscast as the Nazi Commandant.

Angle on:

Niles and Mel and the receiving line. An older woman approaches them.

Mel   Niles, I'd like you to meet Adrianna Pettibone. She stables "General Prescott," the current grand champion right here at our equestrian club.

Niles put his arm around Mel.

Niles   Wonderful. And speaking of grand champions, how about this little filly? And I didn't even have to check her teeth.

He laughs merrily.

Adrianna   You're a lively little cowboy.

Niles   Sorry, ma'am, but I've already got Mel's brand on me.

Adrianna moves off. Mel elbows Niles in the ribs.

Mel   What's gotten into you?

Niles   Sorry, I'm a little nervous.

Roz approaches them in the receiving line.

Roz   *(playing along)* Congratulations, you two. *(Sotto)* God, this is so weird… but I guess you would know that.

Niles   Roz! What are you doing here?

Mel   I invited her. Your side of the guest list was looking a little sparse.

Niles   I can't believe you actually came. You don't even like me.

Roz   What can I say? I'm a sucker for freak shows. Now if you'll excuse me, I'm going to leave my fingerprints all over a martini glass and, with any luck, that rich looking guy in the tuxedo.

She moves off.

Mel   Poor Roz. That's a waiter.

Niles   Yes, but on the plus side, he's the head waiter.

Mel   By the way, if anyone asks about our honeymoon, we're flying to Paris, taking the Orient Express to Venice, and then it's two weeks in the Mansarda Palazetto Suite at the Cipriani.

Niles nods, then is quiet for a beat.

Mel   What's the matter?

Niles   It sounds like a wonderful trip.

Mel   (*softly*) It's not my fault we're not going.

Niles   (*a beat*) I know.

A photographer approaches them.

Photographer Here's the happy couple. All right, you two. Show me those pearly whites.

He brings the camera up to his eye as they smile halfheartedly. Lowering the camera, he tries to lighten them up.

Photographer Come on. Smile. You've got the rest of your lives to make each other miserable.

They smile as he takes the picture.

Photographer There we go. Now how 'bout a kiss?

Mel and Niles look at each other awkwardly.

Niles   Uh… sure.

He turns and gives Mel a rather tepid kiss.

Photographer C'mon, Doc. This is your wife, not mine.

Niles makes this one look like he means it. The flash goes off. The guests applaud. The photographer moves off. Niles and Mel awkwardly separate.

Niles   I'm uh… going to get a drink and see how Dad and Frasier are doing.

He moves off.

Angle on:

Frasier and Martin are talking to a middle-aged couple.

Frasier   Yes, they do make a lovely couple.

Woman   Don't they? I'm sure they'll be happy together for many years.

Martin   You never know.

This grinds the conversation to a halt.

Frasier   Dad…

Martin   Well, you don't, do you? I'm just sayin'… you never know.

Woman   No, I guess you don't.

She and the man move off uncertainly.

Frasier   *(brightly)* Enjoy the party! *(Then to Martin)* What's the matter with you?

Martin   Hey, in a few weeks, I'm going to look like a genius.

Roz approaches them.

Martin   Hey, Roz, how's it going?

Roz   *(annoyed)* You know, they ought to make waiters wear name tags.

Frasier   Yes, carrying trays and taking drink orders still leaves room for ambiguity.

Roz   Shut up.

Niles comes up.

Niles   Well, it seems to be going well. Do you think anyone's suspicious?

Frasier   Everyone seems to be having a lovely time.

Martin   I heard some grumbling about the cash bar.

Frasier   I gave you twenty dollars.

Martin   In this joint that's a beer and a half. *(To Niles)* So, how you holding up, Son?

Niles   If I have to stretch my muscles into a smile one more time, I think my face is going to crack.

Mel   *(o.s.)* Niles!

Niles   *(phoney smile)* Yes, Darling.

Mel joins them.

Mel   It's time to cut the cake. Why don't you go gather everyone around? I need to borrow Frasier for a moment.

Mel takes Frasier by the arm and leads him away.

Mel   I had an interesting phone call this afternoon from Donny.

Frasier Oh?

Mel   He said you'd been by to see him earlier today.

Frasier I may have done so.

Mel   I understand you were a busy little bee before the wedding, first buzzing in Daphne's ear, then buzzing in Niles' ear…

Frasier Let me explain. You see—

Mel   Buuuzz, buzz, buzz, buzz, buzz, buzz. Buuuzz, buzz, buzz, buzz, buzz, buzz, buzz. Buuh…

Frasier Stop that! Please.

Mel   You see, I've been torturing myself trying to figure out how this all happened so quickly. Now I know. I won't forget this.

She moves off to join Niles. Frasier follows and stands next to Martin.

Martin   What was that all about?

Frasier Mel talked to Donny.

Martin   I told you not to go down there.

Frasier All right, Dad!

Mel taps a glass to get everyone's attention.

Mel   Attention, everyone. First of all, my husband and I would like to thank all of you for coming here tonight to share our happiness.

Niles   *(overdoing it)* Yes.

Mel   Before we cut the cake, Niles' brother Frasier has agreed to offer a toast in our honor.

Martin   *(sotto, to Frasier)* I didn't know you were doing this.

Frasier *(sotto)* Neither did I. *(Then)* Ladies and gentlemen. For most of his adult life, my brother, Niles, has searched for the perfect woman. Along the way, he's broken a heart or two, and no one regrets that more than he. But tonight, it gives me great joy to tell you he's finally found the woman of his dreams.

Mel's friends applaud. Mel knows what Frasier is really saying and she's not thrilled though she tries to hide her displeasure.

Frasier She's warm and loving, and my father and I have considered her a member of our family for quite some time. In fact, Dad will be the first to tell you she gives a mean back rub. (*Laughter*) So, if you will, raise your glass and join me in wishing two very special people so close to my heart a lifetime of happiness.

He raises his glass, as do the others. Everyone drinks. Mel and Niles begin to cut the cake.

Mel   (*sotto*) Wasn't that clever of your brother. Too bad your little English muffin wasn't here to enjoy it with you. Speaking of which, you do realize that while we're pretending to be married, you can't be seen with her in public.

Niles   I... I...

Mel roughly shoves a piece of cake into his open mouth.

Mel   I love you, too.

She turns his face to the camera and smiles as a flash goes off and we freeze the frame.

FADE OUT.

END OF ACT THREE

ACT FOUR

SCENE P

FADE IN:

INT. FRASIER'S LIVING ROOM — THE NEXT DAY — DAY 3

The living room is empty. Simon enters the front door.

Simon   (*calling out*) Hello, hello? Anybody home?

He plops onto the sofa.

Martin   (*o.s.*) (*calling out*) Hey, Simon. I'm making some coffee. You want some?

Simon   I was actually thinking of something a bit colder with more of an amber hue.

Martin   (*o.s.*) A beer?

Simon   Brilliant! If you aren't Seattle's finest detective then I'm the Prince of Wales.

Martin   (*o.s.*) So, how did Eddie like his walk?

Simon's brow begins to furrow in slow realization that something is wrong. A thought begins to form, "Where did I leave Eddie?"

Simon   Uh, the little nipper loved it.

He gets up and heads to the front door.

Simon   Uh-oh. I think nature's calling him again. His bladder's worse than mine. Be back in a flash.

Martin   *(o.s.)* Okay.

Simon exits. Martin enters from the kitchen with a cup of coffee. Frasier enters from his room dressed for work.

Frasier   Did I just hear Simon's voice?

Martin   Yeah. He's taking Eddie on a walk for me.

Frasier   It's about time that chowderhead made himself useful.

Martin   Hey, don't be so hard on him. He tries.

SFX: Doorbell.

Frasier crosses to the door.

Frasier   If you're talking about my patience, he certainly does.

Frasier opens the door to Niles

Frasier   Ah, come in, Niles.

Niles enters.

Niles   Thank you, Frasier. Hello, Dad. You know, about a block from here I saw a dog who looked remarkably like Eddie tied up outside a bar.

Martin   Impossible. He was just here.

Niles   So, did you say anything to her?

Frasier   No. You told us not to.

Martin   You want us out of here when you drop the hammer?

Niles   Actually, I think I'll be safer with witnesses.

Daphne enters from her bedroom area.

Daphne   Niles. I didn't hear you come in.

Niles   I just got here.

He gives here a little kiss, then looks to Frasier and Martin. They quickly avert their eyes.

Niles   *(to Daphne)* How are you today?

Daphne   Better, thanks. I realized that postponing our date one night doesn't amount to much in the greater scheme of things. *(Stiffening slightly)* So, how was your wedding reception?

Niles   Just your average evening in hell. The only thing that got me through it was the thought of you and four brandy alexanders.

Daphne	Well, that's behind us now. We have a wonderful evening to look forward to tonight. I bought a new dress, much too expensive, but you're worth it. I'm getting my hair and nails…
	She notices Frasier and Martin exchange glances.
Daphne	Why are you looking at each other like that?
Frasier	We weren't looking at each other like that. Like what. Like anything.
Martin	*(shaking his head)* Nuh-uh.
Daphne	Yes you were. Those darty little glances mean something's up. Niles?
Niles	About tonight…
Daphne	I hate the way this is starting.
Niles	Mel feels that while she and I are acting like we're married, you and I can't be seen together in public. So I'm afraid that means—
Daphne	*(cool)* I know what that means.
Niles	But it's just until the divorce.
Daphne	Whenever that bloody is.
Niles	Daphne—
Daphne	If you'll excuse me, I've got a splitting headache.
	She turns and crosses toward her room.
Niles	*(calling after her)* You know, if you look at it from Mel's point of view, it really does make sense.
	Daphne stops in her tracks.
Martin	Uh-oh.
Frasier	He came so close.
	Daphne slowly turns toward Niles.
Daphne	*(quietly)* What did you say?
Niles	I said, "Damn that Mel."
Daphne	No you didn't. You should have, but you didn't. It sounded to me like you were taking her side.
Niles	I'm not taking her side. It's just that I can see the logic in her request. When you think of what she could put me through, I think she's showing remarkable restraint.
Frasier	*(rising; sotto)* He's floundering.
Martin	*(sotto)* Sit.

Niles	Can we just turn the clock back two minutes and start this conversation over?
Daphne	Why don't we just turn it back to ten minutes before my wedding and save everybody all this trouble.
	Daphne starts away.
Niles	What are you saying?
Daphne	What do you think I'm saying?
Niles	It sounds like you're saying you're sorry you did this.
Daphne	Maybe that's what I am saying.
	Frasier stands.
Martin	*(under his breath)* Oh boy.
Frasier	Now before somebody says something—
Daphne	Butt out! If you hadn't opened your mouth, we wouldn't be in this mess. Donny wouldn't be suing me and everyone in sight. I wouldn't be out two weeks' salary for a new dress I'm apparently never going to wear. *(To Niles)* And you wouldn't be kowtowing to that shrew of a wife of yours.
Frasier	This is all my fault?!
Niles	Oh, shut up, Frasier. The only thing more hollow than your protest of innocence is your big, fat head.
Frasier	I am wounded! I intervened only out of love and concern for two people I—
Daphne	Oh put a sock in it. I'm sick of listening to you yammer on about everything under the sun.
Niles	Daphne—
Daphne	And I'm sick of listening to you, too. *(To Martin)* You got anything to say, old man?
	Martin shakes his head "no."
Daphne	Good.
	She exits to her room. There's a long beat of silence.
Frasier	I'm waiting.
Niles	For what?
Frasier	An apology for that unprovoked broadside you levelled at me.
Niles	You expect me to apologize to you?
Frasier	Expect it, Sir, and demand it.

Niles	Well, here's my answer to that. No.
Frasier	No?!
Niles	No. And furthermore, why don't you take your "broad side," stuff it in a chair, and keep your unlimited supply of opinions, suggestions, proposals, and recommendations to yourself.

Niles crosses to the front door.

Frasier	Well, I never!!
Niles	No, you always.
Frasier	Get out!!!

Niles exits. There is a beat of silence.

Martin	*(rising)* How's a corned beef sandwich sound?

He heads for the kitchen.

Frasier	I am appalled.
Martin	No problem. I think we've got some smoked turkey in there, too.

He exits to the kitchen. Frasier follows.

RESET TO:

INT. KITCHEN — CONTINUOUS

Martin enters followed by Frasier. Throughout Frasier's speech, Martin goes back and forth to the refrigerator taking out bread, luncheon meat, lettuce, tomato, mayonnaise, etc. and begins making a sandwich. Martin occasionally has to work around Frasier, as he moves back and forth, to get into the refrigerator.

Frasier	What is my offense? What egregious sin have I committed that I be so maligned? Was I to just sit idly by and watch those two misguided souls embark on doomed relationships? Would they have thanked me for that? Not likely, I dare say…

Martin's looking in the refrigerator.

Martin	Who moved the mustard?
Frasier	Top shelf, door.
Martin	Bingo.
Frasier	And then, when they were perched on the very brink of disaster, I snatched them from the gaping maw and placed them gently in each other's arms. But am I accorded a hero's tribute for my troubles? Am I hoisted upon their shoulders and paraded about the room?

Martin has been sniffing a jar of mayonnaise.

Martin   I don't have my glasses. What's the expiration date?

Frasier   *(looking)* Last week.

Martin   *(shrugs)* I'll chance it.

Frasier   No! They turned on me like vipers and made me the villain of the piece. Well, hear me now. This is the last time Frasier Crane interferes with those two ingrates. That's it. Finished. Finito. Nunquam postea.

Martin   Huh?

Frasier   It's Latin. It means never again. And I mean it.

Martin   Uh-huh.

Frasier   Oh, I know I've made these declarations before, but mark the calendar. Note the time on your watch. This. Is. It!

Martin gathers his sandwich and a beer.

Martin   When you figure out how to get those two back together, I'll be in my room if you need some help.

Frasier   *(exasperated)* Have you been listening to me?

Martin   I tried not to, but some of it still got through.

He exits. Frasier shakes his head. He picks up the mayonnaise jar, sniffs it, recoils slightly, and throws it in the trash. Daphne enters.

Daphne   *(tentative)* Hello, Dr. Crane.

Frasier   *(stiffly)* Daphne.

He turns and feigns busy work wiping down the counter.

Daphne   Making yourself a sandwich?

Frasier   No. Dad did.

Daphne   I hope he didn't use the mayonnaise. I meant to throw it out.

Frasier   I've seen him eat worse.

Daphne   I'll say. Remember when he dropped his hot dog at the ballpark?

No response from Frasier.

Daphne   Oh, Dr. Crane, I'm sorry I said those things about you. I didn't mean them.

Frasier   I know, Daphne. Come here.

They hug.

Daphne   I guess this all finally came crashing down on me.

Frasier   It's perfectly understandable *(Then)* Listen, I know your date with Niles is off, but that shouldn't stop two friends from going out and having a nice dinner. What do you say? You and me tonight. My treat. You can put on that new dress.

Daphne   Thank you. It's a lovely offer, but I think I'll just stay home and have a quiet night.

They exit into the living room.

RESET TO:

INT. LIVING ROOM — CONTINUOUS

Frasier and Daphne enter.

Frasier   You're sure you won't change your mind'?

Daphne   Positive.

Simon enters with Eddie on a leash.

Simon   Hello, all. My furry friend and I have just concluded our daily constitutional with young Edward, here, dropping a few amendments along the way.

Frasier   Thank you for that civics lesson, Simon.

Simon   It's heartwarming, really. The bond between man and dog. In just a short time, this pooch and I have become practically inseparable.

Simon unleashes Eddie who immediately bolts down the hall to Martin's room.

Simon   And yet he recognizes when I need my space. So, what's on the docket tonight.

Daphne   All I want is a quiet night at home.

Simon   Stilts, we are of one mind. I'll hoist a beer while you get dinner started. Then, after our bellies are full and you've done the dishes, we'll adjourn to the Winnebago where Mr. Jean-Claude Van Damme, the Muscles from Brussels, will ply his trade against the forces of evil.

Frasier   *(to Daphne)* Ready at eight?

Daphne   Make it seven-thirty.

DISSOLVE TO:

SCENE S

FADE IN:

INT. FRASIER'S HALLWAY/ELEVATOR — LATER THAT EVENING —
NIGHT 3

> *Niles and Martin enter from Frasier's apartment. They cross and
> Niles pushes the call button for the elevator.*

Niles   What a good idea, Dad. An evening out, just the two of us. I had
no idea you enjoyed the Natural History Museum.

Martin   Oh yeah, and this documentary on the rain forest is supposed to
be great.

Niles   That's what I hear.

Martin   I hope it has pygmies. I like pygmies.

Niles   I know you do. *(Casually)* So… uh, where's—

Martin   She's at a restaurant having dinner with Frasier.

Niles   Ah. *(Beat)* Did she happen to ask about—

Martin   Sorry.

> *The doors open and they enter the elevator. Martin pushes a
> button. the doors close.*
>
> RESET TO:

INT. ELEVATOR — CONTINUOUS

Niles   Dad, we're going up.

Martin   Aw geez. Guess we'll have to take the long way.

> *A beat.*

Niles   Why do you like pygmies so much?

Martin   They're short and they blow darts. What's not to like?

> CUT TO:

SCENE T

EXT. ELLIOT BAY TOWERS ROOF — MOMENTS LATER — NIGHT 3

> *There is a small raised structure with a door that houses the
> stairwell to the roof. The roof itself is typical of a large high-rise
> building with vents, air conditioning units and the like. We see
> the illuminated skyline of Seattle and the night sky above.The
> door to the stairwell opens and Martin enters. The upper half of
> Niles becomes visible on the stairs.*

Niles   What could possibly be so important for me to see up here?

Martin	The guy in 1708 just got some homing pigeons and he built a coop up here.
	Niles steps into the doorway.
Niles	Pigeons? You dragged me all the way up here for pigeons?
Martin	Trust me. You're going to like this.
Niles	Dad, I don't think I handled things too well today. Do you think Daphne will ever forgive me?
Martin	Why don't you ask her yourself?
	Martin gestures around the corner of the stairwell housing. Niles takes a few steps and looks in that direction. What he (as well as the audience) sees is Daphne in her new dress seated at a table for two. She looks like an angel bathed in the light of many candles. Standing behind the empty chair is an impeccably dressed Frasier, a towel draped over his arm. The table is set with exquisite silver, china, crystal and a beautiful floral arrangement. Champagne is chilling in a nearby bucket. At their places are two domed silver plate covers keeping their dinners warm. Frasier hits the button on a Bose wave radio. SFX: The strains of something soft and romantic and not too hideously expensive begin to play.
Frasier	*(pulling out the chair)* Your table is ready, Sir.
Niles	Oh my.
	Niles moves trance-like to the table and sits.
Niles	*(to Daphne)* You look stunning.
Daphne	Thank you. You look dashing.
	Frasier shows the champagne bottle to Niles.
Frasier	I hope this is to your liking.
Niles	Everything is to my liking.
	Frasier pours the champagne.
Daphne	It looks like we're having that first date after all.
Niles	You went to so much trouble.
Daphne	It wasn't me. It was your brother.
Frasier	Well, you know me. I hate to butt in. I was planning to take Daphne out to dinner when inspiration struck. I figured since you two couldn't go to Au Pied du Cochon, my faithful companion *(indicates Martin)* and I would bring it to you courtesy of their caterer. If dancing at the Starlight Room was impossible

(gesturing to the heavens) we'd give you the real thing.

Daphne   It's all so overwhelming.

Niles   Frasier, Dad, I don't know what to say. I mean, you even got that man to move his pigeons.

Martin   There are no pigeons, Son. I made that up.

Niles   Oh, right.

Daphne   How can we ever thank you two?

Frasier   Just have a beautiful evening.

Niles   I think we can do that. Listen, Frasier—

Frasier   Apology accepted.

Martin and Frasier head for the door. Frasier turns and starts back to them.

Frasier   Don't forget to give the lingonberry sauce a stir before you—

Martin   *(pulling him away)* They'll figure that out.

They exit down the stairwell. Niles and Daphne look at each other realizing that at long last they are alone on a date. They laugh that silly laugh that comes from giddiness.

Niles   Daphne, about today—

Daphne   Let's just forget about that. Why don't we start again from here?

Niles   I'd really like that.

Niles lifts his champagne glass. Daphne follows suit.

Niles   To us.

Daphne   To us.

They clink and sip champagne, then kiss.

Daphne   I usually feel so nervous on a first date. But not tonight.

Niles   I could never feel nervous with you. *(Beat)* Would you like to dance?

Daphne   I'd love to.

Niles goes over and helps her out of her chair. They step away from the table and begin dancing to the music.

Niles   So where are you from?

Daphne   Manchester, England.

Niles   Really. Big family?

Daphne   Hideously. And you?

Niles   I'm from a small mountain village in Tibet.

        Daphne laughs.

Niles   Tenzing Norgay used to carry me to school.

        As they continue their dance, we pull back and:

        FADE OUT.

END OF ACT FOUR.

SLIDING FRASIERS

Written by
Dan O'Shannon & Bob Daily

Created and Developed by
David Angell, Peter Casey, David Lee

Directed by
Pamela Fryman

ACT ONE

SCENE A

>   *Title card: "This is Tricky, So Pay Attention."*

Frasier   *(v.o.)* All right, if you must know, I'm just about to leave for a speed date.

>   *FADE IN:*

INT. CAFÉ NERVOSA LATE AFTERNOON — DAY 1

>   *Frasier, wearing a suit, is sitting at the table with Roz.*

Roz   What's a speed date?

Frasier   Apparently it's the latest thing. There are twelve men and twelve women in a room. You talk to one person for eight minutes, and when the bell rings, you move along and talk to the next one. Essentially it's all the stress and humiliation of a blind date, times twelve.

Roz   Wow, talk about desperate. And you made fun of me for my personal ad. And the matchmaker I went to, and the time I pretended to be born-again so I could go to that mixer. *Now* who's desperate?

Frasier   I'm not sure we have a clear winner, Roz.

Roz   So what brought this on?

Frasier   I'm tired of seeing happy couples everywhere I look. It's time to get proactive. If I have to paint a target on my ass and waggle it in front of Cupid's face, so be it.

Roz   Well, I won't be finishing this sticky bun. *(Then)* When you say "happy couples," you wouldn't be talking about Niles and Daphne, would you?

Frasier   Among others. Don't get me wrong, nobody's happier for Niles than I — but there are days when his "lovesick swain" act wears the tiniest bit thin.

>   *Niles enters. He wears an oversized T-shirt with a picture of him and Daphne, their grinning faces pressed together. He carries a garment bag.*

Niles   Hello all. Notice anything different?

Frasier   *(refusing to play)* Haircut?

Niles   No, I'm wearing a T-shirt.

Roz	I like it.
Niles	Thank you. I've never worn an undergarment in public before.
Frasier	*(re: bag)* Is that my sweater?
Niles	Yes. What's the big emergency?
Frasier	I'm going out, and I'm reconsidering my attire. While the suit projects an air of professionalism — Doctor Frasier Crane — the sweater evokes a more casual image — Just Fras. *(Then)* Thoughts?
Roz	So Niles, I bet you and Daphne have big Valentine's Day plans.
Niles	Oh, yes. She's cooking dinner for me and then I've arranged a big surprise. I've cleared my schedule and I'm flying her to Maui for a long romantic weekend.
Roz	*(impressed)* Not bad.
Niles	I'm whisking her to the airport in a limo filled with exotic orchids. You don't think it's too over-the-top, do you?
Roz	I think that boat sailed with your T-shirt.
Frasier	Here's an idea. What if I wear the sweater under the jacket? You know, best of both worlds.
Niles	*(standing)* Honestly, Frasier, could you be any more self-absorbed? Goodbye, Roz. If you want to know more about our trip, we'll have pictures on our website as soon as we get back.
	Niles exits. Roz sees Frasier staring at the sweater.
Roz	Oh for God's sake, Frasier, why don't you just flip a coin?
Frasier	Roz, this may seem like nothing to you, but the tiniest decision can shape your whole destiny. It's said that when a butterfly beats its wings in China, it sets in motion a whole chain of—
Roz	Pick one!
Frasier	Fine. You're right. I'll go with… the suit.
Roz	That's the one I would've picked.
Frasier	Well, wish me luck.
	Frasier stands and steps away from the table, blocking the way of a guy named Mike, who had been crossing towards the exit.
Frasier	Oh, excuse me. *(Then, noticing)* Don't you work at KACL?
Mike	Yes, I just started. Mike Schafer.
	They shake hands.
Frasier	Frasier Crane. Have you met Roz Doyle?

Mike	No.
Frasier	You are new.
Roz	Aren't you keeping twelve losers waiting? Mike, can I buy you some coffee?

They sit down as Frasier crosses away. As he nears the door, a waitress serving an attractive woman, Monica, spills coffee. Monica jumps back, sending her chair flying into Frasier's path. Frasier starts to fall, then catches himself on a table, wrenching his shoulder.

Monica	My God, I'm so sorry!
Frasier	Quite all right. *(Calling to Roz)* I'm okay.
Monica	You must think I'm such a klutz.
Frasier	*(gallantly)* Not at all. *(Then)* I'm Frasier.
Monica	Monica.

He extends his hand, then winces and grabs his shoulder.

Frasier	I think I wrenched my shoulder. Did you hear a popping sound?
Monica	I'm taking you to the emergency room.
Frasier	That's very nice of you, but—
Monica	I insist. It's the least I can do.
Frasier	Well, how can I turn down such a gracious invitation?

They head to the door and we:
CUT TO:

INT. CAFÉ NERVOSA — MOMENTS EARLIER — UNIVERSE 2

Roz	Oh for God's sake, Frasier, why don't you just flip a coin?
Frasier	Roz, this may seem like nothing to you, but the tiniest decision can shape your whole destiny. It's said that when a butterfly beats its wings in China, it sets in motion a whole chain of—
Roz	Pick one!
Frasier	Fine. You're right. I'll go with… the suit.

He takes a step away from the table, then steps back.

Frasier	No — the sweater.
Roz	That's the one I would've picked.

Frasier takes off his jacket and starts to pull on his sweater.

Frasier	It's the perfect look for a blind date. The wool says warmth, the tailoring says elegance…
Roz	And the tag says, "Dry clean only."

As Roz tucks his tag in, Mike crosses unimpeded behind Frasier. As we stay on Roz and Frasier, we see in the background the waitress spilling coffee, Monica jumping back, Mike colliding with the chair. A bit more nimble than Frasier, Mike manages to avoid hurting himself.

Monica	My God, I'm so sorry.
Mike	That's okay. No harm done.
Frasier	*(to Roz, re: commotion)* Klutz. *(Then)* Well, I'm off, wish me luck.
Roz	Good luck.

Frasier heads for the door, passing Monica and Mike, who are shaking hands.

Mike	Mike Schafer. It looks like you're going to need a little more coffee.
Monica	Would you care to join me?

They sit down as Frasier exits, and we:

FADE OUT.

SCENE B

FADE IN:

INT. EMERGENCY ROOM — THAT NIGHT — UNIVERSE 1/NIGHT 1

Frasier, in shirtsleeves and tie, sits on an examining table, his arm in a sling. Monica stands beside him.

Monica	You know, you're not the first guy I've sent to the emergency room.
Frasier	And here I thought I was special.
Monica	Well, you are my first shoulder. When I was ten, my brother fell off my handlebars and broke his foot. Then in art school, a pottery wheel got away from me and rolled down some stairs. I broke one guy's knee and another guy's hip.
Frasier	So you're working your way up the skeleton.

They share a laugh.

Monica	Yeah, I guess I've broken more than my share of bones.
Frasier	And more than a few hearts, I'm sure.

Monica	*(modestly)* I don't know about that. *(Then)* Listen, I'm so sorry about this. I hope I didn't ruin your plans.
Frasier	Actually, I didn't have anything special planned.
	CUT TO:

SCENE C

INT. RESTAURANT — THAT AFTERNOON — UNIVERSE 2/DAY 1

From Frasier's pov we see the enthusiastic face of Judy.

Judy	So, did you hear about the new pirate movie? It's rated aaaaaar!
	We reveal Frasier sitting across the table from Judy, with other singles in the background. Frasier chuckles politely.
Frasier	Very droll!
Judy	Get it? Aaaaaaaar!
Frasier	*(chuckling, a bit less politely)* Yes.
Judy	That's sort of my test joke to see if a guy's cool or not. Can you believe you're the first one here who laughed? *(Then)* I mean, can't you just see a pirate walking into a movie theater, he's got his eye-patch and his peg-leg and—
	SFX: A bell rings.
Judy	Boy, that did not feel like eight minutes.
Frasier	Indeed it didn't.
	FADE OUT.

SCENE D

FADE IN:

INT. FRASIER'S LIVING ROOM — THAT NIGHT — UNIVERSE 2/NIGHT 1

Frasier, wearing the sweater (and no sling), enters to find Martin watching an old movie on TV.

Martin	*(distracted)* Hey Fras. How'd that speed date thing go?
Frasier	Could not have been worse.
Martin	That's nice.
Frasier	Dad, you're not listening.
Martin	*(turning down TV)* I'm sorry, son. So, did you get any phone numbers?
	SFX: A knock on the door.

Frasier   No, but if I ever need to track any of them down, I can simply write them care of "the bottom of the barrel."

Martin   That's too bad.

Frasier opens the door to reveal Daphne, who is loaded down with grocery bags.

Frasier   Let me help you with that, Daphne.

Daphne   Thank you, Dr. Crane.

Frasier takes two of her grocery bags and they head toward the kitchen.

Frasier   You're really stocking up, aren't you?

Daphne   It's for Niles's Valentine's dinner.

Frasier   But that's still a week away.

Daphne   Yes, but it's a complicated recipe, and I need time to practice. I'm afraid there are going to be quite a few leftovers.

Daphne crosses into the kitchen.

Martin   Who's she kidding? This house hasn't seen a leftover in two months.

Frasier notices something in the grocery bag and stops.

Frasier   Daphne, you weren't planning on using cumin, were you?

Daphne crosses back into the living room to take his bag.

Daphne   Yes, the recipe calls for lots of it.

Frasier   But Niles is terribly allergic to cumin.

Daphne   Oh dear. I knew about the scallops. And the nutmeg. The oat bran, wheat germ, carob, parchment mites…

Frasier   I know. He tried wearing an allergy tag, but his neck was too weak to support it.

Daphne exits into the kitchen. SFX: The phone rings.

Martin   Did you see that? The character in this movie dials a phone, and at the exact same time our phone rings. It's like Montgomery Clift is calling me!

Frasier   That's fascinating, Dad.

Martin picks up the phone as Frasier wanders over to the piano.

Martin   (into phone) Hello?…Hi, Niles… (Sotto) No, she's in the kitchen, she can't hear… Aw jeez, I don't know about that… All right, if it means that much to you, I'll do it. Bye.

He hangs up.

Martin   That was your brother. He wants me to pack a suitcase for Daphne, for their trip to Maui. *(Shuddering)* Now I have to go through her unmentionables.

Frasier   I wonder if I'll ever see another unmentionable.

Martin   Oh Frasier, come on. It was just one bad date.

Frasier   It was twelve bad dates. And another hundred before that. *(Then, Frasier plays the piano and sings mournfully Bing Crosby's "I'm Through With Love".)*

Daphne returns from the kitchen.

Martin   You're gonna be this way all night, aren't you?

Frasier, lost in his sorrow, continues to play.

Martin   *(to Daphne)* It breaks my heart to see him like this. Fortunately, I can't see him from McGinty's.

He goes for his coat as Frasier continues to play, and we:

CUT TO:

SCENE E

INT. FRASIER'S LIVING ROOM — A SHORT TIME EARLIER — UNIVERSE 1/ NIGHT 1

Frasier, wearing his sling, enters to find Martin watching TV.

Martin   *(distracted)* Hey Fras. How'd that speed date thing go?

Frasier   Actually I went to the hospital instead.

Martin   That's nice.

Frasier   Dad, you're not listening.

Martin   *(turning down TV)* I'm sorry, son. *(Then, noticing sling)* Are you okay? What happened?

Frasier   I tripped and sprained my shoulder. But I'm feeling no pain, because in the process I met the most wonderful woman.

Martin   Is she a nurse?

Frasier   No, she's the one who tripped me. Her name is Monica. She's a commercial artist, she's cute as a button, and she's a danger to herself and others.

SFX: A knock on the door.

Martin   Good for you, Fras.

Frasier opens the door to reveal Daphne, who is loaded down with grocery bags.

Daphne   Could you give me a hand here?

Frasier   I would, but I sprained my shoulder.

Martin   *(off her look)* Bullet in the hip.

Daphne   *(to Frasier)* You still have one good arm, Dr. Crane.

Frasier   The doctor told me not to overdo.

Daphne bends over and picks up the third bag from the floor. During the following she crosses to the kitchen.

Frasier   Oh, I met a girl today.

Daphne   So did she.

She exits to the kitchen.

Frasier   I know it's soon, but I have half a mind to call Monica.

SFX: The phone rings.

Martin   Did you see that? The character in this movie dials a phone, and at the exact same time our phone rings. It's like Montgomery Clift is calling me!

Frasier   That's fascinating, Dad.

Martin picks up the phone. Frasier wanders over to the piano.

Martin   *(into phone)* Hello?... Hi, Niles... *(Sotto)* No, she's in the kitchen, she can't hear... Aw jeez, I don't know about that...

Angle on: Frasier pulls a scrap of paper from his pocket. He rests it on his knee, takes out his cell phone, and dials.

Frasier   *(into phone)* Hello — hurt anyone lately? *(He laughs, then seriously)* Really? Well, technically, all you did was leave the rake out... Listen, I want to take you to dinner tomorrow night, if you're free. We could meet at seven at Café Nervosa and head out from there. *(Then)* Wonderful. I'll see you then. Good-night.

He hangs up as Daphne emerges from the kitchen. Martin has already hung up his phone.

Frasier   She said yes! *(Turns on music)* Tomorrow night I have a date with an angel. Dance with me, Daphne.

He tries to dance with her. She brushes him off.

Daphne   Get away.

Martin   *(off Frasier's look)* Bullet in the hip.

Frasier   Fine. Nothing can dampen my spirits.

Frasier moves to the music.

Martin You're going to be this way all night, aren't you?

Daphne *(to Martin)* McGinty's?

Martin Way ahead of you.

They go for their coats, as we:

FADE OUT.

END OF ACT ONE

ACT TWO

SCENE H

FADE IN:

INT. CAFÉ NERVOSA — A WEEK LATER — UNIVERSE 1/DAY 2

Frasier (still in his sling) and Roz are in mid-conversation.

Frasier We had dinner again Thursday and then again Friday. On Saturday she was visiting her family, so to keep our streak alive I sent her a videotape of myself eating and talking to the camera.

Roz That's cute.

Frasier And how are things with you and Mike?

Roz Good. He's taking me to that Heart Association benefit on Valentine's Day.

Frasier I'm going, too. That's five hundred dollars a ticket. He must really like you.

Roz What are you talking about? The station bought us a table. The tickets are free. *(Off his look)* You bought two, didn't you.

Frasier Well, it's a worthy cause. *(Then)* You know, I think this is a first — you and I in happy relationships at the same time.

Roz I know. The planets must be out of whack or something.

Frasier Or maybe they're finally where they should be.

They clink coffee mugs as Monica enters and crosses to them. They ad-lib hellos. Frasier stands.

Monica How's your head?

Frasier Much better. My peripheral vision is back.

Monica I'm really sorry. But I did enjoy the driving range. *(Then)* By the way, I want to thank you for the flowers. *(Kissing him)* Thank you.

Frasier Wait 'til you see what's coming. You won't be able to thank me in public.

Monica Frasier, I hate to break it to you, but you don't have to keep sending me flowers and poetry. I am officially interested.

Frasier beams.

Monica I'm going to get some coffee.

Frasier Please, allow me.

Monica Frasier, you're sweet, but I think I can get my own coffee.

Monica crosses to the counter.

Roz Looks like your hard work is paying off.

Frasier Yes, but I'm not going to stop now. I don't want her to feel taken for granted.

Roz Wow, Frasier, you're going all out on the romance front. You're giving Niles a run for his money.

Frasier Please. In the great golden book of love, Niles will be a mere footnote to my glorious saga. I'm going to take his ball and run it to the end-zone. *(Then)* Is that a thing?

Roz Yes.

Frasier Good.

CUT TO:

SCENE J

INT. FRASIER'S LIVING ROOM — VALENTINE'S DAY EVENING — UNIVERSE 2/NIGHT 2

> *Frasier (no sling) slumps on the sofa, unshaven, wearing sweats, watching TV, and eating from a bag of chips. The table is set for a romantic dinner.*

Martin Frasier, you've been moping for a week. Why don't you join me at McGinty's? It's crazy there on Valentine's Day. Last year, McGinty hired a midget in a diaper to run around shooting people with a bow and arrow. Wait — that might have been Super Bowl.

Frasier You had me right up until diaper.

Niles drags Daphne from out of the kitchen.

Niles Dad, Frasier, you've got to see this. Daphne has sauce on her nose. Have you ever seen anything cuter in all your life?

She starts to wipe it off.

Niles   No, let me.

He kisses it off. They giggle.

Daphne   Oh, you've got some on your neck.

She kisses his neck. He giggles and pulls away.

Daphne   *(delighted)* Oh, is somebody ticklish?

She tickles him.

Frasier   Okay. You love her, she loves you. Point taken.

Niles   *(to Daphne)* Truce. I was going to wait until after dinner to tell you this, but it's just too torturous. Three hours from now, you and I are going to be on a plane to Maui.

Daphne shrieks with glee and throws her arms around Niles.

Daphne   I barely have time to pack!

Niles   Already taken care of. Dad packed a bag for you.

Daphne   Mr. Crane!

She kisses Martin's cheek.

Daphne   I've never been so happy in all my life.

Niles   I feel the same way. In fact—

Frasier   Someone's trying to watch "Behind the Music" here!

Daphne and Niles cross to the kitchen. SFX: The phone rings. Frasier answers.

Frasier   *(into phone)* Hello?… Hi, Roz… No, I'm skipping the benefit tonight… Let me guess: she's got a great personality… No, I think not. Have a good time. Bye.

He hangs up.

Martin   Roz find you a date for tonight?

Frasier   Apparently she's taking some guy who lives in her building and he has a sister.

Martin   You should go. It beats hanging around here feeling sorry for yourself.

Frasier   I don't think so. A blind date's bad enough, but a blind date on Valentine's Day? Frankly I couldn't imagine a worse way to spend the evening.

Niles and Daphne emerge from the kitchen.

Niles   You have to see this. Ready, Daphne?

She nods, and Niles holds up a strand of spaghetti, putting one

> *end in his mouth, the other end in Daphne's. They eat toward the middle.*

Frasier *(picking up the phone)* Maybe Roz hasn't left yet.

> CUT TO:

SCENE K

INT. FRASIER'S LIVING ROOM — EARLIER — UNIVERSE 1/NIGHT 3

> *Frasier is in a tuxedo and his sling. In the background the table is set for a romantic dinner.*

Frasier *(glancing at his watch)* It's seven-forty-five. Right now Monica should be receiving a jeroboam of chilled champagne.

Martin You're really laying it on thick.

Frasier You don't know the half of it. This morning she awoke to a string quartet on her porch. When she got to work, her desk was covered with seven dozen roses — a dozen for each day I've known her.

> *Niles staggers in from the kitchen, gasping for breath. Daphne follows. (She has a spot of sauce on her nose.)*

Daphne I'm sorry!

Martin What happened?

Daphne He's having some sort of reaction.

Niles Were there scallops in that sauce?

Daphne No.

Frasier Nutmeg?

Daphne No.

Martin Wheat germ?

Daphne No.

Frasier Carob?

Daphne No.

Niles Cumin?

> *A beat.*

Daphne Maybe.

Niles This is a disaster. And we have reservations to fly to Maui tonight.

Daphne *(excited)* Really?

Niles	We can't go now. I couldn't possibly sit still on a plane for five hours with this rash you've given me.
Frasier	Now now, you two. Don't let one little mistake spoil the most magical night of the—
Niles	The whole weekend is ruined.
Daphne	I said I was sorry.
Niles	I even had Dad pack a bag for you.
Daphne	You what? You let him go through my things? *(To Martin)* How could you!
Niles	I was just trying to do something nice for our first Valentine's Day.
Daphne	Well what do you think *I* was trying to do? Now I'm going to have to spend the whole night rubbing lotion all over you.

There is a long beat.

Niles	I'm sorry I yelled at you.
Daphne	I'm sorry too.

They hold hands and head off to Daphne's bedroom.

Niles	You've got a little sauce on your nose.

She starts to wipe it off.

Niles	No, let me.

He kisses it off as they exit, and we:

CUT TO:

SCENE L

INT. BALLROOM — LATER THAT NIGHT — UNIVERSE 1/NIGHT 3

Tuxedoed Frasier, a cape draped over his sling, enters with Monica. They spot Roz and ad-lib hellos.

Frasier	Hello, Roz, where's Mike?
Roz	He's parking the car. *(Noticing)* Monica, what a beautiful corsage.
Monica	Thanks. It was a gift from Frasier — along with about a million roses.

Kenny approaches. His cummerbund and tie are festooned with bright red hearts. There is a blinking red heart on his top hat.

Kenny	Hello, young lovers.
Frasier	Kenny, look at you.

Kenny	What can I say? Under this gruff exterior lies the heart of a true romantic. I just love love.
Roz	Where's your wife?
Kenny	She had plans.
Roz	Come on, Kenny, I'll buy you a drink.
	They cross away.
Frasier	I thought maybe after the party we might take a carriage ride through the park and then head back to your place, where I believe there are ten pounds of chocolate truffles whispering your name.
Monica	Ten pounds, huh?
Frasier	Well, your sister told me how much you love truffles.
Monica	Cheryl? You talked to Cheryl?
Frasier	I did my homework. She also told me an adorable story about your first training bra.
Monica	But how? She lives in Wyoming? I haven't talked to her in years.
Frasier	Let's just say there are Internet companies that will track anyone down for the right price. And no price is too high for my little Monica Jean Marie, six pounds, seven ounces at birth.
	He leans in to give her a kiss. She turns her cheek to him.
Monica	I just did my lipstick.
Frasier	I understand.
	And we:
	CUT TO:

SCENE N

INT. BALLROOM — EARLIER THAT NIGHT — UNIVERSE 2/NIGHT 2

	We see Monica and Mike making out in the background. In the foreground, Frasier enters, wearing a simple suit. He passes them by and hears Roz calling to him.
Roz	Hey Frasier. This is Robert, my date.
Robert	Nice to meet you.
Frasier	Same here. *(Then)* Roz, I want to thank you for getting me out of the house. I've been feeling sorry for myself long enough.
Roz	That's the spirit.

Frasier	I have to admit, on the way here I even got a little excited about meeting someone new.
Roz	Oh, here she is now.
	Judy — the woman from the speed date — approaches.
Judy	*(pointing at Frasier)* Oh my God! *(Then)* Aaaaaaar!
Frasier	*(halfheartedly)* Aaaar.
Judy	Aaaaaaaar!
Frasier	Okay.
Roz	Well, I guess you two know each other — you've even got your own language.
Judy	It must be fate!
Frasier	Must be.
	CUT TO:

SCENE P

INT. BALLROOM — LATER — UNIVERSE 1/NIGHT 3

Frasier and Monica are dancing. He reaches inside his tux and pulls out a rose.

Frasier	For you, my sweet.
Monica	Wow. Another rose. Listen, Frasier, I appreciate everything you're doing. The flowers, the carriage ride, the "Love Is…" cartoons from the newspaper.
	Frasier places a finger gently to her lips.
Frasier	Please. It's a drop in the ocean compared to what you deserve.
	The song ends. Applause. During the following Frasier guides Monica to their table, where Kenny is already sitting.
Emcee	That song was dedicated to Dr. and Mrs. Arthur Day, celebrating their fiftieth anniversary.
	They all applaud as an older couple stands.
Monica	That is so cute.
Frasier	I'm glad to hear you say that. Wait right here.
	Frasier bounds to the stage, shares a few words with the emcee, who nods to the orchestra. Frasier takes the mic.
Frasier	*(into mic)* Good evening, ladies and gentlemen. I'm Dr. Frasier Crane and I have a dedication of my own to make.

Frasier cues the band. They start the intro.

Frasier   Normally I devote myself to matters of the head, but tonight I want to share what's in my heart. This is for you, Monica.

The band plays "Oh Babe, What Would You Say." Frasier sings. As he sings, Frasier crosses over to Monica. She sits mortified, a frozen smile on her face. At this point Frasier has leaned down and is holding the mic in front of her. She puts her hand over the mic, which doesn't prevent the following from being heard.

Monica   Frasier, we need to talk.

Everyone "ooohs" and turns away. The whole room winces.

Kenny   Ouch.

CUT TO:

SCENE S

INT. BALLROOM — LATER — UNIVERSE 1/NIGHT 3

Frasier and Monica stand near the door in mid conversation.

Monica   Don't get me wrong, Frasier. Everything you did was nice, it was just too much. You were making me feel like a project and not a person.

Frasier   I can tone things down. We can start fresh. How about lunch tomorrow? *(Then)* See? I was going to say breakfast.

Monica   I don't think so.

Frasier   I see. Shall I take you home?

Monica   No thanks, I'll catch a cab. *(Then)* Bye, Frasier.

Frasier   Goodbye.

As Monica crosses to the coat check, Roz approaches.

Roz   You okay?

Frasier   Well, I'm humiliated.

Roz   Oh Frasier, nobody really even noticed what happened.

Kenny   *(passing by)* Ouch.

Frasier   It's my own fault. I guess I saw what Niles had and I pushed too hard to get it for myself.

Roz   Well if it means anything, I thought what you did was terribly romantic.

Frasier   Thanks, Roz.

Roz   Let me walk you to your car.

Frasier	What about Mike?
Roz	It's just a few minutes. He'll be fine.

Frasier and Roz exit. Angle on: Monica, who gets her coat. As she throws it around her shoulders she hits Mike in the face, causing him to drop his drink.

Monica	Oh God, I'm sorry. I'm such a klutz.
Mike	It's okay, really.
Monica	Let me get you a new drink. It's the least I can do.
Mike	I guess that would be okay. *(Holding out hand)* I'm Mike.
Monica	Monica.

They share a look. She takes his hand.

FADE OUT.

SCENE T

FADE IN:

INT. FRASIER'S CAR — LATER — UNIVERSE 1/NIGHT 3

Frasier, in his sling and his tux, drives down a Seattle street. He turns the radio dial to "The Best of Crane."

Announcer	*(v.o.)* We now return to a previously recorded broadcast of "The Best of Crane."
Frasier	*(v.o.)* Roz, who's our next caller?
Roz	*(v.o.)* We have Phil from Tacoma. He just got out of a three-year relationship.
Frasier	*(v.o.)* Go ahead, Phil, I'm listening.
Phil	*(v.o.)* Thanks, Doc. We've been broken up for three weeks and I'm still miserable. Sometimes I think I'd be better off if I'd never met her.
Frasier	*(v.o.)* Well, Phil, as hard as it may be to imagine, you will get over her…

CUT TO:

INT. FRASIER'S CAR — CONTINUOUS — UNIVERSE 2/NIGHT 2

Frasier	*(v.o.)* At times like this, it helps to remember the old adage: "It's better to have loved and lost than never to have loved at all."

Frasier considers this.

Frasier   I do make a good point.

CUT TO:

INT. FRASIER'S CAR — CONTINUOUS — UNIVERSE 1/NIGHT 3

Frasier   *(to the radio)* What a load of crap.

Frasier   *(v.o.)* The important thing, Phil, is not to give up hope.

Phil   *(v.o.)* I guess you're right, Dr. Crane.

Frasier   *(v.o.)* Good luck. I see we have time for one more call. Hello, you're on the air.

We hear the sound of a lively restaurant in the background.

Rachel   *(v.o.)* My name is Rachel. I just wanted to let you know, I read that Thurber book you quoted from, and man, is he funny.

Frasier   *(v.o.)* Glad you liked it. It's always good to speak to a fellow Thurber enthusiast.

Rachel   *(v.o.)* I also have a confession to make. My sister dared me to call because I have a crush on you.

Frasier   *(v.o.)* I'm flattered, Rachel. But I'm afraid I make it a policy not to date my callers.

Rachel   *(v.o.)* Well, if you ever change your mind, I'm the chef at the Columbia Street Tavern. You should come by sometime.

Frasier perks up.

CUT TO:

INT. FRASIER'S CAR — CONTINUOUS — UNIVERSE 2/NIGHT 2

Frasier perks up.

CUT TO:

EXT. SEATTLE STREET — CONTINUOUS

We see Frasier's car stopped at a light. The car from Universe One pulls up and they become one car. The light changes and the car u turns, heading towards the restaurant.

FADE OUT.

END OF ACT TWO.

THE BEST OF
FRASIER ®

**Vintage comedy for all Frasier fans featuring 15 complete
scripts of the finest Frasier episodes from the first six series,
including all five Emmy Award winners.**

ISBN: 0 7522 1394 6 £9.99

You can order your copies direct from Channel 4 Books by
calling 01624 84 44 44. Postage and packing is free in the UK.